Inside Out

You Can Take the Boy Out of Peckham . . . .

∞

RICK ATKINSON

Copyright © 2010 by Rick Atkinson.

Library of Congress Control Number: 2010917563
ISBN: Hardcover   978-1-4568-2244-6
                         Softcover   978-1-4568-2243-9
                         Ebook   978-1-4568-2245-3

All rights reserved. No part of this book may be reproduced or transmitted in any form or by any means, electronic or mechanical, including photocopying, recording, or by any information storage and retrieval system, without permission in writing from the copyright owner.

This book was printed in the United Kingdom.

To order additional copies of this book, contact:
Xlibris Corporation
0-800-644-6988
www.xlibrispublishing.co.uk
Orders@xlibrispublishing.co.uk
301320

Dearest Pat.

Hope you enjoy the

Book

Inside Out

You have been a

great friend

Love

[signature] 2012.

RIKKI WILSON

Contents

1) BIRDED OFF 1

2) MEMORY LANE 5

3) FRAGGLE ROCK... 18

4) THE ITALIANS 48

5) THE BLOODY PETER... 73

6) PETER 23 78

7) LEADER OF THE B WING FIRM 83

8) MAD MAX IS JEKYLL & HYDE... 93

9) THE KING OF THE TABLE 97

10) NAME AND NUMBER TO THE GOVERNOR........................ 105

11) THE FIVE LITRE CREEPER 109

12) DOWN THE OLD KENT ROAD 112

13) THE PEACH BOYS... 123

14) ASSAULT ON SAINSBURY'S CAR PARK 131

15) PC WORLD... 144

16) KEEPING SAM SWEET 151

17) TOM FOOLERY 155

18) THE JOLLY GREEN GIANT 165

19) DON'T COME BACK 170

20) THE POLICE CAR POUND ROBBERY.................................. 174

21) WHAT GOES AROUND COMES AROUND........................... 183

22) REVENGE PENDING 194

I dedicate this story to my brother John,

He knows why.

and to my Mother for her strength and wisdom.

CHAPTER I

BIRDED OFF

ON THE 8TH of February 1991 I heard those words I had been dreading for the past six months, especially since I had hoped to have a double celebration that very night. It was my twenty-second birthday and instead of sitting at home opening presents in the company of my nearest and dearest, I was standing in the dock of Southwark Crown court waiting nervously for the Judge's verdict. **"I've taken into account all the details and mitigating circumstances of this case Mr Atkinson, but due to the seriousness of the crime you have committed, I have no choice but to hand you a custodial sentence, therefore I sentence you to nine months imprisonment at her Majesty's Pleasure." Take the prisoner away,"** After a collective sharp intake of breath from my family in the gallery, my mother who had a look of shock and desperation on her face had just enough time to lean over and hand me my newspaper before the jailor led me down the stairs to the court cells. I was taken straight to a temporary holding cell where I was to be briefed by my barrister. The sound of the heavy Iron grey door slamming shut behind me and the loud blunt echo of the locks clicking into their closed position left me with an empty sinking feeling. The realisation that I was now in a different world began to sink in quickly, I would now be locked up for at least the next four and a half months within an institution, not knowing what was going to happen next, or what the other prisoners were going to be like, was prison like the violent place that I'd seen in films? A new chapter had begun and I would have to adapt fast if I was going to get through it. Strangely enough by the time my barrister got to my cell to go over the details of my sentence, I was feeling calm and had some sort of inner mental strength building up. It was something I'd never experienced before, like my subconscious preparing me for what lay ahead.

"I have spoken with your mother and she is very upset and wants to know if you are ok," explained my barrister.

"Have you got some paper so I can write her a note? I asked.

Passing me a pen and a page from his notebook I began writing.

Hello mum, I promise you I am fine, I knew that I would be given a prison sentence no matter what all the street experts told me. So I have been mentally preparing myself for this outcome for a while, so please don't worry about me I'll be ok. Give Ben a hug and a kiss for me. I'll see you when you come to visit, love Rikki xxxx

My barrister went on to explain that I was lucky to have only received a nine-month sentence, of which I would only serve four and a half as long as I behaved myself.

"I would advise you not to pursue an appeal since it is quite possible the Judge would double your sentence," he said. I had first met him at a top-notch law firm based in the Temple area of London and it was the first time I ever needed to be appointed a barrister. The building, which was overlooking the Thames, was very Edwardian in its decor and the oak panelled corridors were overloaded with Crombie filled coat stands and umbrella holders. My barrister never minced his words, was very abrupt and spoke like he'd just swallowed a dictionary. After introducing himself he brought me straight down to earth with a thud, "I am going to tell you right now that you will be going to prison, and from this point on my job is to try and make sure you get no more than a nine month sentence, I have dealt with many cases like yours recently and most of my clients have been given eighteen months for this particular crime." I left that meeting in no doubt about my fate and over the following months I always had my barrister's honest and frank statement in the back of my mind no matter how many times my family and friends would tell me I'd get away with it.

His prediction had come true so job done as far as he was concerned, after wishing me luck he gathered up my case files, shoved them in his brief case and gave the screw a nod, he and the screw then left locking the heavy iron door behind them. Any hope of a light at the end of the tunnel or salvation at the hands of my barrister had diminished with the sound of his footsteps fading away into the distance leaving me with deep feelings of abandonment. The noise of other prisoners screaming and shouting in desperation and rage was deafening and made me sick to the pit of my stomach. The damp musky stench of the dimly lit cell triggered memories of the loneliness I had felt when spending the odd night at my local police station in the past. But this wasn't going to be one of those odd nights; there wasn't going to be a slap on the wrist and a caution before being sent home, it was forever, the key had well and truly been thrown away as far as I was concerned. After an hour or so the door was unlocked and I was led down a corridor with other cells to my left and right, The screw searched me and took my lighter but left me with 20 fags and an ounce of Old Holborn which I had been advised to take along with my toothbrush by ex cons from the street.

I was given the choice to go into segregation or join the other birded off prisoners in the Tank, (A large holding cell for multiple inmates). Luckily I opted for the Tank since segregation meant Rule 43.

It was later explained to me by a fellow inmate that Rule 43 was where they kept the Nonces, Grasses, and Rapists segregated from the main prison population for their own safety, so if I had taken option (A) I would have ended up with the scum of the earth and become a target for the razor blade brigade. In other words my mash potato would have had tiny fragments of crushed light bulb glass mixed in with it, and my prison issue soap would have been embedded with broken razor blades.

In the tank there were about 15 other inmates, who were all relaxed and chatting like this was everyday life for them. It was, and the majority had come from prison to court for sentencing after being on remand for a few months, still wearing my suit I felt slightly over dressed as I sat down on a spare seat.

"Fucking hell Rick, what you doing here? I heard coming from a corner of the tank.

It was Terry Galloway, someone I knew from Peckham, I went to school with him and his brother Mickey.

"Terry, how you doing mate," I said relieved to see someone I knew.

"I've been better, that judge in court one is a fucking wanker" he said as he made his way over to me.

"Jump up bruv", he told the wirery looking feller sitting next to me. The feller got up and moved to another seat.

"How long did you get then Tel?

The bastard weighed me off with another six Moon, I've already done six on remand in cockroach alley," he complained. Prison had its own slang with words that you wouldn't hear on the street. So I learned my first two words, Moon meaning months, and cockroach alley was self explanatory for Pentenville prison.

"What about you Rick, how long did you get?

"Nine months, apparently I'll do four and a half if I keep my head down".

"What are you in for then? He asked. For a split second it seemed as though the whole room had hushed while waiting for my answer keen to find out what sort of bloke I was.

"Possession with intent." I replied as I looked around the tank trying to gage what sort of impression I had made with my answer.

"What class B?

"Yeah class B," I said as the hush in the room returned to chitchat.

"You got a right touch, see my mate Gavin over there?" He got 18 moon for the same offence."

"My barrister seems to agree with you," I said as Terry called out to his mate.

"Gavin! This is my pal Rick,"

"All right mate," Gavin said nodding to me,

"He's in for the same offence as you Gav, but they only weighed him off with a shit shower and shave," laughed Terry. A shit, shower and shave meant, on the scale of most prison sentences you were in and out in no time at all, Gavin wasn't sharing Terry's humour and was too engrossed in biting his nails to make any comment,

I took my box of 20 Bensons from my inside blazer pocket, took out a fag and offered one to Terry.

"Put them away for fuck sake," he said pushing my hand back towards my pocket.

"Why? I thought we were allowed to smoke,"

"We are, but if this lot know you've got 20 fags they'll be all over you like a fucking rash mate, fags are like gold dust in here, that's why everyone is smoking matchstick size roll ups," he explained. "I can see I'm gonna have to clue you up on prison politics, aint you got no backy? He asked.

"Yeah I've got an ounce of Old Holborn in my other pocket,"

"Listen," he said whispering, "keep your smokes in your pocket until you get to the nick, all of us in here are going to be shipped off to Brixton prison for re-allocation, you can smoke mine until then and pay me back later, I know quite a few Kanga's at Brixton so I'll try and make sure we get to share a Peter."

"What the fuck is a Peter or a kanga? I asked him.

"Peter Bell means cell, and Kangaroo means screw."

He rolled me the thinnest fag I'd ever seen, and to make matters worse it was pipe tobacco, apparently pipe tobacco was much cheaper than the usual gear and lasted longer. After about 30 seconds of coughing through my now down to the roach roll up, I took my newspaper from my back pocket to have a little read when all of a sudden like flies around shit there was a queue of people all wanting to have a look at it. Puzzled I asked terry what all the fuss was about.

He explained that in some prisons it was rare to get an up to date newspaper, and were usually a week old by the time you'd get to read one. Terry was about my height and stood 6ft tall, with greasy dark brown hair, high cheek bones and sunken eye sockets he wasn't exactly a picture of health. To say he was cocky and a bit of a Jack the lad was an understatement, I remember he always had a mouthpiece on him in the school playground so nothing had changed.

CHAPTER II

OUT
MEMORY LANE

I T WAS PROPHESISED by my step dad, (who we called Deb), that I would end up doing bird at some point in the future. **"He's going to end up in prison"** he used to say to my mother, normally after the police had brought me home for one thing or another. Deb had been in our lives since the very early 70's after meeting my mother at a pickle factory where they both worked. My mother Helen, and father Marcel, separated when I was a toddler and he moved back to Cricklewood north London. The earliest memory I have of my father, was when he kissed me good bye and told me to be good for my mum. From that point we only ever saw him at Christmas and birthdays when he would turn up with a bin liner full of gifts. To me he was just a bloke called dad, and once John and I had finished opening our presents we went out to play. I don't really remember having an emotional connection to him so when Deb came into our lives he was the father figure that we needed and became a round peg in a round hole as far as fitting in with our lives was concerned. Towards the end of my parent's marriage my mother and Deb became quite friendly and would often meet up to take my brother and me to the swing park. We were told his name was Debbie which didn't sound too strange to us since we were still knee high to a grasshopper at the time, so should our father ask us where we had been we would say, "We went to the park with Mummy and Debbie." Anyway the name stuck and over the years it was shortened to Deb. His Real name was Frank and he was from a large Irish family with 3 brothers and 3 sisters. He had a London accent and was quite softly spoken. Deb was a loving caring father to us and set good moral examples even though my mum was the boss. He was about 5ft 8, had a well rounded belly and sported a Bobby Charlton comb over. The four of us were always going out on trips to the seaside or spending days in the countryside with a picnic. Mum and Deb would play scrabble or Cribbage while John and I would go climbing trees in the woods or swimming in the sea depending on where we were at the time. Sadly Deb died when I was 17; he never got to find out that he was right all along about me ending up in prison.

From about the age of 8 or 9 my brother John, our neighbour Derrick and I would steal rolls of lead from the roofs of shops, banks, schools and factories in and around our local area of Peckham South East London, and we would give it all to Derrick's old man who would sell it to the local scrap dealer. We never asked questions and would rub our hands together later on in the day when Derrick would come and give us our share of the winnings. My first payment was £4.00 which made me feel like I was loaded since I'd usually be lucky to get 25p pocket money from my mum if she had a good week. Derrick's old man, who I will call Sid, was over six foot tall and balding, he reminded me of Sid James from the Carry on films which probably had something to do with the way he laughed and spoke with his typical Cockney accent and personality to match. Sid was a keen pigeon fancier and had a couple pigeon lofts in his garden situated at the back of our block of flats. He had about 50 racing pigeons and quite a few of them were champions. As a young kid you never really know much about adults, but I knew that Sid was never far from the road when things were falling off the back of Lorries, so he never asked questions when we'd turn up with trolleys full of lead from time to time. Although we all lived in pokey little flats Derrick's family were never short of a few bob. Derrick always had a new bike, new skateboard etc, whatever he wanted he got. He lived right next door to us, so between him my brother and me we made a bedroom-to-bedroom intercom system by wiring up the speakers and microphones that we pinched from public telephone boxes. We'd power them up using a heavy duty battery which any one of us would nick from the ample road-works lamps that were available locally. Eventually we up-graded the intercom system by swiping the whole ear/mouth piece including the springy wires. So unlike before when we had to hold the mouth piece with one hand and the ear piece with the other, we were now using the whole unit and talking on the phone to each other every night for free. Never a day went by without there being a bike ramp on our street. The seventies were great; we never had computers, mobile phones, play stations, game boys, videos and DVD's. We knocked for our many friends and played out on the street all day usually trying to emulate Evel Knievel by flying over a ramp on our bikes to see who could jump the highest and furthest. When we got bored with that we'd play games like Ting Tang Tommy, British Bull Dog, Cannon, Run outs, Arrows, Chinese football, or we'd race our go-karts against kids from another street. All go carts had pretty much the same design. We would make them using a set of old pram wheels, a length of wood, a milk crate and some string. They were great even if we did have to keep banging extra nails in every half hour to prevent the front axle from falling off. One of our other favourite pastimes was building war camps over the dump. The object of the game was to pick two teams, and then go about trying to destroy your enemy's camp after a long drawn out stone fight. The dump was once called Moncrieff Street and was full of Victorian houses that ran parallel to Raul road where we lived. The houses were demolished and the whole area was fenced off with corrugated iron. There were big holes dotted about all over the place which were once the Victorian coal cellars belonging to the houses that had previously stood there. Some of the cellars were half filled with muddy rain water but others were bone dry and were a great base to build underground camps. The dump remained our playground for about a year. The old Victorian kitchen sinks that lay strewn in amongst the decaying rubble were now filled with green murky rain water and somehow always seemed to be full of tadpoles. There were abandoned mattresses and the remnants of old armchairs everywhere you looked. The whole place was a breeding ground for rodents and inevitably the local blocks of flats and houses became rat infested.

But we were quite happy to continue playing on the dump, which we did until some bright spark decided that they were going to build a new Sainsbury's complete with multi storey car park. One day me and a bunch of other kids decided to make some protest banners and spent a few hours walking around shouting, "Save our dump! Save our dump!" Sadly our protesting fell on deaf ears, after all we were only nine or ten years old and we didn't carry much weight when it come to volume or political influence down at the local town hall.

THE BOOGIE WOOGIE MAN

As well as my brother John and I, our mates were all keen swimmers and we spent half our lives in various swimming pools in our area. Peckham open air swimming pool was great in the summer, our mums brought picnics and would sunbathe near the fountain at the far end of the pool while us kids swam and had fun. The water was stutteringly cold and would always have dead, or half dead wasps and other insects floating around on the surface. There were so many it was hard work trying to avoid swallowing one. If we weren't acting out the crocodile fight scene from Tarzan we would be doing a scene from Man from Atlantis which could go on for hours, so by the time us kids were ready to call it a day our mums would be red raw with sunburn. We had a massive black and white television in our living room, so my brother John and I would always watch the old Tarzan films on Saturday and Sunday mornings. There were a few different actors who played Tarzan but Johnny Weissmuller was our favourite. There were some great programmes and films for kids on the weekend like Champion the wonder horse, the Beachcombers, The Double Deckers, Michael Bentine's potty time, Zorro, and always a Lassie or flipper film too. Laurel and hardy, Abbot and Costello, George Formby, and Norman Wisdom were our comedians; those were times of warmth and security.

Then someone came along who changed my life, it was John Travolta. I was Eight years old when I first Saw Saturday Night Fever by sneaking in the back door of the Peckham Odeon Picture house. The buzz of the music and dancing was hypnotic, also there was something about leather jacket wearing rebels with quiffs that fascinated me like the Fonze, Elvis, Alvin Stardust, and James Dean, so I left that picture house in a trance. I was Tony Manero and he was me, I wanted his life I started walking like him, acting like him, dressing like him, and I would comb my hair in the mirror whilst listening to Night Fever. Then I saw Grease and soon became Tony Manero and Danny Zucco all rolled into one. I went to Peckham Park junior school and during playtime Kenickie (Lee Butler) and I would strut around the playground in our leather T Birds Jackets followed by Rizzo (Tracey Harvey) and Sandy (Karen Pauling). Every Ten minutes Kenickie and I would hit the toilets to add more water to our quiffs. We always kept black combs in our back pockets and would do the summer loving scene on the benches under the rain shelter with the T Birds at one end and the pink ladies at the other. At every school disco or dance event Lee Butler and I would do Tony Manero's solo dance routine. I used the same routine in the Pig and Whistle dance competition at Butlins holiday camp and came 3rd. Even throughout my teens and well into my 20's I would go through the bedroom ritual of blow-drying my hair in the mirror, slipping on my necklace and shirt whilst listening to the Bee Gees. In every nightclub I would be listening to Staying Alive in my head as I approached the dance floor. Even today I get a nostalgic lump in my throat if I watch either of those two films. Throughout my many evenings accompanying some of my past girlfriends while babysitting their younger siblings, and sitting with my daughter night after night, I must have watched Grease a thousand times and it still has an effect on me. Saturday night fever can cripple me with just one song and I have to compose myself. It's weird, after all the shit I've seen and done in my life, one simple film can easily floor me.

OLD ASKEAN

I was fortunate enough to be accepted into the best secondary school in south east London, Haberdasher's Askes Hatcham Boys school. My brother John was in the 3rd year by the time I got there, Askes used to be a Grammar school and turned comprehensive on the year that John started. Nothing had changed though, the strict regime and high standards were still the same. The teachers all wore cloaks and the head master and his various deputies even wore the dodgy hats with the cloaks which added to the air of pompous authority that they carried. Immediate on the spot punishment was dished out if you broke the rules, each teacher had their own preferred method of disciplinary action and some had an array of weapons of which to carry out the castigation. My fifth year maths teacher Mr Kerridge would make you stand at the front of the class and wait while he studiously sifted through the copious amounts of canes and other weapons that were systematically hanging in his tiny storeroom. He would make sure you could see him methodically testing each one out, until having decided which one he thought warranted the right amount of pain to fit the crime. So he would mentally punish you as well as physically, some of his tools would range from the thin end of a 3 piece fishing rod to a Jesus creeper sandal, or a one metre ruler amongst many others. My geography teacher Mr Barber, was also known as 'Psycho,' and trust me, this bloke lived up to his name. He was the head of the geography block, which we referred to as the hut, and during first break or lunch time, if anyone just happened to be hanging about outside or making slightly too much noise, Psycho would randomly come running out of the building and knuckle everyone in his range on the head. He only ever got me once since I quickly learnt to keep one eye on his door. His knuckling really hurt seeing as he hit you really hard and would always have the look of a serial killer etched across his face when doing so.

We would occasionally wind him up on purpose so that he would chase us, it reminded me of a game we used to play on a little housing estate near where I lived, there was an old Staffordshire Bull Terrier who couldn't run very fast but would try it's damndest to catch us when we wound him up. He always hung about in his front garden and would make a dash for us growling and snapping at our ankles as we ran away jumping on to walls and bin sheds just out of his reach. The difference was that the dog would return home after his first failed dash, whereas the Psycho was relentless and used to chase you all around the playground, and he would end up hitting anyone regardless as to whether or not they were involved. Can you imagine something like that happening today in 2010? The teacher would be facing multiple charges of child abuse, and there would be a string of compensation claims. We just soaked it all up, it was part and parcel of life in that school and getting knuckled, slapped around the face, punched or whipped went with the territory. I was a fully paid up member of the Saturday gang, A.K.A the Breakfast Club. I was given Saturday morning detention every week which meant coming to school in full uniform for two to four hours. Whilst there, I was required to either do school work or help moving furniture and stuff around. My crimes would usually be either getting caught smoking or getting two or more Friday detentions in the same week which would then be converted into one Saturday morning DT. The deputy head would read out the names of the detainees during Friday morning assembly. You could practically mime the list of names he read out since they were more often than not the usual suspects made up of members from the Bog posse. The Bog posse was a gang of us lads who were smokers and generally the ones causing a disturbance in class and around the school on the whole. The name came about given that we spent so much time smoking in or around the playground Bog (toilet). I was the Tucker Jenkins of that era in my school and there wasn't a day that went by without my involvement in some kind of scam or skulduggery. Never the less I really liked the school and in between being a rogue I actually learned quite a lot. I was also known for my basket ball skills and my team would often attract a large crowd when playing in a house v house match in the gym after school. A couple of the lads I knew at Askes have made it to the big time, one of them is doing very well in the movie "business" and the other is high up in the music industry, I'm hoping there will be another Old Askean who makes it big in the book writing industry.

THE CHEF HAD DIORHEA

I was one of those kids who had his own distorted interpretation of the rules and used to blur the lines quite often. I was always willing to cut corners and take risks but naturally on some occasions my plans would back fire and I would receive my just deserts. For instance, one Saturday lunchtime when I was about 13 years old I was walking around the East Lane Market with a mate of mine called Jermaine. The market which only opened on a weekend, was always very busy and widely popular. We were hungry and were trying to make up our minds whether or not to buy some food from the Wimpy burger bar. If we put our money together we would have enough for a hamburger and chips each, but the only problem was that this would leave us with no bus fare, and meant we'd have to walk the three or four miles home. We flipped a coin calling heads for food tails for the bus, it was heads so in we went and ordered our food. The usual protocol was to eat your food then either ask the waiter/waitress for your bill or pay at the counter before you left. The Burgers and chips arrived via one of the two pretty Greek waitresses that worked there and after covering the chips in tomato sauce we tucked in. Five minutes later both our plates were empty barring one or two chips and now with a full belly we were gutted about having to walk home. I instructed Jermaine to eat the last few chips slowly while I went to the toilets to see if there was a back way out which would save us having to pay for the food. The men's toilets consisted of two rooms, one had a urinal and a sink and the other was slightly smaller and had a normal toilet for anyone needing to have a shit. The urinal was being used by another diner so I went in the little room and shut the door. Although very cramped the WC had very high ceilings and the walls seemed to go up and up forever. I noticed an open window about fifteen feet up and very near the ceiling so with a leg on opposite walls I straddled my way right up to the top to see if there was a possible way out. The window lead nowhere so my aspirations of escaping without paying were over, or so I thought. Just as I was about to shimmy back down, the door swung open way below me and in walked one of the chefs. He pulled his trousers down and sat down to take a dump and began reading his news paper as he puffed away on a roll up that he had retrieved from behind his sweaty ear. I couldn't believe it, what the hell was I going do now? If he saw me how the fuck was I going to explain what I was doing up there, and the same applied if I simply just climbed down. There was absolutely no excuse so the only option open to me was to stay where I was until he had finished and just hope he didn't look up. Well the chef must have been on his lunch break because he read the whole fucking paper while smoking a couple more roll ups. My arms and legs were shaking violently as they strained to keep me aloft and out of sight in the strangest situation I had ever been in. It was very uncomfortable to say the least and to rub salt in the wound I think he had diarrhoea because the smell of his shit was putrid and raising upwards with a vengeance. I was at the stage where I felt like just jumping down to face the consequences when the chef tore off some toilet roll and started to wipe his arse. I remember the relief I felt as he flushed the toilet and without even stopping to wash his hands made his way back to the kitchen. Back in the restaurant Jermaine was close to panic thinking I had escaped and left him behind with no money.

"You wouldn't believe what just happened to me in there," I moaned.

"I thought you'd fucked off and left me, what took you so long? He said whispering.

"I'll tell you on the walk home, let's just pay and get out of here 'cos I'm feeling sick.

I was dealt instant justice for trying to steal a dinner, my punishment was being forced to watch a man taking a dump and having to inhale the potent fumes of his shit for 15 minutes. Now days it would be called Karma.

BUSHWACKERS FROM JEW BOY HILL

Between the age of twelve to sixteen, every now and then along with a gang of about five or six mates from the Cossal estate, I used to go and watch Millwall FC play football at the old Den. It was about two miles away which would normally be a forty minute trot along the main roads. This could be cut down to half an hour if like us you took a short cut through three or four housing estates. We didn't head towards the turnstiles though because we never had tickets. Instead we made our way to a place known to us as Jew Boy Hill; other official names for it were Beggars Hill and Poor Man's Hill. It was a grassy mound which was situated just outside one corner of the stadium and you could just about see three quarters of the playing field when tip toeing. Jew Boy Hill was quite popular due to its convenient view point and there were always a few young boys watching the match from the lofty heights of their fathers aching shoulders. During this era I was more into girls and getting into trouble than watching footy, but it made a nice change and was a welcome distraction. Even though officially I was a Man United fan, the loud roar of the crowd chanting traditional Millwall songs used to give me a rush of adrenalin and an eagerness to get in amongst the electric atmosphere. Luckily we would only have to wait until half time because there was one small section of the perimeter wire fence, that when pulled to the side provided a gap just big enough for us to squeeze through and gain entry. At half time the stewards would be busy herding the sheep towards the food outlets and making sure the away supporters were kept safe from the infamous Millwall Bushwackers. This provided us with the opportunity to sneak in while their attention was momentarily diverted. We'd split up and mingle in with the crowds just in case we were spotted slipping through the broken fence. As soon as the second half kicked off my mates and I would regroup to watch the rest of the game together. I didn't have to look far to see a familiar face seeing as most people from my manor were Lions supporters. One day we found out that sneaking through the dodgy fence was no longer necessary due to the fact that after half time the officials would often open the main gates and let fans in for free providing there was sufficient space in the stands. So we'd watch the first half standing on the hill and the second half from inside the Den. On a couple of occasions my mates and I would get caught up in clashes with the away fans while walking along Ilderton road on our way home. There was one incident when we literally had to fight our way out of trouble when it kicked off big time outside the Den. There was a frenzy with home and away fans throwing punches at each other and it got to the point when no one could tell who was who, so it ended up with lots of confused lads just hitting out at anyone not wearing colours. There were only a few old Bill who were prancing about on horses, and their scarcity left big gaps which made penetrating the dividing lines easy. Once back on the safety of our own turf on the Cossal estate, we sat around all night telling anyone who'd listen about our big fight down at the Den. Typically by the time we re-ran the story a few times and added arms and legs to it, we had ourselves down as the Bushwackers top boys. Well that's teenagers for you. It would have been more convincing had we returned sporting a few black eyes and a thick lip here and there, since not many people bought our story given that neither one of us had so much as a scratch. I can vouch for at least three of us landing some kicks and punches, so we were lucky, (or unlucky as the case turned out) that all five of us walked away in one piece. The original firm associated with Millwall was known as F-Troop. The Bushwackers were one of the most active firms in the 1980's. Their Primary purpose was to cause trouble and fights at Millwall football matches. On occasion they were blamed for causing some of the worst acts of rioting in British football. They took and adapted their name from groups known as Bushwhackers that would ambush certain individuals and towns during the American Civil War. When sitting in the garden at home on a breezy day, I could tell when Millwall had scored because you could hear the roar of the goal celebration, followed by chants of, "We are Millwall, Super Millwall, no one likes us, we don't care!

SKATE CRAZY

In the early eighties around the time when Break dancing and body popping came to town, the roller skate craze had well and truly kicked in and immediately took over our lives. John, our neighbour derrick and I became accomplished skaters and along with some other lads from our street we'd go everywhere and anywhere on our skates. There were skate parks popping up everywhere and one of them was at the Southbank opposite waterloo train station. It didn't take us long to get there since we used to surf on the back of a number 12 or a 171 bus all the way there. Occasionally when the conductor got fed up with us hanging of the end of the bus we were forced to start surfing vans and lorries in between waiting for another bus to come along. Most Saturday and Sunday evenings a gang of us would go to a roller disco at Crofton Park leisure centre. More often than not John, Derrick and I would always earn free tickets for the following week after winning all our age group speed races. Half hour before the end of the disco the long jump competition would start. This involved jumping over people who were lying down in a row nervously hoping that they wouldn't get hit by a skate. I managed to jump 9 and a half people; John and Derrick could jump 10 or 11. You wouldn't get away with doing that now days with all these health and safety laws. Jumping people soon turned into jumping flights of stairs on our local housing estates. Once a certain flight of stairs had been accomplished we'd move on to find a flight that were more challenging, after all the higher and longer the jump was, the more you were rated. If we jumped stairs forwards we would then have to do it backwards. We had no fear which eventually lead to us pushing the boundaries by jumping from one roof to another. We found a school which had a flat smooth roof with an alleyway at one end. On the other side of the eight foot wide alley, was some residential garages where the small council estate house dwellers could lock their cars up. The garage roofs (although still dangerously high) were slightly lower than the schools and were also smooth and flat. So we'd skate towards the edge of the school roof at high speed then fly over the width of the footpath and land on the garages roofs. This used to terrify the pedestrians who happened to be walking along beneath us. Where ever the skate craze took us we did it with speed and style. The kids today wouldn't understand the buzz that went with street skating, most of them just go to local skate parks to use the bowls and ramps, whereas we did lots of mileage to try different stunts in other areas. It was very important to have the right equipment; we rode on top of the range skates for the time. Bauer boots, ACS500 trucks, lightweight base plates, precision bearings, Sims Street Snake or Power Bones for wheels, and leg warmers to match. If your skates were a load of shit, you'd be left behind and playing catch up while the rest of us where gliding smoothly and gracefully towards our destination.

SPACE INVADERS

Growing up in south east London was never mundane, there were countless derelict buildings, factory's and deserted run down houses which were great places for my friends and I to investigate and seek adventure. Climbing on our local bus garage roof was an exciting, often hazardous undertaking but that was nothing new. It was a massive building and getting up there required little effort since there were iron service ladders bolted to the walls in strategic locations around the outside of the depot. It would lead to a whole host of other roofs belonging to various shops along

Rye lane, Peckham's principal shopping area. The biggest shop was Jones & Higgins, it was a departmental superstore and sold everything from carpets to Haberdashery, furniture, clothes, electrical equipment, you name it. It was Peckham's answer to Harrods and first opened in 1891. It closed in 1980 and re-opened two days later as the Houndsditch but was still referred to by its original name. We pinched so much lead from that roof and all its skylights I'm surprised it never caved in. I used to pay special attention not to walk under the skylights in the toy and sports section on the top floor whilst walking around with my mother. The inside of Jones and Higgins was also a great play ground, at 11 years old my girlfriend Lorraine and I would hide in amongst the endless hanging rolls of carpet which were stacked on long A shaped frames resembling lofty two birth tents. The carpets were all slightly unrolled providing absolute cover from the staff and shoppers, so while cloaked in concealed darkness we'd steal a few innocent kisses before moving on to another den. One day while playing in Jones & Higgins my friend Gary and I were being pursued by the manager of the toy department, he seemed to spend most of his day chucking out naughty kids. Anyway as we sensed him getting closer from behind us we began dragging our feet on the thick plush blue carpet. Between us we had built up and stored enough static energy to fire up a 100 watt light bulb and when he reached out to grab us by our collars we both touched his hand. He received such a jolt it was like a mini bolt of lightning especially since Gary had touched his metal watch. He winced (more in shock than in pain) while shaking his hand which gave us the head start we needed to get to the exit where we made our getaway pissing ourselves with laughter. Roughly four or five years later when I was about 14/15, another good close friend of mine Patrick Galahan and I burgled Jones and Higgins hoping to pinch a load of space invader toys that were all the rage at the time. I knew getting inside would be easy since the skylights had been relieved of their lead fixtures a few years earlier by my very own grubby little hands. So we slid the glass pain along its runners and dropped straight into the toy department. It was about a 12-foot drop and we never thought about how we were going to get out. We had the whole store to ourselves and plenty of time to get what we wanted, or so we thought. We filled up two carrier bags with space invaders then went down stairs to see what else we could find. After negotiating our way through the hanging chandeliers and lamps in the home section we ended up at the jewellery counter, which was full of watches, Parker pens and lighters. We were about to start filling our bags when we heard the jingle jangle of keys coming from the adjacent department where the carpets were, and a waft of pipe tobacco filled the air.

"Shit it's a security guard, whispered Patrick nervously.

"Fucking hell it's Steptoe let's get out of here, I said pulling his arm.

The security guard was more like a caretaker who would be responsible for minor odd jobs around the building during open hours, and had often tried to throw us out of the shop in the past to no avail since he was quite old and unfit and we would run rings around him. We used to call him Steptoe because he was scruffy and missing a few front teeth. His Pipe was a permanent fixture of his mouth whether lit or un-lit, smoking laws were different in those days and people often smoked while walking around shops.

We legged it back up the stairs towards our entry point and were quite happy to just get out with what we already had. Alarm bells started ringing when to our horror we realised there was no way of getting to the opened skylight seeing as it was in the middle of the room and very high up.

"We're fucked, said Patrick.

I could smell his fear and he could smell mine.

"What are we gonna do now Rick?

"Shhhh, listen," I said as we hid in the dark behind some bikes whilst nervously looking at the doorway waiting for Steptoe to come in. There was no jingle jangle of keys, no sound of heavy footsteps coming up the stairs and no stench of tobacco. Maybe the old goat was more frightened of us than we were of him and had gone to the safety of his basement office to ring the old bill. Patrick, called Pat for short, was about an inch or two shorter than me and carrying a bit more weight around his waist than I was, I remember we were in hysterics one day when I had to roll him around his living room floor to enable him to fasten the top button of his jeans. Although slightly rotund, he was still quite agile and we had both been in a scrap or two so I wasn't too worried about us taking on Steptoe if we had to. On the other hand I knew he would recognise me and that's the last thing I needed while walking around the store with my mother on another day. So with plan B out of the question we had to find a way out as quickly and quietly as possible. I remembered passing a stepladder which was propped up against the wall near one of the chandeliers in the home section down stairs. I suggested to Pat that we should go down and get it given that it was our only hope of getting out. So off we went creeping slowly back down the grand staircase which had been there from the Victorian days. It was oak panelled with hand crafted oak banisters and had old wooden steps which meant that every tip-toed step we took creaked like the knee caps of a group of arthritic pensioners doing squats. It didn't bother us when we had thought we were alone but now it seemed to be amplified and was in danger of grassing us up. So we slid all the way down to the ground floor on the banister. There was no sign of Steptoe and although the waft of pipe tobacco was still lingering in the air the home section was eerily quiet and vacant. Pat and I got either end of the thankfully long stepladder and made our way back up to the skylight not worrying too much about the creaky steps now that we had the ladder and were sure to escape. We opened the ladder which fell about 4 foot short of the opening so still had to work hard to get back out on to the roof. Pat went first and I had to give his podgy arse a shove from half way up the ladder. After passing him the bags I pulled myself out making sure I kicked the ladder away. We then slid the pane of glass back to its original closed position trying to conceal our escape route. As we looked around we noticed about half a dozen police panda cars in the car park with their doors wide open but there was no sign of any coppers even though we could hear the white noise of their CB radios and the odd call of Mike Mike Oscar Bravo. They must have just entered the store to look for us and didn't have a clue we were on top of the building rather than still in it. If it came on top we didn't want to get caught with any evidence, which would give us the excuse that we were only up there climbing around, so we hid our bags in one of the many service cupboards hoping to come back to retrieve them in a week or so when the dust had settled. Luckily I knew every inch of the local elevated geography so Pat followed me as we hastily made our way through and over a labyrinth of dips and curves on the bus garage roof to a metal engineer's ladder attached to the wall at the high street end of the building. We quickly negotiated the thirty or forty foot decent then ran into a nearby housing estate and fell about laughing, more in relief and the realisation at just how close we came to capture. A few weeks later I went back to the spot on the roof where we hid the bags of games only to find they were no longer there.

About five years later we did another job together pinching power tools from a plant hire outfit in Peckham (which I go into with more detail later on in this book) then Pat took it a step to far by getting involved in an armed bank robbery with some crack head Yardie's. He was only there as the lookout on the door and to make sure that nobody tried to be a hero. Although not armed for real he was feigning to have a gun in his coat pocket by making a pistol shape with his hand and fingers. It all went smoothly and if my memory serves me right they walked away with around £25,000. Pat's cut was about £7,000 and he couldn't wait to go around buying expensive gifts for himself and Jane (his missus). Jane was doing her fair share to bring home the bacon too, she was part of a small team of women who used to go up town to a very well known posh department store and steal rich Arab women's handbags which on most occasions proved to be very lucrative. This is how it worked, the leader of the gang who was an attractive glamorous looking 35 year old blonde woman called Angela had a contact deep inside the management of the famous store. The contact would tip Angela off every time a party of super rich Arab wives were due in from one of the middle eastern country's to have a spend up while their Sheik husbands were here on business. Sometimes Angela and Jane would do a sting on their own while the rest of the team were working in another store or department. The wives would usually be carrying a new credit card and the pin number would be written on a separate piece of paper within the same purse. Also in the handbag there would usually be rolls of cash and very expensive jewellery. The women's shoe section had two rows of chairs which were always set out in a back to back fashion and while the wives were trying on shoes they would usually put their bags on the floor. Assumingly the thought of worrying about becoming victims of theft never crossed their minds since it was hardly going to be an issue in the ridiculously lavish world that they had come from. Angela and Jane were also very elegantly dressed as part of their gig. Angela was the "Kicker/slider" and would sit amongst the rich wives and try on some shoes herself while Jane would sit with her back towards them. When the right opportunity came along Angela would kick or slide one of the Arab handbags under the chair towards Jane who would pick the bag up like it was her own and head for the exit. If the gang were three handed then Angela would kick/slide two hand bags under the chairs. It was a low risk sting because there would be at least ten hand bags laying around and the wives were so indulged in chatting and comparing shoes that there was no way on earth they were going to notice one or two missing handbags until they were ready to move on. The Arabs could spend anything up to an hour trying on shoes, after all there was no need for urgency given that they had the whole day to shop which gave Jane and Angela plenty of time to leave the area. The gang didn't just pick on the Arabs since they were fully aware that it wouldn't take long before the store noticed a pattern emerging so they staggered their visits and stung rich American women too. One hand bag could easily net them up to five grand each keeping them happy for a good couple of months. I remember going to a few different cash points with Patrick to draw out as much as he could from the stolen credit cards. It was easy money which contributed towards their new champagne lifestyle. But that all came to an abrupt end when Pat had to go on the run to Ireland after the old bill had arrested his two Yardie accomplices. I remember driving him to Victoria to get a coach that would take him to the ferry port. Jane was in pieces and crying her eyes out since she wouldn't be going with him and was terrified that he would be caught or would have to remain in Ireland for a long time. But after staying with friends in Dublin for a couple of weeks Pat returned to London to lay low at his dads' house near the river Thames. A few months had passed before it was assumed the old bill were not looking for Pat and had probably closed the case since they had successfully prosecuted the two crack heads for 6 counts of armed robbery on various banks and building societies. They both received a 12 stretch for their crimes.

CHAPTER III

INSIDE
FRAGGLE ROCK

L ATER THAT DAY me Terry and a few other convicts were handcuffed and led along another corridor towards the courtyard.

"What Happens now Tel?

"They're gonna load us into the sweat boxes, and we'll be driven to Brixton, It's a right shit hole but we should only be there for a week or two before we get shipped out to another main stay."

The sweatboxes I soon found out, were tiny secure cubicles in the back of a lorry situated either side of a footway in the middle. Like miniature prison cells they were around three feet wide and three foot long and about five foot high with a one way tinted Perspex window, when sitting on the miniature bench type seat, your knees would be pressed up to the front wall. After10 minutes on the road the sweat box began to live up to its name, it was getting hot in there but I couldn't remove my blazer due to her Majesty's bracelets on my wrists. It was pouring down outside and everything looked dull and depressing, worsened by the fact that the small square cubicle window had a dull tint to it. But I would have given anything to be one of the rain sodden people I saw walking freely down the wet and gloomy street. I remember thinking how privileged they were to be at liberty to end up at whatever destination they desired, they were civilians and I was a criminal not fit to be in their company. Despite being handcuffed I managed to light up a fag with some Swan

Vesters that Terry had given me earlier whilst in the tank, and soon learned this was a bad move since there was no escape route for the smoke, so coupled with the overwhelming heat it was an uncomfortable journey to say the least. It wasn't long before we were entering the gates of Brixton prison, known to its inhabitants as hells waiting room. One by one the Kanga's marched us out of the sweatbox and into a processing area, where we were made to strip naked and squat. The squatting was to make sure we weren't smuggling dope up our arses, (known as bottling) and was also a way of humiliating you and letting you know you were no longer a civilian. It was a very degrading experience standing stark bollock naked in front of other prisoners and half a dozen screws. Any ounce of dignity you were still desperately clinging on to disappeared when they took away your name and reduced you to a mere number like how a farmer would stamp a brand number on the arses of his cattle with a piping hot iron.

"Atkinson! Step forward," said the head screw in an authoritative military voice.

"From This point on you are just a number, you will be addressed by this number throughout your sentence, do you understand?

"Yep," I said nodding to him.

"Yes Sir, is the phrase you are looking for," he barked.

"Yes Sir," I shouted back.

"Your number is, W0290, Make sure you remember this number because you will need to use it until you are released, so tell me, what is your number boy?

"W0290 Sir! I answered. One of the other screws put my suit and possessions into a tray and pointed me in the direction of the stores where I picked up my new prison clothes, bed sheets and blanket. After getting dressed in my prison stripes, I was ushered into a large waiting room with other inmates who had come from various other courthouses that day, Terry was chatting to one of the screws just outside the door before he joined me in the holding room.

"Sweet as a nut Rick, I've squared it with the Kanga's so that we can share a Peter,"

"Result," I said feeling strangely optimistic and slightly exited, Terry was so relaxed and cock sure of himself, I imagined this was going to be a giggle and an adventure. It wasn't long before I was brought back down to earth with a bang. Terry and I were escorted to our Peter on the four's, (4th floor) the wing code in all prisons was, if any inmate saw a screw coming on to your wing they would shout out the floor number to warn other inmates of his presence in case they were smoking dope or breaking other rules, for example if the screw is spotted entering the 2nd floor landing, "On the two's! Would be the shout. The ground floor was always known as the ones so the two's would actually be the first floor and the three's would actually be the second floor etc.

"Is this a fucking wind up guvnor? Terry asked the screw in anger.

The screws liked to be referred to as guvnor, probably for empowerment reasons.

"It's only a temporary measure; we've had a big intake today and are over crowded."

"So why can't you put some other mug up here and give us a peter on the three's?"

"Because you two just happened to get the short straw," explained the friendly screw whilst opening the door to our new 12 by 8ft home.

"If any of them lot see us up here they'll fucking carve us up by the morning," complained Terry with a tinge of fear in his voice while pointing down to the lower floors.

"Look, you'll just have to suffer it for a couple of days and I'll do my best to get you moved," the screw said as he locked us in.

"What the fuck was that all about Tel? I thought it would be better up here, less crowded, out of the way."

"Rick mate, they've lumbered us in Fraggle Rock," he said nervously looking out of our peephole to see if anyone was being busy about our new abode.

"What does Fraggle Rock mean?"

"It's Rule 43 where all the mental cases, nonces and grasses get segregated from the rest of the prison population, on the fours is Fraggle Rock no matter what prison you get banged up in, so come dinner time when they let us out to collect our grub, the other prisoners will see us coming down from the fours and think that we are nonces or grasses."

"Great, we're right in Shit Street then," I said as I slumped deflated on to my bunk.

"Do you know what happens to nonces and grasses in here Rick? He then explained about the extra portions of mash, and the special bars of Imperial leather that turned your skin red.

"Have you got any more Fucking good news to tell me?

Silly question, he had loads more good news to share, and for the next couple of hours he clued me up on all the ins and outs of prison politics, and what he didn't tell me I would eventually have to work out for myself, but at least he had given me a head start. Our next mission was to get our food, and get back to our cell without getting carved up or an extra large portion of mash to go with our mushy peas.

"Right, this is the plan, when we get let out to go down and get our dinner I'm gonna have a chat with a couple of bods I know on the two's, I'll clue them up on our situation, and hopefully they will spread the word that we are on a level."

Apparently these blokes he knew were lifers and literally ran our wing, and nothing went down without their say so. We were the only inmates to be let out on the four's since the others (the Fraggles) were let out after the main population were safely locked up in their Peters.

On the outside apart from the odd nights out up the Old Kent, road I use to spend most nights in my local snooker club on Rye lane called Pockets, and had lots of criminal and non-criminal friends in there. There were some real hard cases and plenty a thief would come and sell stolen car radios or whatever they had nicked that day. There was no oxygen circulating since the air was a thick cloud of cannabis, and every half hour or so there was the loud thud of some low life smashing his fist into one of the many robbing bastard fruit machines. Bodies of blokes high or low on drugs would be laying in every orifice available sleeping off whatever they had been taking; half of them just couldn't be bothered to walk home. And every couple of hours a fight would break out over a foul shot on the green baize or someone sharking the one arm bandits, so I'd seen and been in plenty of ugly situations, but nothing could have prepared me for what was to come in the following 15 minutes.

HELLS WAITING ROOM

On our way down the main staircase from Fraggle Rock every fucker in the block was screwing us out, and as we reached the second landing Terry peeled off and disappeared into one of the cells leaving me to make my own way down to the ground floor. I was getting daggers from every angle and felt like a Rapist walking along death row towards the chair. After what seemed like half an hour to reach the ones, I can't begin to explain the feelings of dread about my immediate future that were going through my head. I had my prison issue blue plastic plate, cup and plastic knife and fork in my hands, and couldn't cover my mouth as I let out a nervous cough while negotiating the last flight of steps with my now jellified legs. Just then I heard a deep voice with a Jamaican accent growling from behind me,

"Oi, white boy, Stop, Coughing your Fucking germs all over the place," I looked round to see a Mike Tyson look-alike flanked by 3 or 4 other ferocious looking black guys bearing their gold teeth like rabid dogs.

"Sorry mate," I said with a whimper while refocusing on the last few steps to the safety of the ground level where there were about five or six screws.

"You Fucking will be, and I aint ya fucking mate you CUNT!" he snarled as I tried to remain as insignificant as possible while joining the cue to the bay-marines. He did have a point, although could have been a bit more amicable about it, (had we been in a Samaritans seminar). Not wanting to cause any more friction by mistakenly coughing over their food I stepped back and gestured that he and his pack of wolves could have right of way in the dinner queue, and they promptly barged in front of me. I'd sooner have them ahead of me rather than behind me. I took a rain check on the mashed potato and nodded to the guy serving up the sausage and beans, after pouring tea into my cup from the tea urn I grabbed two slices of bread, and an apple, then made my way back to our cell keeping my eyes down whilst trying not to cough. The sausage and beans were cold and you could almost pick the whole lot off your plate like a slice of pizza since they were welded together after being on the hotplate for so long. By now although relieved at getting back to the Peter without further confrontation I had lost my appetite, boycotting the bean supreme I lit up a fag and sat on my bunk drinking my sugarless tea while trying to remain calm as I took it all in. Our Peter had a bucket for a toilet, which we would have to share and slop out every morning, a bedside cabinet, and a 1-foot square glass window secured within 4 vertical iron bars. The beds were either side of each other instead of the usual bunk bed style, and consisted of a flimsy metal sprung frame and a wafer thin mattress that had seen better days. Terry soon arrived with his dinner giving me a quick wink while nodding his head back at an angle to let me know we had company. A Kanga poked his head in the door.

"Bon appetite," he said grinning sarcastically, and then slammed the door shut before locking us in for the night, simultaneously we both gave him the middle fingered salute.

"What did your mates say Tel, how did it go? I was anxious to find out if our predicament was going to improve. Terry cheered me right up when he smiled and said,

"Sweet as a nut mate, I had a good chat with them and explained the situation, luckily they both remembered me from when I did a two month stretch here on remand last year, so don't worry Rick by the time we go down for breakfast the rest of the inmates will be in the loop, and anyway no one would try to make a move on us without them two knowing about it."

As you may have gathered Terry was always in and out of prison, he was a thief with a heroin habit and was doing time for handling stolen goods. He was looking rougher than he did the last time I saw him on the out. I didn't know just how ill he was until he started pissing blood in the bucket, maybe he'd been given extra portions of mash at some point while doing bird, whatever the reason he didn't appear to be too worried about it. I grabbed a half-ounce lump of Old Holborn from my pouch and said,

"Here you are Tel; stick that in your tin,"

"Don't be silly Rick, You've only had a couple of mine, and you're gonna need that,"

"Take it Tel, Fuck knows what I would have done if you weren't here,"

"I'll tell you what, I'll have this bit," he said splitting the half-ounce lump into two halves,

"And you put that bit back in your pouch, listen mate you're a Peckham bod, and you will probably bump into plenty of other geezers from our manor as you get moved around and you will learn we all watch each other's backs, unless you are one of the cunts from Fraggle Rock."

Still feeling somewhat shaken up about the coughing incident on the stairs I laid down on my bed and lit up a normal cigarette hoping it would help calm me down, compared to the matchstick size roll ups we'd been smoking all day it felt like I was smoking a cigar. We sat there chatting for about an hour while smoking my fags and drinking tea that we had been given from the nightly tea round. All the excitement and tension of the day had tired us out so it wasn't long before we got our heads down and went to sleep.

I must have woken up on the hour every hour hoping to be in my bedroom and getting a reassuring and forgiving lick on the nose by my loyal dog Ben who would always curl up next to me on our sofa bed at home. But all I would see was the sinister shadow of the cold iron bars encaging the cell, cast by the ever vigilant exterior flood lights that were never off guard. The occasional distant screams would echo around the prison corridors steering your thoughts into wondering what they were screaming about, were they just mad or were they being tortured. It was easy to imagine all sorts of twisted scenarios whilst acclimatizing to your new environment.

The next few days had passed by without drama, I followed Terry's lead by making sure we kept the friendly screw on side since he was giving us first go on his newspaper once he'd finished with it. One late evening whilst sitting in our cell Terry was in the middle of teaching me how to split matches with the razor blade of an old prison issue Bic when we heard the sound of Blakied footsteps and the jingle jangle of a bunch of keys approaching our cell door. Terry raised an eyebrow as our door was being unlocked since it was outside any normal activity schedules. The door swung open, it was the friendly screw, he stuck his head in the door and announced,

"Right lads pack your shit up you're being re-located first thing in the morning"

"About Fucking time guvnor, where are we going, on the two's or the three's? Asked a relieved Terry.

"Not quite, you are going back to the Vill, (another slang name for Pentenville) and he's getting shipped out to Wandsworth" (a.k.a. Wanno).

"How come we are getting out of here so soon? asked Terry. It usually took a few weeks sometimes months before they processed the short term inmates and shipped them out.

"There's nowhere else to put you and we can't keep you up here for a week, it's against our safety policy, so your cases got rushed through, replied the kanga.

"Nice one guvnor, you're a diamond," said Terry. The kanga left locking the door behind him, Terry looked at me holding his index finger on his lips saying shhhh as he waited for the sound of keys and blakey's to disappear into the distance. As soon as we heard the gate at the end of our landing creek open and shut Terry produced a folded up piece of paper from his crotch inside his trousers, and unravelled a layer of silver foil and a brown substance, (smack). He rolled the paper into straw stuck it in his mouth and began heating up the smack on the foil from underneath with one of his Swan Vester matches. Within seconds the smack was liquefied and he began chasing the liquid over the foil with his straw sucking up the fumes at the same time, (a.k.a. chasing the dragon).

"That kanga is the only decent one I know," he said while slowly exhaling a lung full of heroin smoke.

"Yeah he seemed alright, "I answered edging further back on my bed so as not to breathe in any of the fumes.

"I got this bit of brown from a mate on the three's, I did bird with him at the Vill before he got moved here for cutting some cunt." Terry said before chasing more smack around the foil.

"He sounds like a proper charmer," I added sarcastically.

"He's as good as a gold mate, the geezer he cut up was a Nonce pretending he was doing bird for robbery, but someone recognised him from his time on rule 43 in another nick, so he had it coming to him anyway."

"Great, with all these nut cases floating about my future is looking rosier by the minute, so what's Wandsworth nick like, have you ever been there?

"Yeah mate, I did a stretch there about 3 years ago, it's better than this place but the Vill is my favourite, the scrubs (Wormwood Scrubs prison) aint bad either."

"Don't worry Rick, you'll probably do a month or two in Wanno and then you'll get shipped out to a D cat." Said Terry as he inhaled the last suck of fumes from the now empty piece of foil. His speech began to slow down, his eyes were half-mast and his pupils had shrunk to the size of a full stop. He rolled the foil into a tiny ball and flicked it out of the window through the iron grills. D cat meant category (d) which would be much more laid back in terms of how secure the prison and it's regime was. So a D cat was an open nick for non violent short termers.

"D cat is like an 'olliday camp, as soon as you get to Wanno ask for an application form for a transfer to an open prison and when you fill out your application form write down Stanford Hill or Ford as your first choice, it's a fucking piece of cake at ford,"

Those were Terry's last words before he let out a big sigh and fell back on to his pillow. I rolled up a fag and sat there for about an hour trying to take everything in, even though Terry had been a great help and an asset to have around I was still finding it hard to acclimatize to life behind bars. I still hadn't mentally let go of the outside and before I could get settled in we were being moved on, and to make matters worse I wouldn't be able to rely on Terry anymore and would have to start learning to stand on my own two feet.

OUT
TRACKS OF MY TEARS

A year before my arrest I had been living with my then girlfriend Maria Bosco, her 5 year old son Jason and our 6 month old puppy Ben. Maria and I got together shortly after I had been dumped by my long time girlfriend Lorraine. We were both separately invited to the same party and knew each other vaguely from the past. She was very pretty with blue eyes and natural blonde hair. I was quite a bit taller than her and a year younger. From the moment I clapped eyes on her I knew I had to make a play for her, she was an incredibly energetic dancer and every tiny movement she made just oozed sexiness. The way she flicked her hair, and the seductive way she tilted her head showing her kissable neck sent a rush all over my body, and to my delight she was just as attracted to me as I was to her and we flirted and danced around each other all night. After the party had finished in the early hours of the morning it was time to go home, just as I was preparing to leave Maria asked if I would like to go over to her place later that day to share a bottle of wine. Thrilled at her invitation I accepted and went home with a spring of jubilation in my step. That evening I arrived at her flat which was situated right next door to a pub in another part of Peckham, Maria opened the door looking a million dollars and showed me into the living room which was minimally furnished and spotlessly clean. There was music playing softly in the background as I made myself comfortable on her sofa while she poured two tall glasses of wine. We laughed and giggled as the wine kept flowing, the music which was a compilation of sixties, seventies and eighties love songs added to the ambience. Being in Maria's company felt like the most natural thing in the world and I was already falling in love with her. The merrier we got, the more touchy feely we became with each other and soon slipped into an amorous clinch. After each pause for a sip of wine the clinches grew to be more erotic, our hands were all over each other, and devoid of sexual apprehension our inhibitions were now lying at the bottom of the empty wine glasses. I slid my hand inside the top of her low cut red dress and brushed my fingers over her silky perfectly formed breasts. Her pert nipples welcomed every tender stroke with anticipation. That first touch of her bosoms sent waves of arousal straight to my erogenous zones, which also became apparent to Maria's investigative hands as she unzipped my flies and released the top button of my jeans freeing my throbbing pride from its clothed restraints. Feeling the grip of her cold sensual hand as it moved gently up and down was sending me wild with desire. I moved my hand down to her now wide open legs caressing the top of her thighs before running my fingers along her knicker line making her quiver whilst letting out a cute intake of breath. With that Maria took me by the hand and led me down the hall to her bedroom where we tore each other's clothes off and made love over and over again, I was even more turned on after finding out that she liked to take control when she straddled me, pinned my arms behind my head, and started to thrust herself up and down slamming her firm bum cheeks into my lap. While sliding up and down with a lubricious rhythm she kept teasing me by lowering her boobs so that her nipples were an inch away from my mouth, occasionally allowing my eager lips to make the briefest of contact before pulling away, She did this again and again until we both exploded with orgasmic pleasure. After an hour or so of lusty passion we laid cuddling in bed while listening to the compilation of love songs from earlier, taking turns to get up and turn the cassette tape over. Maria had borrowed the tape entitled, Tracks of my Tears, earlier that day from the library and the songs became part of the love bond that was growing rapidly between us. We repeated that night for the next four or five days, the wine the music and the erotic passion. I was under her spell and completely in love. We made copies of the tape before returning it to the library. At the end of the week Maria's young son Jason was due home from his dads, it was the summer holidays and he had been staying with his father's family for a fortnight. He didn't take too kindly to his mum's new boyfriend and rebelled by kicking me in the shins every now and then. I soon won his respect after a few days of paying him plenty of attention and would spend time with him in the swing park right next door to their flat. In a short space of time I moved in with them both and things were really good for a while. Maria's dad had a four month old puppy called Ben who was a German Shepherd crossed with a Border Collie, he wanted to get rid of the dog after falling ill and could no longer take care of him so we were more than happy to take him on. When Ben was about a year old and much bigger, I used to take him and Jason down to the play park and I invented the lion game. Jason (who was still only about 5 yrs old) and I would call Ben and then we'd run to the nearest obstacle to escape the chasing lion (Ben). I would always make sure we nearly got caught as we scrambled onto the slide or roundabout, causing Jason to scream with excitement, and Ben was always true to his role as the fierce lion whilst relentlessly pursuing us all around the park. I always took Jason on adventures inventing other imaginary scenarios as we played sword fencing made from sticks we found along the way, pretending we were fighting off imaginary enemies whilst riding on our magic invisible flying horses. Jason had more respect for his sword/stick and other stuff I made for him, than he did for any of the expensive toys that lay scattered around his bedroom. His sword took pride of place in his toy cupboard. I think our relationship worked because I was still a child at heart and had just as much fun as he did while playing our games. Mine and Maria's partnership went from strength to strength and we were very comfortable together for a long time. We would always fall asleep listening to the same love songs until the day we watched Dirty Dancing together, we were crazy about the songs from that movie so we bought the sound tracks. I became Johnny and Maria became Baby which injected fresh passion into our nightly goings on. We were having the time of our lives until the day we decided to dabble in smoking Wacky Backy for a laugh. At first it was all fun, we enjoyed giggling all night and it added a new zest to our love making. But after a few months the dreaded Paranoia started to rear its ugly head and our daily lives became strained.

LEATHAL LEATHER

I'd just been given the sack from a big leather company where I had been working for about six months. They imported leather skins from an Italian Tannery and sold them to the copious leather and suede coat manufacturer's who had hundreds of retail shops spread around the Brick and Petty coat lane area of the east end. It was a very busy concern also feeding other suppliers in London and Essex. The company and the rather large building were owned by an elderly very affluent Jewish chap who was referred to as "the old man". There were many staff including the main sales manager who was also the hirer and firer. He was as smooth character in his fifties and claimed to be half Italian and half Turkish and like a typical salesman he had the gift of the gab. Anyway he fired me after I got caught and arrested by the old bill leaving a cannabis outlet whilst purchasing an eighth for his son. Little did he know that along with himself and one of the other salesmen, my mate Tim, I had been earning a substantial amount of money selling skins on the sly to one of our biggest customers. The skins were wrapped up in large cigar shaped bundles tied at each end with ribbon and came in boxes of 12. I was the only delivery driver on the firm and would sneak 6 or 7 extra bundles of leather on to the van and drop them off to the buyer at a much reduced price netting me around £500 quid per trip. The company were turning over about half a million pounds of leather a week and stock checks were rarely taken since the manager was up to his neck in dodgy deals and it wasn't in his interest to order a stock check. Tim, who had got me the job after the last driver left, was a few years older than me and we had known each other for about 8 or 9 years. Like the manager he was also of mixed race, half English and half Indian but spoke with a proper cockney accent, he was slightly shorter than me and built like Bruce Lee. Tim didn't have any idea that I was stealing leather, I had no idea he was stealing leather, the manager had no idea we were stealing leather and Tim and I had no idea the manager was stealing leather. The only one who knew anything was the dodgy customer who was buying it from all three of us. Although on the odd occasion I did find it suspicious after delivering a "legitimate" order, and was instructed to collect a sealed brown envelope and give it directly to the manager, mainly on the old man's day off. My weekly wage was a measly £90 after deductions and since I seemed to be the only person doing any hard work, earning an extra monkey a week in perks sat ok with my conscience. Strangely enough no one asked any questions when I started turning up in the staff car park with a sports car, a Lancia Beta two litre coupe. In fact the whole company car park was like a show room for sporty motors. There were Porsche's, top of the range BMW's, a Rolls Royce, a Mercedes, and Tim's RS 2000, among others. Everyone must have been on the take at the old man's expense, but there was so much stock coming in and going out each week it would have been nigh on impossible to keep track. One Friday morning after four days anxiously trying to sneak my usual £500 worth of leather out of the building, I had to resort to desperate measures since oddly Tim had been helping me to load the van for most of the week. I took six bundles of skins into the toilet in order to drop them out of the window knowing they would land in a concealed unused pathway at the back of the building close to the staff car park, giving me the chance to pick them up when the coast was clear and load them into my car if necessary. I was horrified when I realised the bundles were too big to slip through the security bars just outside the window, especially since a queue was beginning to form outside the toilet door. There was no feasible excuse for me to be in the toilet with bundles of leather and I was put under more pressure when the manager, the old man, and Tim began knocking on the door complaining about the time I was taking.

"Hang on I'm having a shit, I had a dodgy curry last night," I pleaded, hoping to buy myself some sympathetic time. I quickly worked out that the only way I was going to have a chance of getting them through the bars was to un-wrap the skins and re-roll them into 12 smaller bundles, so in a frenzy I began unravelling and re-tying until I had twelve thinner rolls of leather. By now the queue of colleagues outside were losing their patience and started complaining ardently since 10 long minutes had passed and my duration in the carsey was in danger of appearing very suspicious, to make matters worse, uncharacteristically there was going to be no stench of a dodgy curried shit lingering in the air.

My next problem was trying to disguise the loud thud of the bundles landing 3 stories below into the narrow alley, so whilst trying my hardest to at least muster up a smelly fart I began loudly reassuring my colleagues that I was nearly finished as I frantically pushed the rolls of leather through the bars, upping the volume on each predicted thud. Finally fifteen minutes later after all 12 rolls were lying in the gutter it was safe for me to vacate the toilet.

"About bloody time, what have you been doing in there? Groaned the angry queue collectively.

"I wouldn't go in there without a gas mask," I joked while feigning a gut ache. Luckily the old man was first in and believe me, his shit did stink. The Toilet episode was too close for comfort, in my greedy desperation to make sure I went home with my weekly perk I got sloppy and nearly ended up blowing my whole operation.

Every fortnight we would unload close to a million pounds worth of stock from the delivery truck which would park right outside the main entrance to the building. A friend of mine from Peckham who I had previously shared this information with, approached me with an offer. He had connections to a well known underworld family who liked to capitalise on robberies when they had someone with inside knowledge of how the setup worked.

He explained that a gang would show up just as the lorry arrived, they would wait until the driver and his mate jumped onto the back of the lorry preparing to unload, two of the tooled up gang would climb in the back with them, tie them up and blindfold them, then give the keys to one of their men who would lock the four of them in the back and drive the truck to a designated spot where they would unload the goods onto their own smaller lorries. All they wanted from me was to make myself busy somewhere else when it kicked off and make sure that none of the other staff would be there to foil there plan. They also wanted to know the build, names, and character of the two drivers, and what time they usually arrived. For my small part I was to receive £30,000. I agreed and wrote down all the information they would need after he assured me the drivers would be un-harmed. A week later my friend phoned me to confirm it was on, and was going to take place the following Wednesday, our usual delivery day.

I arrived for work on the day of the planned robbery feeling nervous but excited at the prospect of getting thirty grand and spent half of the morning in and out of the toilet unloading what felt like a volcano brewing up in my back passage. The delivery was expected at one o'clock as always, I tried hard not to arouse suspicion whilst constantly looking out of the window hoping to see the lorry pulling up in order to carry out my part of the plan. Right on schedule I spotted the truck turning into the far end of the street and was a minute away from parking outside. Our company was based on the 3rd floor above two other companies on the floors below. The building had a goods lift that everyone used rather than walking the many stairs to get up and down. I quickly walked down to the second floor landing and jammed the lift door with a simple trick I had learned in the past. By placing a folded up piece of cardboard under the door mechanism which sat above the outer meshed gate, the lift would think the safety gate was open and would cease to function. This would buy me at least three or four minutes before anyone thinking of going down realised the lift wasn't working. I walked down the three flights of stairs to the first floor and looked out of the small window in order to monitor the robbery from a safe distance and not get seen by the driver, giving me the option to play dumb and use the excuse that I was on my way down when it all happened.

I saw the driver and co-pilot get out of the cab and make their way to the back of the lorry; here we go I thought as they opened the big swinging doors. I was shaking and my breathing became decreasingly shallow while anticipating the events that were about to unfold. My eyes were darting all over the place covering every angle of the view through the now steamed up stair case window. A couple of minutes had gone by and still no action, I could just about hear the shuffling of boxes on the back of the truck and the odd giggle of banter between the two drivers. Instead of sheer chaos and commotion there was calm and tranquillity, the main driver appeared at the rear of the truck simultaneously checking his watch and looking up at the third floor window wondering why no one had come down yet. By now they had been there for at least ten minutes and it was at the point where if I didn't show my face it would have looked odd, so I removed the card board from the lift door and made my way down to greet them.

"Fucking hell, where have you been? "We've been here for half hour," moaned the driver exaggeratingly.

"Sorry mate, we've been having problems with the lift again."

"Come on then let's get a move on, I want to get home to night, and where is Tim, picking his nose and sitting around doing nothing I suppose?

"One sec I'll give him a shout," I walked back to the lift feeling slightly relieved since I was close to having a heart attack, but also gutted that I wasn't going to get my thirty grand realising the gang had obviously pulled out.

Tim came down and for the next hour and a half we unloaded the lorry without a hitch and sent them on their way. That evening I phoned my friend to find out why the gang never showed up, he was just as surprised as me and said he would make a few phone calls then let me know. The next day we were expecting a delivery of French leather from a separate transport company who used to deliver once every couple of months since the French skins were not as sort after as the Italian variety we usually sold. The consignment was worth about fifty grand and consisted of 30 or so boxes. Each box was about the size of an old fashioned treasure chest and required 2 people to carry. The Lorry had already parked by the time I got to the ground floor of the building where I was met by two hefty aggressive looking blokes. One of them blocked my exit to the door and with a hostile tone he asked,

"Are you Rikki?

"Yeah," I answered, wondering how he knew my name.

He took out a fifty pound note and shoved it in the top pocket of my shirt, then giving me a couple of light but significant slaps to the face he said.

"Fuck off over the cafe and get yourself some breakfast for half an hour, we are unloading your lorry." I stood there for a second in complete shock trying to gather my composure and understand what was going on since this was all out off the blue and wasn't the original plan. The other bloke confirmed I needed to fuck off without delay by pulling out a flick knife and growling, "It's the cafe or the fucking basement, what's it to be?

"The cafe," I croaked as I promptly walked passed them without a backwards glance. As I exited the building onto the street the driver must have already been on the back of the truck since the back doors were open and I noticed 3 blokes were already unloading the heavy boxes onto a large sack barrow. Whilst having a cardiac arrest on my way across the road towards the cafe I remember thinking that the gang must have done a recce on the building, how else would the knifeman have known that the descending two flights of stairs from the ground floor led down to a dark and creepy cul-de-sac, an abyss absent of any life or existence? Still in a state of confused panic I ordered 3 smoked salmon bagels and a crusty cheese roll from the ever cheerful Greek chap in the bakers whilst trying to appear relaxed and unfazed. Even though my mind along with my heart was doing somersaults I still managed to come up with a self-preserving plan in a short space of time. Every day at lunch time I was usually sent out to get fresh filled bagels for the manager, the old man, and Tim. I was hoping that if I turned up with the food, (which I often did without prompting), my colleagues would have little reason to doubt me when I explained that the shop was very busy and I got held up in the queue, totally unaware of the events occurring outside our firm. Whilst waiting for the food and watching the events unfold across the road I was trying to work out why they had chosen the French lorry as their target since the value and quantity of leather was miniscule compared to the amount they would have gained from yesterday's delivery. They knew my name, so surly they must have been the same gang my pal had connections to and not just some thieving opportunists. If they got away with all 30 odd boxes, the black market value would have been around twenty five grand. Split five ways would be £5,000 a head so there was no way they were going to look after me. It quickly dorned on me that the Bull's Eye in my top pocket was more than likely all I was going to get out of this, and I, being the middle-man was now taken right out of the equation. I started to feel quite annoyed at being threatened with a knife and the fact they were more than likely prepared to stab me leaving me dead or fighting for life in the desolate murky basement, all for fifty quid. In a brief moment of stupidity fuelled by my new feelings of resentment I even contemplated putting the mockers on their venture but soon came to my senses when I weighed up the pro's and con's. I had a crisp bully in my pocket and more than enough money at home amassed from my weekly perks. There was no need to be greedy, besides I was quite impressed at their bravery and the brass neck way they went about their work. I left the bakery with a carrier bag full of food and drinks and ambled slowly back over towards the truck but staying at a safe enough distance to monitor the situation. I noticed Tim pacing up and down the street with one of the office cordless phones pressed firmly to his ear. He was talking to who I assumed was the old bill since he was waving his free hand about as though mimicking the information relayed to him by the driver. The driver was on the other phone obviously talking to his bosses. He was noticeably very shaken up, his hands were trembling and was lobster red in the face.

"What's going on? I asked on approaching the scene.

"We've been robbed," replied Tim,

"I knew there was something iffy about them bastards," grunted the now vexed driver.

The robbers who were pretending to be members of our staff told him that the boxes had to be loaded straight onto our truck since they had been pre ordered and were going to be delivered direct to various clients throughout the day. The driver had only ever been to our premises on one previous occasion so had no reason to disbelieve them. But after disappearing around the corner with the third trolley load of boxes the driver did begin to get suspicious and soon came to the conclusion something dodgy was afoot. He went round the corner to see where they were taking the boxes and found the men acting very shifty whilst loading the goods onto a white Luton van, so he decided to go up to our office to determine if everything was all above board. As soon as the gang realised he had gone into the building they made the decision to abort. Not wanting to get caught red handed with the goods the robbers obviously elected to leave the leather behind, and dragged their stolen cargo from the back of the van leaving the 6 or 7 boxes strewn across the street and pavement as they sped off. So in total they got away with sweet F A and ended up fifty quid out of pocket. The police turned up 15 minutes later, after taking a statement from the truck driver they began asking Tim and I if we had witnessed any of the robbery. I kept a cool head while explaining I'd been buying bagels in the busy bakers and the first thing I knew about anything was when I saw Tim outside our firm.

The only evidence the police had was the vague descriptions of the gang given to them by the driver, and the sack barrow they had left behind. I'm pretty sure the old bill never did find the culprits since a few months down the line we were told they found no telling finger prints from the trolley and were no nearer solving the case. My mate who started this whole thing played dumb under my questioning and was adamant it had nothing to do with his contacts. I knew he was covering his and their backs so I never mentioned it again. About a year later after Tim was no longer working at the company either. we were having a drink down our local when I confessed to him that I used to steal leather on a weekly basis. I gave him a cocky smile thinking he would be shocked at my confession, but he looked me in the eye and as cool as you like he said. "How do you think I paid for my house? His retort left me stunned, apparently he had been stealing at least a thousand pounds worth of leather every week for the last year and a half, then he told me the manager was stealing even more than him. We laughed when we realised we'd been both selling to the same guy. I never let on about my part in the attempted robbery though, because although Tim was a mate he was also a slippery fucker and couldn't be trusted with such sensitive information.

DE JA VOUS

My brother John had been head hunted by a bloke called Bob who was about to open a new Pie & Mash shop in Sydenham South east London, and although he had friends in the trade Bob didn't have the first Idea about the pie & mash game, but he knew there was money to be made since it was a very popular cheap meal. John had a bit of a reputation for his pie making abilities and was also very knowledgeable about all the other ins and outs to do with running a pie & mash shop, John suggested that he employ me too since I'd had plenty of experience myself, so he did. Along with Bobs two sons Robert and Dave John would make the pies and prepare all the other ingredients for the day. They would start about six o'clock in the morning and I would start at 10 o'clock and begin serving up the food at 11.am. The shop layout was no different to your run of the mill cafe, the only difference was we had a set menu of pie and mash. The attraction to pie and mash was in the secret recipe of pies with minced lamb being the main ingredient. The liquor was also a key factor in the overall package and also had a secret recipe of its own. Traditionally the liquor was made from the water that the stewed eels were boiled in, then some parsley was added along with one or two spices which I will not divulge, in more modern times some flour was added to thicken the texture making it more like a sauce. We also sold jellied or stewed eels which were normally only consumed by customers over sixty years old since pie and mash and eels were a cheap meal for Londoners during the war. The origins of pie and mash can be traced back to the 18th century with its roots firmly stuck in the East end of London. Early pie and mash was very much different to the dishes we enjoy today, the first pies were filled with eels as these were cheap and plentiful and caught right from the river Thames. I had to take two buses to get to work and after getting off the second bus at Cobbs Corner I would have a 15 minute walk along the high street.

During this period the ambulance service were on strike and there were groups of paramedics protesting outside their depot on the high street. A few of them were holding collection buckets and shaking them up and down so the loud jingle of the coins wouldn't fail to grab people's attention, they held placards with something along the lines of WE ARE UNPAID PLEASE HELP WITH A DONATION: written on them. I used to chuck a few bob in their bucket every day on my way in. One morning, just 20 yards after passing their depot I looked across the street where the start of another road lead off from it. As I read the sign with the road name on it (Hazel Grove) I suddenly stopped dead and came over with a strong sense of de ja vous which sent me into a trance like state. Whilst in this state I saw a vision, there were five blokes all leaning over a railing which I can only describe as like the Iron railings you get on the pavement of a busy main road or pedestrian crossing, only this railing was inside a building and had a type of landing just above the five lads heads, a bit like the landing on certain blocks of flats. The dimly lit vision would then start to come towards me in a camera zoom like fashion, and as it neared, the four lads either side of the bloke in the centre would slow up and fade away leaving the one in the middle to become prominent with all attention on him. During this episode I would get a very intense feeling of connection with him, like a strong brotherly love and I felt I knew him, but the closer he came towards me the more blurred and unfocused the image would become. At this point the vision faded away and I automatically snapped out of the trance and carried on walking to work. I just put it down to tiredness and thought nothing more of it. Word had got around and we had quite a reputation for our pies so come lunchtime the queue was already very long and I was busy cheerfully serving up food to the hungry customers when out of the blue I went into a trance again. It was exactly the same experience that had happened that very morning, I found myself desperately trying to recognise the face of the man in the middle as it zoomed in towards me. As I became aware of coming out of a trance I found myself standing there staring through the next customer and off into the distance with a plate in one hand and a mash potato scoop in the other. "You ok mate? Asked the first 2 or 3 baffled and concerned queuers. "Yeah, sorry about that, two pie and single mash weren't it? I asked the man in the front of the queue vaguely remembering the order. "Yes mate that's right, and loads of liquor please, are you sure you are ok, you were miles away?

"Yeah yeah, I'm fine, how long was I like that then? I asked him, I was still confused myself as to what was going on. "About 30 seconds," he said.

I gave him his plate of food took his money and carried on serving as usual and the rest of the day went by without any dramas. I mentioned my two strange trances to Maria and we laughed whilst trying to predict what the queue of people must have been thinking while I just stood there like a zombie staring into the oblivion. The very next morning I chucked my customary few bob into the jingling buckets of the striking ambulance personnel and headed for work. This is where it started to get weird, at exactly the same spot I looked over at Hazel grove then came over with that de ja vous trance like feeling followed by the five men vision. Again they were leaning over a railing and looking directly at me, no matter how hard I tried I could not put a name to the face of the guy in the middle as he zoomed into a blur before fading away. After three or four days of repetitive morning and lunch time trances I started to take notes down of times and made descriptions of the recurring vision, I also noted how it made me feel during the episode. As each day went by it seemed like I was getting nearer and nearer to recognising the face, the feeling of connection to him had grown stronger. During this period my 21st birthday had come and gone, life went on as normal apart from these two particular times in the day and I was starting to think there was something seriously wrong with my head, or something was trying to give me a message about the guy in the vision, if I could only bloody work out who he was! This all went on for around two-three weeks until one late night around 2.am approx, I remember sitting bolt upright in bed, the otherwise pitch black dark room was lit up with what appeared to be three bright lights shining straight in my eyes. I came over with a very strong sensation of de ja vous followed by the vision which seemed to be more intense and pressing than ever before. The very next thing I remember was coming slowly back to consciousness on the floor next to our bed, I felt an uncomfortable pain in my mouth and as I started to open my very painful eyes I saw blurry green coloured silhouettes of people and heard the muffled sounds of voices and white noise from radio's which grew louder and clearer as I started to regain my senses.

It was morning and the sun was coming through the window, I started to freak out when I noticed I was surrounded by a load of blokes dressed in army fatigues one of which was holding the end of a metal instrument that was wedged deep into my throat and making me gurgle as I desperately pleaded to know what was going on. After removing a spoon from my mouth the soldier began to ask me questions, "Do you know what your name is? "Rikki," I answered nervously, I looked round to see Maria sitting on the bed who had just started stroking her fingers through my hair, "what happened to me, what's going on, why are you here?

"Can you tell me what year it is? Asked the soldier whilst shining his pen type torch into my eyes. "1990, Maria what the fuck is going on? I demanded.

"You've had a fit babe, you were having really bad convulsions, your eyes rolled to the back of your head so violently I couldn't even see the whites of your eyes," Maria said with concern in her voice. Still confused and in shock I asked, "what's the bloody army doing here then?

"We are filling in for the ambulance service while they are on strike, how old are you Rikki?

"21, what do you mean I had a fit, I'm not epileptic, I don't suffer from fits."

"Well you were convulsing violently when we turned up so I had to use the spoon to stop you swallowing your tongue," said the soldier who was obviously a trained medic. Apparently He took over spoon duties from Maria's brother Pete who lived in the flat below us with his missus and their two kids. Whilst having a fit on the bedroom floor I was making so much noise that Pete thought we were having a fight, and after hearing Maria screaming "Rikki!!! He came running up to find out what was occurring and on noticing my predicament he immediately knew I was in danger of swallowing my tongue and choking. "We are going to take you to Kings College A&E now Rikki." It was at that point I realised that I was already lying on a military stretcher and the soldiers secured the safety straps around my arms waist and legs before carrying me off down the stairs and out of the building and onto the street where there were three army trucks one being a small army ambulance. At the hospital they wired me up to various monitors and machines and I spent most of the day on a bed in the corridors of A&E before the doctors deemed me well enough to go home. I had been given an appointment to return for an ECG brain scan to check for any abnormalities like epilepsy. Back at home I had my first chance to look in the mirror my eyes were severely bloodshot and the skin under my eyes had thick red blotches caused by the trauma from my eyes rolling back so aggressively.

A few weeks later I went back to hospital to have my brain scan where they attached about 30 or 40 probes to my head and chest. They asked me some simple questions and before long the test was over. I waited in the waiting room for the specialist to give me the results, three crosswords and a Whizzer and Chips later (about an hour) I was called back into the surgery. "Have a seat Mr Atkinson, when you are comfortable I will read you your results," said the specialist who sounded a bit too serious which put me right on edge since that statement usually preceded bad news, "There is absolutely nothing wrong with you, the results of your brain scan have given us no reason to be concerned."

"So I don't have epilepsy then doc? I asked, now feeling much more optimistic.

"No, you have perfectly normal brain activity.

"Why did I have a fit with severe convulsions then, any Idea?

"It must have been a one off fit, I have no explanation, sorry." I left the hospital with mixed feelings, on one hand I was happy that I wasn't suffering from a serious illness and had been given a clean bill of health, on the other hand I was still no nearer knowing why I had had such a violent fit in the first place and whether or not it would ever happen again? Well it never did, I stopped having de ja vous and recurring visions and stopped working at the pie & mash shop too. My mother sent my brother John and I on an all expenses paid trip to Italy to help me get over the trauma since she was convinced it was caused by stress and was very worried about the state of my health. We had a good couple of weeks away staying in Venice, Padova, Bologna and Crespilano. It wasn't long before the whole episode was firmly behind me and life went on as per usual.

THE ROCKY ROAD TO CAPTURE

In 1989 my brother and I were keen to get our feet on the booming property ladder, it was at the start of the buy and sell quick era and people were making money hand over fist. Our plan was to purchase a property with a mortgage, let the rooms out, then sit and wait for a year or two for the value to increase by at least twenty five to thirty thousand pounds, and then sell making a quick profit and move on to another property. The mortgage was going to be paid by the rent received from our tenants. We had an offer from an old friend who had converted his family home into two flats after moving into another house he owned. He had already sold the ground floor flat and was looking for a buyer for the flat above. At £64,000 it was £10,000 below the going rate so we decided the flat would be an ideal start to our venture. At the time I was earning a pittance working nights at my local snooker club and my brother was still making pies in the pie and mash shop so we were earning far too little to get a mortgage the conventional way. So with a dodgy mortgage broker and a written affidavit from the seller stating that we had given him a £10,000 deposit we were soon granted a mortgage by one of the high street banks. The flat consisted of two double rooms and a box room, an average size kitchen, a bathroom and separate toilet. After furnishing the three rooms it wasn't long before we had rent paying tenants occupying all three rooms. We mounted a pay phone on the communal hall wall which made us an extra tenner a week, so along with the rent we were able to cover the mortgage with a few bob to spare. By 1990 Although still living with Maria our once close loving relationship was beginning to show deep cracks, mainly due to the fact she was now drinking heavy on a daily basis and was very insecure which caused her to become paranoid and violent. I often arrived home from work to find she had kicked the dog out to spite me and I would go trawling the streets looking for him expecting to find him dead in the gutter since he was young and wasn't fully road trained. One night after smoking a joint and downing a bottle of wine the paranoia got the better of Maria and she became convinced I was having an affair with a neighbour called Candy who lived downstairs in our block. I had gone to bed earlier than usual after an argument, leaving Maria in the living room to indulge in her intoxication. Some time later I was woken up with a large kitchen knife pressed into my throat that was millimetres away from severing my jugular vein. Sitting on my chest with her legs either side of my torso pinning my arms down, Maria with blood-curdling venom in her eyes hissed,

"Tell me the fucking truth you bastard, are you screwing Candy?

"Of course not babe, don't be silly, I'm with you aint I?

"Don't fucking lie to me, I know you are fucking her," she snarled, putting more pressure on my neck with the razor sharp knife. The room was pitch black apart from the flickered illumination of the full moon that crept through slightly opened curtains adorning the window. The curtains caught a gust of wind every now and then allowing the light to emphasize the irrational crazed look on Maria's face. I realised at this point there was going to be no negotiating with her.

"You've got ten seconds before I ram this fucking knife in your neck, now tell me, are you shagging that dirty cunt downstairs?

"You're paranoid babe, I swear I aint been near her,"

"One, Two, Three, Four, Five, I'll fucking do it, Six, Seven, . . ."

My heart was beating like a piston, I had to act fast since I had no reason to doubt her intentions to cut my throat given that this wasn't the first time she had come at me with a kitchen knife, so when the count reached 8, I rapidly arched my body upwards causing her to bolt forwards over my head. Being launched at speed towards the wall meant that Maria had to use both her hands to prevent her face smacking into it, giving me the opportunity to grab her wrists and disarm her, which I managed to do eventually after a frantic struggle. You may be thinking that the logical thing to do was get the fuck out of there and don't come back, but naively I stayed. After calming down she kept apologising and begged me not to leave her, blaming the joint for her paranoia and the bottle of wine for her violent behaviour. She promised to try and give up the drink, and as for smoking dope, it wasn't a regular thing so wasn't going to be hard to quit. I loved her and decided to give our relationship another chance because away from the drink and drugs she was a gentle, kind, and beautiful girl who always smothered me with love which I craved after having my heart broken by Lorraine. She stayed off the booze for a couple of days and things were getting easier between us although I still slept with one eye open. It wasn't long before Maria's will power caved in and she started hitting the bottle in secret and all that anger and paranoia began to resurface. Once again I was being accused of fancying Candy and it all came to a head when Maria rushed downstairs and pounded on Candy's door screaming,

"Get out here you fucking slag." I locked the front door and wasn't going to let her back in until she calmed down and saw sense. After five minutes of trying to get Candy to come out she gave up and stomped back up the stairs. Locking Maria out only served to fuel her rage, she began kicking ferociously at the door until the locks gave way and the door swung open with a bang causing the complete chubb lock unit to rip free from its chasm. At this point I'd just about had enough and didn't want to put up with anymore of her crap. I would never lay a finger on a woman and was damn sure I wasn't going to take it from a woman either, so I told her I was leaving her for good this time.

"You're fucking mad," I shouted, "you need fucking psychiatric help." I grabbed Bens lead and after finding him quivering in terror under the coffee table I headed for the door which by now was hanging on one hinge. Fortunately her son Jason wasn't there to witness the chaos, he had been out with his dad for the day and wasn't due back until that evening.

"I'll be back to get my stuff in a couple of days," I said while carefully steering Ben through the splintered debris from the front door and door frame that lay scattered across the hall floor. Realising I was serious this time, Maria quickly changed her tune.

"I'm sorry, I just got crazy, it won't happen again I swear, I love you, Please don't go," she sobbed. "Don't go, let's talk about it, please." I had heard it all before, my heart was breaking listening to her desperate plea's but my mind was telling me the sensible thing to do was leave her. I stuck to my guns and with tears welling up in my eyes and a big lump in my throat I walked out onto the stairway with Ben. Then as quick as a flash Maria switched from a heart broken girl to an aggressive monster telling me I was all the cunts under the sun. She picked up the chubb lock and as the dog and I were making our descent down the first flight of stairs Maria threw it as hard as she could in my direction. It hit me on the back of my head causing a deep gash and blood to spurt out all over the walls. Now in severe pain I ran down the remaining steps, out of the door and onto the street urgently trying to stem the blood flow from my head injury with one hand whilst holding onto Bens lead in the other. Just as Ben and I began crossing the road I heard a crash and a thud coming from behind us. Maria was chucking my stereo and other stuff out of the window effing and blinding with every throw. I continued walking away, I needed to get to my mum's house (about half a mile away) as quickly as possible so I could get my head wound sorted out since I was losing lots of blood and feeling dizzy. My eyes were clouded with a mixture of tears and blood and along the way people constantly stopped to ask if I needed help. I declined and carried on walking. I had just got to the bottom of my mother's road when all of a sudden, as much as I was upset and in pain, this amazing feeling of freedom swept over me, like the world had just been lifted from my shoulders. It may have been due to the fact I was feeling a bit giddy, but strangely I was filled with elation and felt like I was on my way to paradise after being in hell, I was walking into the future, the unknown, and the past was back along the trail of blood that I had left behind me.

My mother was a nervous wreck when she saw the state of me, I looked like I'd been in a car crash since my head, face and hands were completely covered in claret. After cleaning me up mum and I decided not to go straight to casualty providing the wound stopped bleeding and I was feeling ok, we would reassess the damage the following morning. Although not over the moon about having a dog in the house my mum allowed me to keep Ben there for a couple of days, after which I'd either have to find him a new owner or move out with him. It turned out that one of the tenants in our flat was due to vacate the next day after having previously given my brother a weeks' notice, so Ben and I moved in to one of the double rooms. I still had fleeting contact with Maria when she began coming to my flat with Jason to visit me and Ben. Her excuse being that Jason was missing the dog. The visits soon fizzled out after I paid little or no attention to her when she came, making it quite clear there was no way back for us and that I had moved on. Sadly I still loved and cared about her and missed the good times we had in the beginning, but too much water had gone under the bridge and I knew I could never go back. As the months went on Maria met another guy and I was firmly back on the pull resulting in a string of one night stands. My brother was now living in the single room and his ex girlfriend Janet was renting the other double room after our other tenants moved out. Janet who had always been a good friend of mine started dating John when they were teenagers. They split up after nearly three years but remained friends. Our mum treated her like a daughter and she was always welcome in our home. So it seemed like a natural thing to do having her move in with us. Janet and I were partial to smoking the odd joint and would often share a spliff while watching a film together giggling and getting stoned. But it wasn't all fun and games and we did have the occasional fall out over trivial things like her cats litter tray for example.

John and I were struggling to pay the mortgage on our wages and to top it all the housing market crashed soon after the interest rate exploded and went sky high. The result was, our monthly mortgage repayments doubled from £400.00 to £800.00, we were going to lose everything. The Value of the flat decreased rapidly to £46,000 leaving us sitting on negative equity. If only we could ride the storm until the interest rates dropped and the market grew strong again. But we were barely able to pay the four hundred a month let alone eight hundred. We were on the repossession train with no return ticket desperately trying to halt the ride. After getting in touch with the DHSS hoping they could help, we were informed that no help with Mortgage payments would be granted until six months had passed. So in a desperate attempt to keep the wolf from the door we decided to try and make some money selling cannabis since I had loads of contacts and associates in the spliff smoking community. Also I had a good vantage point working in the snooker club given that nearly everyone who frequented the place were either stoned or getting stoned.

We managed to raise the £600 needed to by a soap bar of Rocky, using the money we had put by for that months mortgage and a loan from John's boss. A soap bar of Rocky was slang for a nine ounce lump of Moroccan made cannabis that came in the shape of a bar of soap. We got it from a long time friend of ours who had his fingers in many pies and was knee deep in the stuff, so getting more was never going to be a problem. We chopped and weighed it all into eighths and sixteenths before wrapping them in Clingfilm. I managed to sell half of it down the snooker club and the other half was sold to my mates and other people Janet knew. Word spread fast and before long we were buying and selling two bars a week. The only pitfall was the amount of punters turning up at our door every day since it was bound to arouse suspicion amongst our many curtain twitching neighbours. Within six months we had other local dealers buying a few ounces at a time from us on a daily basis and our operation was expanding fast. It soon got to the point where we were buying kilos instead of soap bars and the number of dealers we were supplying just kept growing. Dealers were coming from all over London and some were making regular trips through the Blackwall tunnel to buy from us when a cannabis drought hit parts of the east end. We were so busy trying to keep everyone happy that things were spiralling out of control. I grew extremely cautious and was forever casing our immediate area with binoculars from every window in the flat trying to find any old bill staking us out. John kept telling me I was paranoid and told me to stop worrying. I wasn't paranoid, I just knew that there was far too much action at our doorstep and the police and our neighbours weren't stupid enough not to recognise the signs. Even though we'd stopped selling petty Eighths and sixteenths which stopped all of the small time smokers turning up, our flat still resembled Piccadilly Circus and I wasn't happy. I told John we would have to put a limit on the amount of people who we let come round.

So from then on apart from a selected few, every time a dealer would ring up with an order we told them to pull up outside a phone box next to a couple of disused prefabs at the end of our road, give us a ring and one of us would run their order down via a pedal bike. Eventually we had four local drop off points at various phone boxes in the local vicinity and we'd arrange to meet each customer at different locations eliminating curiosity from the people living near the rendezvous points.

There were two lads who we did let come round, a black guy called Anthony which was shortened to Ant and a white Scottish guy called Mark who were roughly the same age as us. They both lived in a half way house in Victoria where people with no fixed abode would be sent after being released from prison or out on bail, it was generally referred to as a Bail Hostel. Being the only dope dealers in the building which housed about 150 people, meant they were sitting on a goldmine and were sent to us by a business associate of ours who could vouch for their reliability. Their usual supplier had moved up north and they had spent the profit previously made on day to day living expenses. So we agreed to let them have 2 ounces on the slate just to get the ball running. The next day they turned up with our £180.00 (the price of two ounces), so we gave them another two on the slate. This continued every day for months and even though the dope was always on tick until the following day, we trusted them and they were making us money. One day John and I came to the conclusion that they were earning enough dough to clear up their slate and start paying up-front for the Merchandise, so later that day when they phoned to say they were on their way I explained the new rules. "Yeah no problem Rick, we'll be there in an hour." That was the last we heard from them for over a week, so John and I decided to pay them a surprise visit one night and drove to the hostel in Victoria. After telling the receptionist that we were popping in to see our cousin Mark she buzzed us through the security door and gave us directions to his room. "Number 37 on the second floor, go half way down the corridor and it's on the right." We thanked her and made our way up the four flights of stairs and soon found Marks room. We heard about four voices coming from behind the door including marks. John looked at me and asked if I was ready, we both mentally and physically prepared ourselves for a fight since we didn't know what sort of reception we would receive. John knocked on the door.

"who is it? asked one of the voices.

"John and Rikki,"

"what do you want?"

"A quick chat with Mark," after a moment of whispering and shuffling about, a lad opened the door wide enough to show his face.

"He aint here mate, he went to Glasgow two days ago," we knew he was bull-shitting us.

"When is he due back then? I asked.

"Next week sometime, I'm not too sure, When's Mark due back? He asked one of the other lads behind the slightly opened door.

"Next week I think," came the reply, a strong stench of cannabis came wafting out from the Smokey room.

"So you won't mind if we come in and have a look then? Asked John as we pushed our way past the lad holding the door. Like a gutter rat Mark was hiding in the corner curled up behind two of his mates who were sitting on his bed smoking a joint. John grabbed hold of him and pushed his face up against the wall, I grabbed the doorman by the scruff of his neck. "What was all that crap about Glasgow, I thought you said he weren't here you lying cunt," I growled. He tried to struggle free and get out of the door but I shoved him onto the armchair in the corner of the room then closed the door. The other two lads were stoned off their heads and just sat there saying, "Sweet mate," hoping to appear as insignificant as possible, so all the attention turned back to John and Mark. Still forcing his face into the wall John asked him,

"Where have you fucking been and where's our fucking money?

"I aint got the money, It was Ant, he took it and fucked off to his Nan's I swear."

"Don't fucking lie, Growled John pressing Marks face harder into the wall, "why were you hiding then? "Why aint you been answering my calls?

"Cos I've had no money, Ant took all the puff money, and I aint seen him for a week."

"Let him talk bruv." John released his grip on Marks face allowing him to straighten himself up and sit down, he could barely look us in the eye as he sat on the edge of the bed. "I swear I aint got your money, Anthony was supposed to go to your place that day and give you the money, then buy another two ounces up front like we agreed, but he disappeared with the £360.00, I've been left in the shit too." He appealed, hoping to gain our sympathy.

"So why aint you been down to his Nan's house then to look for him? I asked

"I don't know where she lives, all I know is that it's in Camberwell somewhere."

"Why should we believe you, what if we find Ant and he tells us it was you?

"I swear on my life I'm telling you the truth, I wouldn't knock you I swear."

"If we find out you are fucking lying Mark we'll hunt you down and next time we won't be doing any talking," warned John. We searched his room for money and dope and only found a small bag of weed and about £2.00 in change. Although we knew that Mark more than likely played a part in trying to rip us off, there was nothing we could do to prove it until we found Ant. So we left and drove home after giving him another warning.

We never did find Anthony but knew that one day we'd bump into him when he least expected it.

MY THREE LEGGED BEST FRIEND

Up 'til now we were paying the mortgage with the profits, the pie & mash shop no longer needed John to work for the full 10 hours a day since they were cutting back on staff after trade had dropped off. He did however work for a couple of hours in the mornings to help make the pies and was usually home by 10.30 am. I stopped working the odd nights at the snooker club after finding it impossible to get any sleep during the day with all the activity going on. The DHSS informed us they were going to start paying half of the mortgage costs, so we gladly obliged given that if we declined they may have started looking into how we were able to afford the mortgage repayments whilst unemployed, along with the fact that it was too tempting to turn down. You could say we were damn right greedy and there is an element of truth in that, but it was just so simple to go with the flow at the time. I am a creature of habit, so every morning I would go and play snooker then straight to the pie & mash shop for brunch, double pie, double mash and liquor six days a week. I was never short of cash and was surrounded in wacky backy so it was easy to get stuck in a rut. Paranoia did start to creep into my life style and I could quite easily slip into mild depression from time to time. As the money kept rolling in I grew even more convinced we were being watched which stressed me out severely. It got to a point where I couldn't relax being at home so started spending more and more time at the snooker club, only coming home to walk the dog or to sleep. One day whilst in the middle of a frame of snooker I got a phone call from Janet who was in complete distress.

"Rikki come home quickly something has happened to Ben,"

"What do you mean, what's happened to him?

"I think he's been Run over,"

"What, how the fuck has he been run over, how did he get out?!!!

"Please just come home Rick, he's on the door step screaming, he can't stand up."

The club was a ten minute walk from the flat, I slammed the phone down and left. As I ran down the road as fast as I could all sorts of horrible pictures were racing through my mind, what sort of state was I going to find my best friend in? Was he crushed? Would he still be alive? I ran faster and faster taking a short cut through a local housing estate, I jumped over walls darting through peoples back gardens, ran over the bonnets of parked cars obstructing my path, I didn't care about the consequences I just wanted to get to my boy. I could hear his yelps and screams from 200 yards away making me run even faster in sheer terror. On arrival at my front door I found Ben lying on the floor wailing in agony. I could see his right hind leg was snapped at the thigh, my heart was in my throat at this point and I tried my best to comfort him, although in excruciating pain he seemed pleased to see me letting me know by licking my face in between yelps. Janet was standing there in shock with her hand over her mouth looking like a geisha girl, the blood having already drained from her now chalk white face. Calmly I told her to go up stairs and phone blue cars, "ask for Lenny and tell him the cab is for Rikki and it's an emergency,"

She ran into the flat and made the call.

"He's on his way, I told him what has happened and he said he'd be here as soon as possible." I continued to comfort Ben whose screams had calmed down to a continuous whimper. If I could have swapped places with him right there and then I would have done it in a heartbeat just to take away his pain. I asked Janet how the hell this all happened, she started trying to explain whilst trembling and stuttering her words. Apparently Someone who had been round to pick up some puff left the door open on his way out and she never realised Ben was missing until she heard his blood-curdling screams outside the front door. A bloke who claimed he had witnessed it all told Janet that Ben was crossing Heaton road (a busy main road approximately 400 yards away) and got hit by a motor bike. The rider stopped to see if he was ok but Ben got up and limped off yelping whilst trying to make his way home. The witness followed him wanting to make sure the dog was ok and got the help he needed. According to him Ben crawled the last 50 yards to our door whilst squealing in pain.

Lenny the cab driver turned up in mere minutes, We knew him well and always asked for him when using Blue cars. He drove a Granada estate so there was plenty of room in the back to lay Ben down without too much discomfort. I got in the back with him and tried my best to re-assure him. Lenny drove us at speed to a private vet practice about a mile away who he was certain wouldn't turn us away so late at night. He pulled up outside and opened the boot to let me out before scurrying up the garden path of a big old Victorian house and thumped frantically on the old wooden door. A lady opened the door and the two of them had a brief conversation before he shouted,

"Bring him in Rick," After gathering Ben up in my arms as gently as possible we made our way through the garden and into the house. The bottom half of the house had been converted into a veterinary practice and looked very professional, the practitioner directed me into the surgery room and instructed me to place Ben down on a large sponge topped table. Another lady appeared wearing a white coat and escorted me back into the reception area leaving the first lady to tend to Ben who was still whimpering loudly. She produced a clipboard and began writing down the details while I explained as much as I knew about what had happened. After giving her all the facts she informed me that it was going to be a costly procedure to sort his leg out. I told her money was no object, I just wanted him to be ok. She went on to explain that they would keep him sedated over night since he was suffering from severe shock, and they would operate on his leg first thing in the morning.

I left feeling confident that Ben was in good hands and would soon be free from pain. Lenny dropped me off home after a quick visit to the snooker club to pick up my cue and bike. I thanked him for his help and gave him a ten pound drink and booked him for the morning to take me back. The surgeon phoned me the next morning to say Ben had a very comfortable night and was just coming around after a successful operation. I could pick him up in an hour and would have to pay £280.00. An hour later Lenny came to picked me up and took me back to the house. I walked into the surgery to find my boy standing on 3 legs wagging his tail with a big smile on his face. He hopped over and gave me a big kiss as I cuddled and made a fuss of him. After expressing my sheer and utter gratitude to the vet I paid the bill and took Ben home. Still very upset I started to feel anger mixed with guilt that my dog had gone to hell and back all because some wanker coming to buy dope couldn't even be bothered to close the door behind him. This just added to the fact that I didn't want to live like this anymore. On the face of things I acted like everything was ok but in secret I wanted out, I wanted an end to our operation. The money and the mortgage was the only thing that persuaded me to carry on.

IT'S A WRAP

A few months later we went through a cannabis drought and under pressure from our many clients we were forced to look elsewhere to buy our merchandise. After putting the feelers out and searching high and wide for another bulk supplier we eventually found a guy in Brixton who could only get a nine ounce soap bar instead of our usual one or two kilos. The phone was ringing off the hook with small time dealers hoping we could supply them with their usual quantity. We couldn't cater for all of them, so I explained it was now on a first come first serve basis, and when it was all gone we couldn't give guarantees on getting more anytime in the immediate future. So as soon I arrived home after collecting the soap bar from Brixton, I chopped and weighed it into nine separate Cuban cigar size ounces. It wasn't long before the first local petty dealer turned up to buy a couple of oz, he was known by his nick name Digger and dealt on a small scale from his flat on a rundown council estate just up the road. He was a well built bloke who liked to think he was a bit of a hard man and had many small time criminal friends. I gave him two freshly cut ounces, he paid me then he and his mate who had been waiting for him outside skulked off back towards the shit hole they had come from. John was out making pies, Janet had a half oz lump in her bag and was on her way out to her friend's house, and I had Ben and my mate Ginger Tony keeping me company. I was 20 seconds away from stashing the other 6 chopped ounces in my secret storage place which was in a crevasse behind a wooden door frame in my bedroom. I would gain access to the crevasse which was totally concealed to the naked eye by pulling out a loose part of the frame then slotting the lumps of dope one by one inside the hollow chasm. After every piece was neatly piled up on top of each other I would replace the section of frame. Once back in place you would never know that the door frame could be manipulated. Anyway before I had a chance to carry this out I heard Janet shouting my name from outside on the street, just then there was loud bang as my front door was kicked in. I heard the rumble of what sounded like twenty elephants stampeding through the downstairs hall. Ben was now at the top of the stairs barking and growling whilst bearing his teeth. Then came those ominous words I had been foretelling for the past six or seven anxious months.

"POLICE, STAY WHERE YOU ARE, THIS IS A RAID,"

Ben, bless his heart, held them off at the bottom of the stairs by inching slowly down towards them snarling and snapping at their every move, buying me just enough time to throw the dope and the scales under a wardrobe standing in the hall of the top floor landing next to the wall mounted phone.

"THIS IS THE POLICE, CONTROL YOUR DOG, CONTROL YOUR DOG."

After I gave him the nod Tony went down and put the lead around Ben's neck and walked him back up and into the kitchen. Once they were sure the dog was secured six or seven plain clothed policemen then came charging up the stairs.

"Are you Rikki Atkinson? Asked the first copper.

"Yes, why, what's this all about?

"We have reason to believe you are in possession of a class B controlled drug with the intention to supply!

"That's Rubbish, I don't sell drugs, I said defensively. I was noticeably trembling and in complete shock since it had all happened so quickly, their surprise SAS tactics worked. Speed Aggression and Surprise definitely rendered me senseless. I was trying to catch my staggered breath, as they spread out to search the flat. To make matters worse I noticed that in my panic to hide the drugs I had left a corner of the digital scales sticking out from under the wardrobe and was covered in Cannabis crumbs. It was screaming out,

"Here's the Drugs, look under here, are you blind or what? After a brief search of my room and the rest of the house the first copper took of his jean jacket rolled up his sleeves and said,

"Right, you can either tell me where the drugs are, or we will get the drug squad up here with their dogs and turn this whole place upside down, then we will examine all of your electrical equipment and run the serial numbers through our database, anything without a receipt will be confiscated"

Every video, television, and stereo in the house was hooky, and I knew it wouldn't be long before the scales gave me away so I took his first offer.

"It's under the wardrobe," I murmured. The copper got on his knees and found the six ounces of puff, a set of digital scales, a kitchen knife used for chopping, and the £180.00 from Digger who had left 10 minutes before the raid. Another copper began bagging up the evidence while the first copper read me my rights. I told him that Tony was just a visiting mate so they let him leave with the dog. They had already arrested Janet after finding the half ounce in her bag. Tony immediately phoned John to give him the bad news and it wasn't long before he came through the front door.

"What's going on?

"Who are you? Asked one of the old bill.

"That's my brother John, he's got nothing to do with any of this," I said, loud enough for him to hear. I wanted to let John know that he wasn't in the frame, hopping he'd play dumb, after all I had already been arrested for it and there was no need for both of us to take the rap. But they arrested him on conspiracy charges. I explained that we all lived separate lives in our separate rooms and the dope was my personal stash that I was going to share with a couple of mates. But they had an ace up their sleeve and I didn't find out exactly what it was until they ferried the three of us down to the nick.

DIGGER SQUEALED LIKE A PIG

At the police station John, Janet and I were processed then locked up in separate cells and left to stew for a couple of hours. Sitting there in the cramped dirty police cell I wondered if I would ever see daylight again before my imminent trail, which left me feeling lonely and desolate. On the other hand I also felt a sense of relief that all the stress of worrying whether we'd get caught was finally over. My turn for questioning had arrived and just as I was being led along a corridor to the main interrogation room I noticed another prisoner who was being directed into one of the other holding cells after leaving an interview room. It was Digger, I remember thinking, what the fuck is he doing here, it didn't occur to me that he might have something to do with the raid until I was shown the arresting officer's report after I denied that I had been dealing. The chief interrogator who had been writing down my statement asked, "So Mr Atkinson, are you denying the fact that you were in possession of six ounces of cannabis with the intension to supply?

"Yes! I replied vehemently.

"Read this," he said, handing me the officer's report which read something like this.

> *My colleagues and I were driving in our street patrol vehicle when I spotted Mr Diggins and another male walking south along Lindhurst grove. Mr Diggins was known to me as a local criminal who I had arrested on a prior occasion with a quantity of Cannabis resin in his possession, so we initiated a stop and search. On searching both men I found what I believe to be two, one ounce lumps of cannabis resin in Mr Diggins coat pocket. I then asked Mr Diggins where he had obtained the Cannabis and he replied, 397A Consort road.*

> *"Who sold it to you?*
> *"A bloke called Rikki."*
> *"Is he at the address now?*
> *"Yes, I've just come from there about five minutes ago.*
> *"Is this person Rikki alone in the premises?*
> *"No, there is another bloke, a girl and a dog."*

I couldn't believe what I was reading, Digger had grassed me up, he could have said anything else but that, he could have simply said he had bought it from some guy down the frontline of Peckham. The Frontline was on the high street and had drug dealers spilling out of every pub and seedy corner shop strewn along the road in that run down area of Peckham. It was a known Afro Caribbean pocket of Peckham and weed was constantly offered to passers by. You didn't know their names or anything about them so the police would have never followed it up. But without a split second of thought he ratted me out to save his own stool-pigeon arse. I had never been arrested for anything as serious as this in the past and with hind sight I realise I acted naively during my interrogation. I should have said no comment to all their questions and waited for my solicitor to arrive. Instead they laid on a duty solicitor who allowed me to sell myself well and truly down the swanny by owning up to the charge after reading that Digger had squealed. It turned out that we weren't being watched, or under suspicion of supplying. The copper told me that I was just unlucky that they happened to spot Digger that day, since they were CID and not the drug squad on a planned raid. During questioning they asked me where I had bought the puff from. I gave them the answer that the dirty Grass Digger should have given them and claimed I had bought it from a guy with Dreadlocks down Electric Avenue in Brixton. Electric Avenue was the equivalent of Peckham's frontline only twice as long and a hundred times busier. There were so many dreadlocked dealers it would have been impossible to identify anyone in particular. Knowing this fact gave me the lead and put a halt to the police's questions about any 3rd party involvements. They told me that John had owned up and confessed that he too was involved in the dealing, so I may as well tell them everything. Bullshit! I may have been naive about their interrogation tactics but I knew my own brother too well to believe that croc of shit. I was charged and held in police custody until the following morning when I would have to attend court to either get bail or be sent on remand until my trial. John was released on police bail pending further investigation. Janet was released and bailed to appear at Tower Bridge Magistrates court the following day. Apparently Digger the rat was also allowed to go home due to a "medical condition", the old bill must have cut him a deal, or he was already on their payroll since for him it was all over and he was a free man.

Janet and I were in the dock together the next day. The judge gave Janet a severe telling off and fined her £150.00 for possession. After pleading guilty I was given bail to appear at Southwark Crown court on the 8th of February 1991. My mother had put up the £50,000 bail money based on the equity on her house. Thanks Mum.

Just happy to be back in the fresh air of freedom, and with more pressing things to worry about I put getting revenge on Digger on the back burner, although I did let a few gossipers know about his loose tongue. I didn't think it at the time but with retrospect he did me a right favour by snitching, I mean who knows where it would have all lead to? I could have been caught sitting on a few kilo's, or ended up being shot dead somewhere along the line, since meddling with any type of drugs meant that more often than not you had to rub shoulders with some very dangerous, power hungry people. So thanks Digger.

CHAPTER IV

THE ITALIANS

JUST PRIOR TO being jailed I was back working with an Italian Fine art and antiques shipping company owned and run by a close friend of our family Franco fratelli. I was holding on to the slight chance that the judge may be lenient if I was in a full time employment. I have known Franco from the age of ten. In the summer holidays I used to travel with him in his lorry over to Bologna Italy, and would stay at his home with his wife Rafellina and their child Fabrizio who was about 7 yrs old. Their home was at the top of a luxury block of apartments within a large complex, which had two warehouses on the land with offices used for the shipping business. Elsewhere within the complex were chicken coops, and various other bird enclosures in and around farm like area. Their apartment was always busy with family members and work associates always coming and going. None of them spoke any English so at eleven years old I began learning to speak Italian. I had to, since spending a few weeks there without being understood would be a nightmare. Well I couldn't expect them all to start learning to speak English. Anyway Rafellina loved to sit with me whilst going through a picture book; it had the Italian meaning and the English meaning for each object. It was great we taught each other how to pronounce the words in both languages. So it wasn't long before I could ask for basic things like milk, shirt, cup, plate, water, and food etc. I had some good times in Italy and being so young, everything was an adventure and the weather was always hot. I would zoom around all day on a fifty cc motor cross bike, or just wonder around the fields with Fabio and his cousin Andrea, who lived in the apartment underneath us. I taught them how to make peg guns, which they loved since having never seen anything like it. They were rich kids who had always been bought anything they wanted, they played and grew up within the safe confines of the complex, where as I was a poor kid from the streets of Peckham who would be grateful for a pair of skates at Christmas. One Christmas, I had to share a second hand fold up girl's bike with my brother. Mum didn't have much money even though she worked very hard. So we used to make our own toys like Peg guns and go-karts. Don't get me wrong, this aint a sob story, we did have toys, and were very happy, well fed and looked after by our ever-loving mother. I just wanted to give you an Idea of the diverse worlds my new Italian brothers and I had been raised in. They knew a few English words like, Football, The Beatles, and Maggie Thatcher, and would giggle naughtily when I taught them some swear words. Fuck Off, and bastard for instance were words they had already come across, but Cunt, Wanker, and bollocks were new words that they could share with their school friends. I made them promise not to tell any of the adults about the new additions to their English vocabulary, well at least not until I was safely back home and could deny the charges. I loved being in Italy and have some fond memories, it was all a new experience for me since I was learning about a whole new culture and way of life; I was discovering new tastes in food that I had never eaten back home. I loved going into all the little old towns when Rafellina took me out to the shops. The buildings were old and were architecturally diverse from anything I'd seen in England. There were armed guards outside the banks and Rafellina had to pull me away when I stood there staring gob smacked at their holstered guns. I also had some great evenings out; one in particular was when I was 13 years old. Franco, Rafellina, and eight other members of their family and friends took Fabrizio and me to an outdoor festival. It was an old school Italian event with mainly old couples dancing to classic Italian songs in an open sided wooden gazebo. There were tables Spread all around filled with families tucking into their food and the wine was being passed around like there was an endless supply. I walked around hypnotised by all the activity. We all sat down to eat on a long table close to the open air bar, and before long there were waiters filling our table with various bowls of pasta and meat dishes. Soon the wine and conversation began to flow, the whole atmosphere was relaxed and jolly. I had my first ever taste of alcohol after mistaking a glass of wine for my lemonade, I quivered and pulled a face like a bull dog chewing a wasp, nobody had noticed since they were all engrossed in deep conversation and banter. The after taste was quite nice though so after a few more sips I didn't feel the need to gurn anymore. Before long I had downed the whole glass and began to feel very giggly, it was a great feeling and I wanted to keep it so I started looking for a refill. I managed to fill up another glass without anyone noticing, I was going to play dumb if I got caught and pretend that I thought it was water. After downing my second glass I was so merry and giggly that I was in danger of giving myself away, so I left the table and went over to the dance area. Happy and filled with bravado I began asking some of the women for a dance they took up my offers so I danced with a

string of different ladies one after the other, which amused everyone since I didn't
know the steps and kept bumping in to people. After a while I went on the hunt for
more wine and found some, it was free on tap from a big wooden barrel that had a
small queue of people in front of it having their glasses re-filled by one of the waiters.
I grabbed a couple of glasses and joined the queue trying to conceal the fact that I
was pissed. I pointed to our table and told the waiter the wine was for Franco and
his wife, he filled up my glasses and I walked off looking for a place to hide. I found
a little corner behind the bar and downed both glasses quickly while smoking a
fag I had pinched from one of the many cigarette packets lying around un-guarded
on the tables. I was lagging drunk and couldn't stop laughing, I walked around the
festival looking for adventure and found a swing park. The rest of this little story was
recounted to me by Franco the next day since I don't remember much about what
happened after finding the park. He was sitting talking with the family at the table
when one of the festival staff came over and asked if the English boy was part of his
group. After confirming that I was with him Franco was urged to come and have
a look at something by the staff member who then led him to the park. On arrival,
Franco found me slumped on a spinning roundabout whilst giggling uncontrollably.
He was told that I kept going back to the wine barrel for refills and saying that
they were for the adults at our table, and this had happened three or four times in
between embarrassing myself on the dance floor. Franco and his brother had to pick
me up and put me in the car, Rafellina drove us all back home and the next thing I
remember was being dumped in the bathtub and put under a power shower to sober
me up. Franco was a diamond and took it all in good spirits, the shower only served
in cleaning me up because I was still pissed, so after repeatedly telling everyone that
I loved them Rafellina put me to bed and nursed me until I fell asleep.

   After a few summers spent in Italy my command of the language had improved
so my mum started taking me to Italian lessons at night school to learn how to read
and write it. At fifteen I often went to work with Franco during school half term,
eventually after a few other failed jobs I started working with him full time when I
left School at 16. I did leave to go and try other jobs from time to time in my late
teens, but always ended up back at Vero ltd (The London side of his company). After
my Prison sentence I was re-employed immediately and was quickly promoted to
manager. We used to export antiques to Italy, and import modern Italian furniture
for various clients. So I spent quite a bit of time in and out of auction houses such
as Sotheby's, Christies, Phillips, and Bonham's. Another part of our work was
International removals, which would often take me into very affluent abodes with
a variety of pomp and splendour. With my colleagues and clients my nickname
was Ricardo Cuore de Leone, (Italian for Richard the lion heart) and my trust and
integrity were never in question. You may be thinking after reading this book that I
was a thieving little Git, once a thief always a thief blah blah blah. But I have never
had that thieving instinct, most things I nicked where on the back of an adventure
or revenge plot, never for greed. Being trusted was important to me and it felt good.

If I had wanted to, over the on-off 20 year period I worked with Franco I could have easily got away with stealing thousands of pounds worth of silverware and other goods, but that thought or the temptation never once crossed my mind.

I couldn't write a chapter about the Italians without mentioning what I call the Chinese mosaic story. It started on a warm summer's morning around midweek in 1986 when the van driver Mario and I were picking up a 500 year old Chinese cabinet from a high end antique shop in Notting Hill. The shop owner called Mr Sarti had sold it to one of our clients and was very anxious about the cabinet remaining in one piece and rightly so in view of the fact that it was worth about £50,000. It had two front doors set beneath about twenty small draws which were all decorated with ivory, onyx, and other precious stones. The main bulk of the cabinet was made from ebony and was adorned with marble columns and ceramic figurines. It was a really busy piece of furniture with a Mosaic style mixture of materials. True to form Mario and I managed to get it on the van without any drama's and covered it in blankets before tying it up securely and making our way to the next collection point on our list. Mario was a very friendly 30 year old Italian feller who was about 5ft 9 with black curly hair. He spoke fluent Italian with a queen's English accent due to the fact that he had been brought up in London. He came across as very camp which provoked plenty of gossip about his sexuality, but trust me, he was a red blooded heterosexual. I wish I had a penny for every time someone took me aside and whispered in my ear, "Rick between me and you, is he a bender?"

Anyway we got on like house on fire and worked well together. After collecting one or two other bits of furniture from other antique shops in the area we made our way back to the warehouse. Franco and his old business partner Michael Woods were waiting impatiently at the warehouse shutters in order to help unload the van as quick as possible. It was lunchtime and Michael was especially fond of the popular rump steak sandwiches that were served down at the local pub, and he liked to get there before it got too busy. The four of us managed to unload the van within a quarter of an hour and I was left behind to man the phones while the other three sped to the pub in Michaels BMW. The warehouse was fairly big and was now half empty after we had loaded and sent a full articulated lorry to Italy the day before. With all that space the temptation to fly around on our meaty old forklift truck was overwhelming. The others would be gone for at least an hour so I had ample time to fill my boots. After making a miniature Brands Hatch with rolls of bubble wrap and corrugated cardboard I started her up then accelerated my way around the course doing handbrake skids at every bend and chicane. Ten minutes in to my mini grand prix I started to get carried away by pushing the boundaries of my driving ability to the very edge and taking too many risks. This inevitably came to an end when I lost control and ploughed into the £50,000 Chinese cabinet with the heavy Iron forks at speed. The blood drained from my face like a car having an oil change as I watched this 500 year old piece of important Chinese history collapse into a hundred pieces before my eyes. Just when I thought it couldn't get any worse, it did. As I reversed the forks back out from within the cabinet it folded even more and by the time I could finally take stock there were bits of ivory, onyx, ebony, marble and ceramic figurines spread far and wide across the warehouse floor. Franco was going to fire me, the client was going to have me whacked and Mr Sarti was going to have a fucking major heart attack. Short of a miracle happening I was bang in trouble no two ways about it. I had to think on my feet and come up with some sort of solution but I only had fifty minutes to find one. I remembered that along with the shipping documents was a photo of the cabinet for the benefit of customs and excise, so I began gathering up all the pieces of the puzzle that lay strewn across the floor. There were plenty of restoration materials to hand since we were used to making occasional minor repairs to the odd piece of furniture before sending them out. So with some rapid drying wood adhesive I started gluing the two front doors back together. The fresh cracks and deep crevasses were screaming out, "Look at me I've just been hit with a fork truck." So I stained the wood with a mixture of mud, some old engine oil and a black felt tip pen. Then with the help of the photo and some super glue I began painstakingly sticking the mosaic style pieces of onyx and ivory back in their original positions using everything available to help disguise the faults and flaws. I kid you not, by the time I had finished with the cabinet it was upright and looking just like the one in the photo, but only from about 10 feet away, any closer and you could clearly notice it had undergone a complete cosmetic face lift. I guess I was hoping that if I could get through the day without anyone realising that the cabinet had been murdered, someone else might get the blame when I wasn't around. It was a long shot I know, but it was the only option I had. Right on schedule Franco, Michael and Mario had returned from lunch at the pub where they would normally consume a couple of glasses of wine each to wash down the steak sandwiches. Mario and I were due to deliver a pallet full of boxes to an address in Kensington so we opened up the front shutters while Franco started up the fork truck in order to load the pallet onto the van. Uncannily as Franco turned the fork truck around, one of the forks feathered the Chinese cabinet with the slightest of contacts. With that the cabinet completely disintegrated and caved in spewing hundreds of pieces of marble, ivory, onyx, and ceramic figurines all over the warehouse floor in a cartoon style cloud of dust, causing Michael, Mario and myself so scream "NOOOOOOOOO" whilst holding our heads. Franco was still on the truck in a state of total and utter shock, his foot was still pressing urgently on the brake while his leg was visibly shaking.

"How many fucking glasses of wine did you drink? Asked Michael.

Franco just couldn't understand how such a glancing blow could have caused such devastation to the 500 year old £50,000 historic Chinese cabinet. My prayers for a miracle had been answered and had come to fruition right before my very eyes. I mean what were the odds of that happening? After gathering the pieces together and accumulating them into one pile, Mario remarked how the cabinet looked like it had already been badly restored at some point in the past. Strangely enough and lucky for me the normally very astute Franco didn't put two and two together and point the finger at me, instead he took sole responsibility even though he could never quite get his head around it. I suppose it was just too far fetched even for Franco to assume that in an elaborate plan to get off the hook, I painstakingly restored the whole cabinet, while hoping someone else would just happen to randomly crash into it. Franco would have to give the client free shipping until such time that he covered the cost of the restoration which in this case ran into many thousands of pounds. Did I feel guilty? Nah not at the time but I'm sure that I more than paid for it in blood and sweat and unpaid overtime during the twenty years of my employment at Vero ltd.

COSA NOSTRA

Due to the fact that we had clients from Sicily, Napoli, and Rome who dealt in fine art and antiques at the top end of the market it was inevitable that we would be dealing with various Italian mafia families along the way. Some of them were very serious characters who demanded respect, not in a vocal way but by the manner in which they carried themselves. A few of them were glorified waiters who had watched to many gangster flicks and were sound-alikes with nothing to back it up. Others were more laid back and jovial for example there was one client who for the sake of protecting his identity I will call Vincenzo, he would turn up at our premises in a top of the range Mercedes which was driven by one of his four henchmen. He hated flying so each visit to London would involve a nonstop 36 hour drive across Europe with each of his men taking turns at the wheel only stopping to re-fuel. The driver always got out first and would open Vincenzo's door before helping him up since he was in his late 60's and could do with losing a few stone. The other three minders who by now were sporting three day old growths, would walk around for a minute stretching their legs while yawning and furiously scratching their nuts before escorting Vincenzo to our office. He always wore a cream coloured suit with fedora hat to match and was a dead ringer for Don Fanucci (the black hand) from the Godfather movies, in fact their whole gig had Mafioso written all over it. He was very loud which matched his personality, he was constantly telling jokes and swapping banter with his sidekicks. But behind his relaxed appearance Vincenzo was a hard businessman who took no prisoners. For the many years that we did business with him there were a few occasions when Vincenzo and his Hench men would use one of our offices to have private meetings with a couple of serious looking Sicilians who wore the sharpest black suits I'd ever seen. There was something very different about these guys, they had heavy duty written all over them. They didn't make small talk and never uttered a word to anyone who wasn't connected with whatever business they were conducting with Vincenzo. They would always arrive in a top of the range car that was oozing class but not overtly attention grabbing. The silent and meaningful manner they went about their business spoke volumes about what type of people they were.

All of my children's Italian family in Bari Italy

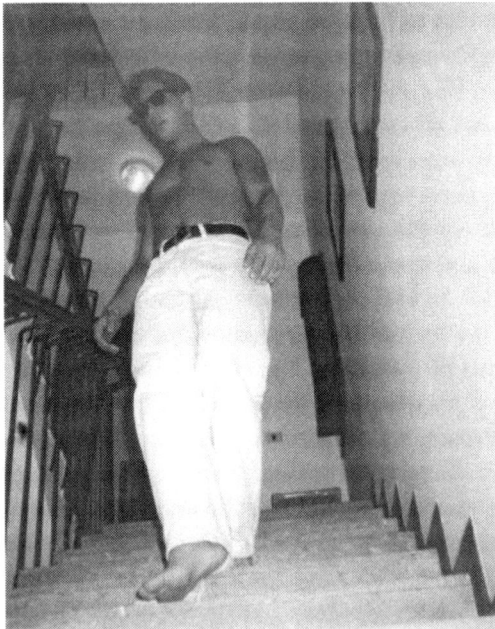

me in Venice Italy

my younger brother Ryan

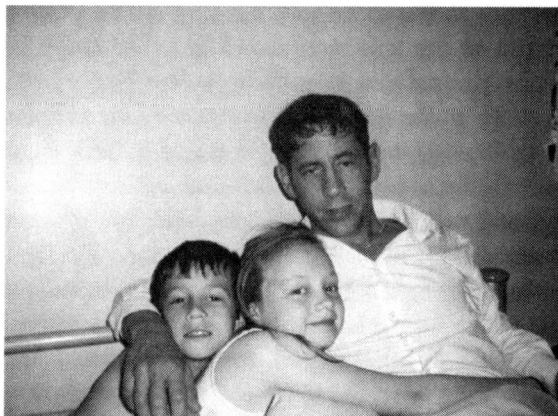

Me and my precious Children

Me and Mattie a.k.a. Bros

One of my more sinister encounters with an Italian gangster was with a guy who always seemed to be pissed off with everyone and everything. He had a very intimidating stance coupled with a threatening tone of voice. In mafia terms he was lower down in the pecking order and more of a rogue soldier. For the same reasons as before I will call him Salvatore, he was fairly tall and quite broad with shoulder length greasy black hair. To say he was highly strung and a bit of a live wire was an understatement. Fortunately he only turned up three or four times a year since my boss hated having anything to do with him and would always try and keep things above board. One day when Franco was away on business in Italy Salvatore had bullied Anna our timid secretary into sending me to pick up a package from a lorry owned by another Italian shipping company. I was sent to an address in Essex where the Italian driver was in the middle of making a delivery to a modern furniture company. The driver and I were already acquainted since we'd worked with each other on a big household removal in the past. So after a brief period of catching up he pointed out a wooden case in the corner of the lorry.

"Sta li dentro," (it's in there) he said handing me an electric drill. The crate which was of interest to me was surrounded by other much larger and heavier crates. The driver who seemed to want nothing to do with the package continued off loading three-piece suits to the warehouse lads leaving me to struggle with opening the wooden crate which was well and truly wedged in between the other crates. I managed to remove the lid using a power drill and noticed that stacked inside were about 6 or 7 boxes and various other packages. Through past experiences I knew that Salvatore always sealed his packages with duck tape and signed his name over every strip of tape in order to tell if it had been opened or tampered with. I could see Salvatore's box which was about the size of a portable television. It was at the far end of the crate next to other "legitimate" parcels, but I just couldn't stretch over enough to reach it. So I decided to try and grip it somehow with the crow bar and hopefully drag it up towards me and free it from the crate. It worked but then my worst nightmare happened, whilst pulling it towards me the crow bar tore its way through the box ripping a sizeable hole in the side. I grabbed the box and after wishing the driver well I hurried back to my van. There was no way I could disguise the fact that Mr Angry's box had been penetrated so I thought I might as well have a quick peek inside. I could only see what was in the top two thirds of box which happened to be filled up with used 100,000 Italian Lira bank notes wrapped in elastic bands, I couldn't see what was underneath the notes but was able to investigated with my fingers. It felt malleably soft and was weighing the box down. I was sure it could only be bags or packets of powder. I was now getting really worried seeing as Salvatore would know that I would have more than likely seen the contents of his box and could possibly expose him. I phoned Anna the secretary and told her what had happened with the crow bar, which only served to make me more nervous when she wailed "OH, MY, GOD, "and this was before I had even told her what it contained. She went on to explain that Salvatore would be at our office in an hour expecting to collect his box. I drove like a man possessed and managed to get back to the office in 55 minutes. Anna had a panic attack when she saw the state of the box and nearly keeled over after finding out what was inside it.

"Quick lets tape up the hole and pretend it was like that when you collected it," she said before taking big nervous gulps from her bottle of Evian. I taped up the box with the same colour duck tape hoping he wouldn't notice anything until he had left. We sat anxiously awaiting Salvatore's arrival for what seemed like ages, it was 5.30pm and already dark outside by the time he pulled up in his Jag. He was his usual arrogant pissed off self continuously muttering swear words to himself in between asking for his box and moaning about the traffic. The box had been smuggled into the country so I had no official paperwork for him to sign. I brought his box over on a wheelbarrow and helped him put it in the boot of his car. He gave me a pat on the back and said "Bravo Rikki" as he handed me a fifty pound note from his full to the brim money clip. I thanked him whilst shuffling off as fast as I could towards the office when I heard,

"MA CHE CAZZO SUCCESSO QUI? He had rumbled me and was shouting "What the fuck has happened here? Whilst pointing to the taped up hole in his box. So in Italian I began explaining how his box had ended up with a hole in the side.

"Oh that was me, I did it while trying to grab the box with a crow bar."

"Why the fuck were you grabbing it with a crowbar? He growled.

"It was stuck in the middle of other boxes and I couldn't get to it, the only other way would have been to wait for at least an hour while the driver finished unloading the other goods before we could access the crate with your box in."

"Did you check inside to see if anything was broken? Asked Salvatore while attentively checking out my facial reactions for any signs of deception.

"No I didn't, I'm sorry, I was in a rush because I wanted to finish early this evening, so I just stuck some tape around it and put it on the van. Was there something fragile inside? I asked, pretending to be concerned.

"Yes some glass and porcelain ornaments, but don't worry it doesn't sound like anything is broken," he said, as he gave the box a little shake while pretending to listen for shattered glass.

"Next time pay more attention, do you understand!

"yes I understand Mr Salvatore, I'll be more careful in future."

I'm not certain that he totally bought my story but I think due to the fact that I apologised for not checking the box for damages may have convinced him that I'd seen nothing. Besides as far as Vincenzo was concerned he had bought my loyalty with the nice crisp fifty pound note that was now safely tucked away in my back pocket.

Once again he began muttering swear words to himself as he got in his car and sped off. Anna breathed a sigh of relief when I walked in the office smiling and re-assured her that the whole episode was over. We both agreed not to mention it to Franco as we locked up and headed off home.

There were many more colourful, exiting and precarious adventures during my employment with Franco, but to write about all of them would take me a lifetime. Nevertheless I just have to tell you about this particular very nerve wracking event I got involved in after being made an offer I just couldn't refuse.

One morning I turned up at our Battersea warehouse to start work and was greeted by Franco and one of Franco's closest friends a Neapolitan feller called Antonio. Franco was acting oddly out of character and had a fixed nervous smile on his face which was making me feel a little un-easy. He asked me to sit down explaining that he wanted to make a deal with me, a deal which could possibly change all our lives forever. He began unwrapping a blanket from a painting that he had fetched from a remote corner of the warehouse. Franco and I only ever spoke in Italian but he went on to explain the history of the painting in his broken English accent. He only ever did that when he was trying to convince me of something or give off the impression he was telling the truth. I asked him to start again only this time to speak in Italian since his broken English wasn't very accurate, and as you will soon find out I needed to know every precise detail of what he had to say. It turned out that the painting was an old master and had been painted by none other than William Turner, a famous painter from the mid 18th to mid 19th century who was mostly known for his many paintings of venetian scenery. The story goes that the painting had been stolen from a famous London art gallery in the early 70's by the father our Neapolitan friend Antonio. The next part of Franco's speech turned my legs to Jelly, he went on to explain that the painting could be worth anything up to thirty million pounds but no less than ten million. This would be split three ways between Franco, Antonio and myself since the original thief (Antonio's father) had died in the eighties. To earn my stake all I would have to do is turn up at either Sotheby's Bond Street, Christie's st James, or Philips Bond st with the painting and submit it for their next old masters sale.

"You are fucking crazy! Was my initial response, I knew that the worlds press and the police would be all over this like a rash and would all want to know how a multi million pound Turner ended up in the hands of a scruffy lad from Peckham. Franco and Antonio had already thought of that, I would tell them that I bought the painting from a stall in Bermondsey market in south east London. Legend had it the local law stated that anything bought at Bermondsey market before 6.am was deemed to be a legitimate lawful transaction regardless whether or not the item was stolen and would become the legal property of the purchaser. My cover story would be that I had no idea it was a Turner and bought it for £100.00 because I simply liked the picture. By the time Franco had finished the debrief my mouth was as dry as a nun's crotch and the blood had completely drained from my face. I mean this wasn't like selling a bit of hooky gear to the local fence, this painting was so hot it was on fire. Then I started thinking about the prospect of being an instant multi millionaire, with such a mixture of nervous emotions my bowels were getting the better of me so I went to the carsey to take a dump. I sat there trying to juggle the pros and cons of the offer that had just been laid out before me and as much as I didn't want the obvious heat that would be coming my way, the prospect of never having to work or worry about money ever again was overwhelmingly attractive so I decided I would take them up on their offer. After smoking a whole packet of fags and guzzling a few cups of tea we went over the story one more time before I loaded the painting in my car (Franco didn't want to link the company van with me or the painting). I set of for Philips Bond st since their next old masters sale was just around the corner, also either one of the top auction houses would suffice since the painting's reputation was of key importance and not the venue.

Walking into Philips holding this 3ft by 3ft piping hot masterpiece I was a nervous wreck, one way or another the events about to unfold within the next ten minutes were going to change my life forever. Either my story would be celebrated and I would be rich beyond belief, or I would be interrogated by the police then charged with handling stolen goods, and the painting would be returned to its rightful owners should my Bermondsey alibi fail to hold water. I did have a brief wobble and contemplated aborting the whole mission but soon got a hold of myself and headed for the lift which would take me to the old masters department on the 3rd floor. Philips had three separate auction houses in London, one in Bayswater W2 near Paddington which dealt with the bottom end of the antiques market. Another was situated in Knightsbridge just opposite Harrods which dealt with the higher value bracket of antiques. The third being Philips Bond street was full of toffee nosed art and antique dealers, it had many different departments with experts at hand to value goods and advise on sales. The porters were all posh ex Eton students trying to make their way up through the ranks. On a normal day when collecting for our clients I would never normally feel intimidated by all the pomp and upper class atmosphere that filled every inch of the building. But this time I was there on business and was stepping into their territory. With me being a scruffy working class cockney lad from Peckham I was already feeling like I was out of my depth. While travelling in the lift on my way to the 3rd floor the dread I was feeling can only be likened to my first journey down the stairs from Fraggle rock in Brixton prison, I was shiting myself. I walked into the cramped foyer of the art department. Behind the un-manned counter were three doors, one for each art department. There were three door bells on the counter and each one had a sticky label with a name next to it, Modern art, Old masters, and Miscellaneous. I rang the bell named Old masters and within seconds a pretty blonde girl came out and in her posh private school accent asked, "how can I help you?

I'd like to have this painting valued and placed in your next Old masters sale please," I blurted out nervously. I removed the blanket and laid the painting on the counter. The Girl reached for her glasses that were hanging on a string around her neck and began examining the painting closely. There was no turning back now, it was a shit or bust moment and I would now have to go with it no matter what. After mumbling and making some cooing noises she looked up and said.

"I'm just going to get one of my colleagues to have a look I won't keep you a minute."

I nodded and smiled in agreement since by now my mouth and throat had dried up and I could barely speak. The girl disappeared back through the door taking the painting with her so I poured myself some complimentary water from an urn in the corner and sat in one of the green leather upholstered chesterfield armchairs. I must have sat there for five minutes and still no sign of the blonde which sent my mind into working overtime. What was taking her so long, have they called security, are they talking to the press, are they phoning the police? With each passing minute I grew more and more paranoid and had nothing but negative thoughts swimming around in my head, "don't worry just stick to the story and nothing can go wrong," I kept telling myself.

If the painting had only been worth a couple of grand I would have been as cool as a cucumber, I think the fact that it had a multi million pound price tag and was a very famous master piece was the reason why I was a crumbling wreck and melting like an ice cream on a hot day. When the blonde did eventually resurface she was accompanied by a curly haired guy who also looked and sounded like he had swallowed a full set of art encyclopaedias. "Sorry to have kept you," said the blonde who had an expression on her face akin to someone who was about to tell you your house insurance didn't cover burglary just after you had been broken into.

"We've had a detailed look at it and also asked the head of The Old masters department to give his opinion and we are all in agreement that it is a fake," explained Blondy. Then Curly informed me that it was a good copy and would probably fetch around £150-£200.00 for its decorational value if I were to put it in a sale at their Bayswater premises. He asked me how I had come across the painting so I gave him all the patter about Bermondsey market and told him how I was advised by some respected art dealers to bring it to the Old Masters department. Curly and Blondy both gave me the same look that the sympathetic woman in a hardware shop had given me after being sent in to ask for a tin of tartan paint and a left handed screw driver when I was a kid.

I couldn't comprehend what they were telling me, surely they were mistaken, they must have got it wrong. I had been assured by Franco and Antonio that the painting was the real McCoy. They were adamant it had definitely been stolen from a famous art gallery twenty odd years ago by Antonio's old man, or had it? While loading the painting back in my car I went over everything that had been said. I knew for sure that Franco would have never knowingly lied to me and risk bringing any heat on himself. Antonio wasn't the type of feller to make this whole thing up either, so was his father the source of misinformation? I phoned Franco and explained word for word how the scenario had panned out, he was baffled and convinced that the experts at Philips must have got it wrong. I drove away feeling quite relieved that the whole thing was over, but on the other hand I was gutted, all those fantasies I had of sailing around the Mediterranean in my new luxury yacht were going to remain just that, a mere fantasy. Back at the warehouse the three of us tried to work out what went wrong, Antonio was scratching his head in utter bewilderment, he couldn't believe that they thought it was a fake. He claimed that his father had absolutely no reason to lie about the painting. After lengthy discussions the three of us decided to leave it for a few weeks before trying again at one of the other auction houses, besides my arse couldn't take any more pressure that day. Franco and I came up with the conclusion that either the painting was real and the experts were mistaken after making the assumption that it was too good to be true. Or that at some point in the 70's the real painting had been switched with a fake either before or after it had been stolen. Whatever the answer was we were probably never going to find out given that a couple of weeks later I tried again at Christies South Kensington. Yet again I got a sympathetic smile and walked out with a fake Turner. In the end I think Antonio sent the painting back to his family home in Napoli. Maybe it will be discovered in another 100 years or so and be worth a few million in its own right as an antique fake Turner, or it might even be accepted as the real thing. It's a mystery to me.

By the time my first child was born when I was twenty-eight years old, I was speaking nigh on fluent Italian, I even thought in Italian. Even to this day people still think I'm an i-tie even though I swear blind I'm English. So I'm known affectionately as Ricardo by most of my friends. Speaking Italian had many advantages and if used with a bit of guile could sometimes turn out to be very lucrative, for example there was a period in 1993 when Franco employed an old feller as my new right hand man. His name was Mick and he was the 67 year old father in-law of one of our other drivers. For a man of his years he was still very fit and loved to sing and dance for a laugh and was often fun to be around. On the other hand he was very shifty looking, like an 'Honest John the car dealer' type of character. He could go all quite and be constantly looking out of the corner of his eyes. To look at, he was the kind of bloke you would automatically be suspicious of and would never trust with the safe keys. We got on like a house on fire and laughed our way through most days. On this one particular Monday morning Mick and I were sent to a multi million pound mansion on Tite Street in Chelsea to wrap and collect a number of boxes and a few sticks of antique furniture. Usually I would always introduce myself in Italian to put the client at ease, but I was still slightly hung over from the previous night and was in no mood to make an effort, so when the house owner opened the front door I said in my brain cell deficient Cockney accent, "hello guvna, we've come to collect a few bits and bobs for shipment to Italy." The Client who was part of the Italian aristocracy took one look at us and our ropey old van then shut the door after telling us to hold on a minute.

A few seconds later he re-appeared holding a phone to his ear while talking to Gerardo, (the manager of our sister company in Italy). The client demanded to see our official paperwork which happened to be a tatty Vero job sheet which had only the address, 5 Tite street, written on it diagonally across the page and in Franco's scruffy 3 year old handwriting.

"What is this? Asked the client while continuously turning it over from side to side as though more information was going to miraculously appear on it. He was clearly un-impressed at our lack of class and didn't trust us from when he first clapped eyes on us. Gerardo must have talked him round because after confirming that I was Rikki he invited us in. As expected the interior of the house looked more like a museum than a home. There were Louis XVI style French Giltwood Consuls propped up against every available wall, Georgian Mahogany Chippendale Bureaus sat back in every alcove, many a Persian Rug covering the chessboard marble tiled floors, and everything else you'd probably find in a stately home. Nervously the client ushered us into one of the ample reception rooms and pointed out which pieces we were to take. After collecting our materials from the van Mick and I set about wrapping the furniture under the ever vigilant beady eye of the untrusting aristocrat. Before long he called out to his wife and when she arrived he ordered her to keep a very watchful eye on us since we were not to be trusted, while he went into to his office to make a phone call. Naturally they spoke to each other in Italian, after all they didn't want these two scruffy cockney crooks knowing what they were discussing. Mick looked at me with a wry smile, but I continued to chit chat with him in English. Her Ladyship had run out of things that she could pretend to be doing, like straightening the curtains or plumping pillows or moving books into some sort of order on their huge Georgian bookshelf. She called out to the young Italian au pair/maid, and just like her husband she told the au pair to watch us because we were dodgy and might possibly steal something. Timidly the maid agreed and promptly started to look for something tedious to do. Anyway the husband relieved the maid from her lookout post, and again the wife took over from him etc. This went on for the next forty five minutes and at each change of guard some derogatory remark about our integrity was made. Mick looked at me as if to say when are you going to turn this situation on its head Rick? I winked at him and then went over to the client and his wife who were about to swap places and said, "Signori, e' mica che l'avete un paio di forbiche per favore? Ce ne abbiamo un paio nella forgone se no. (I don't suppose you have a pair of scissors handy do you? We have a pair in the van if not) Dumbfounded it took them four or five seconds to register what had just happened and in her complete state of bafflement her ladyship still tried to answer my question in English. When she came to her senses she asked, Ma, parli Italiano? (Oh, do you speak Italian?) To which I replied, Si, certo,(yes I certainly do) and looked at them both as if they were now the ignorant ones. His Lordship was still silent with his mouth stuck wide open as though in mid speech. The blood began to rush to their cheeks as it dorned on them that I had understood every cruel remark they made about us over the past forty five minutes. With that the whole atmosphere changed from one of hushed severity to one of polite smiles and generous hospitality. They were so embarrassed and felt they had to somehow make it up to us, so out came the tray of cakes and posh biscuits, followed by continuous cups of tea and coffee. Mr and Mrs snooty turned into Basil and Cybil Fawltey trying to be nice to their unfortunate hotel guests. By the time we had finished wrapping and loading Mick and I walked away with a belly full of gateau, and fifty quid each for a drink. They even waved us off like we were relatives who had been visiting for the day as we drove away down the street.

OUTSIDE THE BOX

It was the summer 2002 and I was given the reigns and the responsibility to over-see and manage a very sizeable removal from a millionaire apartment in Holland Park W11. The client who was moving to Rome, was an Italian diplomat who until now worked at the Italian Embassy in London. Vero were short staffed due to the fact it was August and our temporary van boys were off on holiday, so it was left to me to recruit a team who were up to the job.

This was going to be a three day event so I needed an efficient, professional and trustworthy bunch of lads. My pal Mattie was already my regular side kick and was first choice based on his knowledge and experience in the field. Ginger Tony was recruited based on the fact that he was a right laugh and would be the chief spliff roller. Finally Jason the barman from the Railway Tavern was recruited simply because we had no other choices available, also he talked his way into the team by giving us a load of flannel about how he had once worked for a removal company for seven years. He was roughly the same age as Tony about 37 and had only been on the scene for the past six months. He was a very amiable feller who rented a room above the pub, but was always a bit sketchy when asked about his past, so he gave the impression he was a bit of a bull shitter. Mattie and I had been mates for ages, he was about 5ft 10, extremely skinny with blonde hair and blue eyes. I had grown up around Ginger Tony seeing as my step father Deb was his uncle so we were practically cousins, at around 5ft 9 with a stocky build he would be relied upon to help with the heavy lifting. The first day went as well as could be expected for a hand-picked motley crew from the pub. I made sure all the glass and delicate objects were packed properly into boxes with bubble wrap, Tony made sure that the four of us were stoned and giggling all day, Jason the barman made us sure that he'd never done a removal in his life, especially after I had to teach him how seal a packing box with duck tape. Mattie made sure he got the light boxes when it came to lugging them down the stairs to the van, (an old trick he learnt from me). On the upside we did manage to get a lot of packing and preparation done so that night after Jason had resumed his position behind the bar we all made a toast to our productive day.

By the time we were mid way through the second day we were falling behind schedule, I realised it was the continuous walking up and down the six flights of large Georgian stairs that was slowing us down. It played the biggest part in depleting the energy levels of my team of spliff smoking bar props. So I came up with a cunning plan that would halve the distance we had to cover and reduce the amount of effort required to get the goods from A to B. I covered every flight of stairs with flat packed cardboard boxes in a tongue and grove fashion enabling us to simply slide the boxes down to each other, so each man would only have to police two flights each. The only lifting involved would be from the apartment to the start of the slide just outside the apartment door, and from the ground level to the van. We introduced a rota system so that everyone did their fair share. The removal had now gone from being a laborious drudge to being fun and resembling an adventure playground, even the client's wife joined in the fun when she slid giggling from top to bottom on our make shift slide every time she went out to the shops. There was a small passenger lift but it was strictly out of bounds for anything commercial, given that it was nearly as old as the building and also unpredictably temperamental. So day two just got better and better and once again that night we found ourselves in the pub patting each other on the back and toasting another productive day with the free pints of lager served up by Jason. In fact it went so well that we were now way ahead of schedule, my slide idea had knocked at least a couple of hours off our loading time. I phoned Franco to let him know that everything was going smoothly, and to reassure him that we would be finished by lunch time the following day. Most of the boxes and two thirds of the furniture had already been taken to our warehouse over the last two days, so on day three of the operation we were required to finish wrapping and packing the last few boxes and the odd stick of furniture. The only snag was a couple of three seater sofas which would not pass through the front door, so would have to be taken out of the window via a series of ropes and pulleys. Over the past 17 years that I had been working with Franco this type of problem had cropped up on numerous occasions, so I was more than confident that between the four of us we could manoeuvre the sofas out of the living room window and lower them down 50 odd ft to the pavement below without any complications. During the morning Franco phoned and told me to get one of the lads to take the van and pick up some boxes of silver from another client in Kensington. The goods were part of another consignment due to be loaded onto a lorry which was leaving that lunch time. I couldn't send Mattie or Tony since neither of them held a full driving licence, so I sent Jason who was more than happy to go. I made the decision to crack on with the other items that could be carried down through the building, and leave hauling the sofas until Jason had returned. I knew from experience that it would take every inch of four men to execute the tricky procedure of abseiling two large sofas down the face of the building. With no van to load we began stock piling the goods inside the spacious foyer on the ground level. It was around 10.30 in the morning and I guesstimated that Jason would be gone for about two hours which would make it close to lunch break by the time he got back. Anyway Tony Mattie and me were more than able to cope without him for a couple of hours seeing as he had only been contributing about 15% to the overall effort.

Just after midday Franco phoned to see how we were getting on, he needed us to be finished by 3.pm since there was going to be another lorry at the warehouse that he would need help loading. I told him that we had everything apart from the sofas piled up on the ground floor, and we were just eating lunch while awaiting Jason's return. Loading the van would take the four of us half hour tops, and then another hour and a half for the sofas, so we should be back before the deadline. He told me that Jason had just pulled away and was on route to us with the now empty van, Franco's final comment was one he frequently used, "quickwy eh!

Half an hour later at 1.pm the three of us had long finished eating our filled crusty rolls from the local bakers and were now twiddling our thumbs. At 1.30.pm Tony had started cracking jokes after a couple of reefers were passed round, but still no sign of Jason. By 2.pm it was getting to the point where I would have to phone Franco since Jason wasn't answering his mobile phone and should have arrived over an hour ago. It was embarrassing though, seeing as I recruited him and vouched for his professionalism. The journey from Battersea to Holland Park would normally take 20 minutes, even on a bad day so I was now beginning to worry. At 2.30.pm I was pulling my fucking hair out and had to phone the boss in view of the fact that he was expecting us to pull into the warehouse at any moment with a full van. Franco wasn't very happy when I told him we'd lost our driver, naturally he went berserk and was blaming me for hiring an idiot. Jason eventually turned up at 3.pm and nonchalantly jumped out of the van like nothing had happened.

"Alright lads?

"No we aint fucking alright Jase, we've been waiting here for nearly three hours, where the fuck have you been?

"Nowhere Rick, I left the warehouse and drove through Victoria, then drove up Park Lane, I turned left onto Bayswater road and came straight here."

"And that took you three fucking hours did it? come on Jase don't mug me off mate, it takes half hour at the most to get here from the warehouse, now where the fuck have you been? I could smell alcohol on his breath and he was shifting about nervously.

"Rick I swear, I left the warehouse and drove through Victoria, then drove up Park Lane, I turned left onto Bayswater road and came straight here." For some reason he was trying to push this particular Victoria and Park Lane route on me, like he was steering me away from the real route he'd taken. I continued to grill him about the missing few hours knowing full well he was blatantly lying, but he stuck to his ridiculous, nonsensical, and well rehearsed version of events, only this time he remembered that the traffic was diabolical. To be honest a Jumbo Jet could have crash landed in the middle of Park Lane and it still wouldn't have taken him three hours. An hour later we had finished loading the van and were hoisting the last sofa out of the apartment when I looked over and noticed there was a fresh, rather large dent on the box of the van just behind the passenger side door. It was a Luton van so the box protruded about six inches further out on either side than the actual cab did. The dent was about waist high and was covered in dark blue paint scratches which had obviously come from the other party involved in the collision. The deep scratches continued at the same height for about a meter or so beyond the impact point.

Once the second sofa was safely on the ground I called Jason over again.

"How did that happen Jason? I asked while pointing at the dent.

"Fuck knows Rick, I aint got a clue mate, It must have been there already, unless someone hit the van while I was in the shop buying fags just before I got here?

Mattie and Tony agreed with me that the dent definitely wasn't there before Jason left with the van that morning. Jason was digging himself into a hole, and it was getting deeper every time he opened his mouth. I remembered him poncing a cigarette from Mattie just after arriving and at the time he claimed that he was dying for a fag.

"Let's have one of your snout then Jase, come on mate flash the ash." I said.

He pretended to be surprised when he patted himself down but couldn't produce the said packet of fags. Next came the pantomime of being concerned that he may have dropped them somewhere. We all knew that he was hiding something and was lying through his teeth. He was taking me and the others for right mugs, but he was such a likeable feller it was hard to stay pissed off with him for too long, and besides I had done some of my own lateral thinking and mental calculations. I had my own idea of what I believed actually happened but was keeping it to myself until the right time. These were my deductions: Judging by the height and location of the dent, the only thing that could feasibly cause that type of impact was some kind of small post or bollard about waist high. After racking my brains I couldn't think of any bollards that Jason could have hit along the route that he had tried so hard to convince me he'd taken. Also there was no doubt he had been drinking so I tried to think of a pub local to Battersea where he might have stopped, since going to a pub north of the river was out of the question and highly unlikely. I knew that like the rest of us, Jason would prefer a working man's pub with cheap beer, a cheese n pickle roll and a game of pool to boot, rather than a trendy bar with a glass of wine and a smoked salmon baguette. I knew it would also have to be far enough away from the warehouse that there was no risk he'd get noticed by any Vero staff who might happen to be passing by. Then it came to me and it all started to make sense. There was a boozer called the Prince which was situated on Albert bridge road about 500 yards before the approach to the bridge. Also, before crossing there were a couple of width barriers to negotiate which to my memory were dark blue. Vans weighing 3.5 tons or more were prohibited from using the bridge, but I had driven through those bollards hundreds of times when trying to save time and knew that the van would just about pass through with barley an inch to spare on either side. So I'm going to sum it all up in true Velma from Scooby Doo fashion. *(Jason left the warehouse and thought he'd nip in the pub for a drink believing that we'd all assume he was still busy back at the depot. True to form he more than likely got chatting to some other punters or whoever worked behind the bar. It was lunch time so he buys a cheese n pickle roll and orders another pint before joining the queue to play pool. He's having so much fun with his temporary new mates that he doesn't realise 2 hours have flown by. "Fucking hell is it half two already? He asks while legging it out of the door to the van. Jason knew that if he took the risk of driving over Albert bridge he would knock ten minutes off the journey. After three or four lunch time pints he was more than likely slightly tipsy which would have already impaired his judgement, let alone the fact that he had never driven the van before. So he crashes into the bollard and in his blind panic just forces his way through. Going by the depth of the dent he must of being doing at least 10-15 mph when he hit the bollard, rather than the 1-2 mph required speed. Once over the bridge he began rehearsing the spiel about his fake route along Park Lane, just in case someone noticed the damage.)*

After loading the last odds and sods onto the van it was about 4.30.pm and Franco had already been on the blower screwing about having to load the lorry on his own. I asked Jason to sit in the back of the van to make sure nothing fell over, because at the death we ended up loading plant pots and lamps in haste without tying them up. Whilst heading back to the warehouse, without going into too much detail I explained to Tony and Mattie that I had a theory of my own about what really happened to Jason and the van. I drove straight to the south side of Albert Bridge and parked just around the corner from the bollards. I went to the back, opened the shutters and asked a confused and disorientated Jason to jump down and follow me. My first stop was the dent in the van, without saying a word I measured the height of the impact against my body with my hand, which was at about the same spot as my hip, still puzzled Jason followed me as we made our way past Tony and Mattie who were sitting in the cab anticipating something, but still weren't sure exactly what. It wasn't until we had turned the corner and were face to face with the width barrier that the penny had dropped. Jason's shoulders dipped and his posture sank with the realisation that he had been rumbled.

Still holding my hand to my hip, I walked over to the bollard which happened to be exactly the same height, and to eliminate any remaining doubt I pointed out the remnants of turquoise paint from our van that were engraved into the bollard. Without further ado Jason threw his arms up in the air and confessed,

"You've got me Rick, sorry mate."

As we walked back to the van I gave Jason my best Velma impression, and summed up what I believed was his every move after leaving the warehouse. He was astonished at my accuracy, and again threw his hands up while apologising and shaking his head in disbelief. Tony and Mattie were puffing away on a couple of large spliffs and were still in the dark about what was occurring on the bridge. The very next thing they saw was Jason coming back around the corner with his arms aloft in a surrendering type gesture. They cracked up with laughter, and were so tickled by what they had seen that they were rendered incoherently useless for at least five minutes. Jason still couldn't believe how I came to know word for word everything that happened, especially after his efforts to throw me off the scent with the Victoria and Park Lane cover story.

"You should of just come clean in the first place Jason, it's the fact that you blatantly continued lying that's pissing me off, you must think I'm some sort of mug if you thought I'd suffer your sketchy account."

"I know mate, I was wrong, I should have just been honest from the start, I know you aint no mug Rick, even more so now."

Tony and Mattie still hadn't gathered their composure and continued to do Cheech and Chong impressions in the cab while Jason and I were at the rear of the van talking. Jason was so apologetic that it was hard not to feel sorry for him, so I didn't keep on breaking his balls about it. I took the wrath of Franco in my stride, because after 17 years I was too long in the tooth to let it bother me. Later that evening we were all laughing about it down the pub. Jason was still apologising and insisting on buying my drinks all night. He was visibly pissed and his speech slightly slurry when he started warning everyone in the pool bar, "don't ever try to lie to this man, he'll fucking catch you out, Sherlock Holmes has got nothing on him."

Speaking Italian and knowing so many Italian antique dealers and restaurant owners in and around the west end of London had its perks. We used to have many clients who did business with a very well known antique dealer called Chino. Along with his young wife he owned a shop and a restaurant on opposite sides of the same street just off Lancaster gate. So this meant paying frequent visits to his premises to collect furniture and silverware. Chino was getting on a bit and was already pushing seventy when I first met him in the early 90's so he had seen and experienced a great deal of life. He was an old school Italian and loved nothing better than treating people to a slap up meal in his restaurant while recounting stories from his adventurous life. So as you can imagine my co workers and I would usually make sure we planned our route so that we'd end up at Chino's at lunch time. The restaurant called La Trattoria, was very popular with Italian runners who would always be conveniently hanging around just as lunch was imminent. A runner was someone who drove around visiting second hand shops, car boot sales and flea markets picking up cheap antiques at bargain prices before running around London selling them to various dealers. I got in on the act too at one stage and good old Chino would always buy the stuff that I hadn't sold elsewhere, even on the rare occasion when I made a mistake and paid over the odds for something he would always buy it from me at cost price as a way of encouraging me to learn and get it right without losing money. Looking back though as much as I appreciated his generosity he should have let me learn the hard way like he had to. Sadly Chino died in the late 90's and doing business with his widow was a non runner since she was a damn sight tougher than chino who had obviously mellowed in his old age. I missed him, not for the business crutch he provided me with or the many free lunches, but for his wisdom, charm, and his general nice natured personality.

Another restaurant owner was a guy called Pucci who had a Pizzeria on the popular Kings road in Chelsea. He was a very flamboyant character and rather like a local celebrity. Pucci Pizza was the place to be and you would often see the likes of George Best and other famous faces sat outside eating or just having a coffee during the summer months. On the ground level inside the restaurant were tables full of people tucking into their pizza's or plates of pasta. They were surrounded by millions of photos of customers arranged in large collages that were hanging from the walls. The rest of the decor was made up of typical Italian designs painted on the doors and mirrors and had Italian themed table cloths. Downstairs in the basement was a funky wine bar with a disco and dance floor which came alive in the evening. Pucci was a friend of Franco's and used our company to ship furniture to his many holiday homes dotted around the Adriatic coast of Italy. He had his fingers in lots of other pies and had dealings with many of the local Fagin's. Rumour has it that he was also well connected in mafia circles too. Over the years I had built up a good trusting relationship with him and he often gave me surplus gifts like brand new designer shoes and coats. His Pizzeria made the best pizzas in London and he always made sure I never left with an empty stomach. He even invited me to join him and some of his friends on his luxury yacht for two weeks, promising me that there would be plenty of sexy women to keep us all company. The Yacht, he explained was moored just off the coast of Ancona and we would cruise around the Adriatic sea occasionally stopping over night to party at one of his beach properties. Although it sounded like a dream holiday for a lad in his 20's I had to politely refused since my brother and I had already booked a holiday for Venice which fell bang in the middle of Pucci's offer, so I was gutted about that.

One Saturday night my brother John and I decided to go out for a drink down the Kings road for a change. We tried a couple of bars and eventually ended up in a trendy pub which was ok but had no spark or atmosphere. It was about 10.30 pm and John was getting hungry so I suggested we went to get a take away pizza. After finishing our drinks we left the pub and walked the hundred yards down Kings Road to Pucci's. As we arrived we noticed there was a queue outside that stretched at least 50 yards back up the road and went around the corner.

"Sod that Rick, we'll be there all night queuing to get in, let's just go to the drive in McDonalds, and then we might still get in a club down the Old Kent Road."

"Hang on John, follow me," I said while making my way to the front of the queue. There was a bouncer and a woman standing behind a rope gate, the woman was holding a clipboard with a list of names on it.

"Hi, your name please," she said before glancing down at her clipboard expecting me to be on the V.I.P guest list.

"I'm not on your list darling, but could you ask Mr Pucci to come out please?

"Who should I say wants him?

"Tell him it's Rikki from Vero." She went inside and I could see her announcing me to Pucci while he was sat chatting to some diners.

"Rick what are you doing? Asked John who was starting to feel a bit uncomfortable since the queuers were grumbling about us trying to push in. Just then the door swung open and out came Pucci who was as flamboyant as ever when he flung out his arms and yelled,

"**Rikki** !!! Come sei Bello sta sera, look at you looking like a million dollars." He said while pretending to straighten my collar as he looked me up and down. He instructed the bouncer to let us through and after a couple of Italian cheek kisses he invited us in. Johns bottom jaw was already on the floor in awe after the fuss Pucci had made of me in front of the moaning queuers, but he was even more impressed when inside the restaurant Pucci clicked his fingers at one of the waiters and said,

"Prendi un altro tavolo Enzo," and just like a scene from the film Goodfellas Enzo and another waiter produced a table for two and found a nice corner of the restaurant to place it. Within seconds it was dorned with a clean table cloth, a vase of flowers and a small wicker basket full of sliced French bread. Pucci made a big fuss of us by laying on the proper V.I.P treatment, we felt like a couple of movie stars and I guessed most of the other patrons were trying to work out who we were. It was a very busy night as usual and we were advised that our pizzas may take up to 40 minutes to arrive. Jumping the queue outside was one thing, but there was no way Pucci would blatantly serve us before his other waiting hungry clients. So he invited us to have a drink downstairs in the wine bar while we wait for our food. It was buzzing down there and the disco was in full swing. The dance floor was packed with trendy people of all ages from footballers to actors and rich kids from the local area. The atmosphere above and below ground was electric and our night out had improved 100%. Pucci told the barman that our first drink was on the house then he disappeared back upstairs to entertain his expectant diners. Time flew by and after about an hour we were called back upstairs to eat our pizzas. John was driving seeing as we were never initially planning to get pissed up, so once we'd finished eating we thanked Pucci for his colourful hospitality and left heading for the car. There was no need for loads of drink since we were still on a high from the spontaneity of the last couple of hours. We even managed to get into a club back in our manor and bumped into a few of our pals. Both of us were visibly pumped with adrenalin and eager to relay the eventful time we had down the Kings Road, and our mates were duly impressed wishing they had been there with us. John could now let his hair down and have a drink since we would be getting a cab home which made the perfect end to a great night. So like I said, speaking Italian and having some good Italian contacts does have its perks and that was just a couple of examples from hundreds of others.

FIFTEEN MINUTES OF FAME

I attended a very good acting school in the west end when I was about 23 yrs old and stayed for two seasons. The teachers saw potential in me and I was invited back on a scholarship for another season. Those acting lessons came in very handy when at 28 years old I signed up with a couple of television acting agencies. One of them dealt only with commercials and pop videos and the other dealt with movies and television programmes. Franco was very understanding giving me time off when an acting job came up. In total I did around 150 jobs and thoroughly enjoyed them all, most of which were walk-ons and background work. One of my favourites was when I got sent to Pinewood studios to do a walk on role in a Christmas W.H Smith advert. Shortly after arriving I was sent straight to one of the many make-up studios where there were two hairdresser type chairs. Before long I was being made up by one girl and noticed that 3 other make-up and hair girls were fussing over another guy in the chair next to me. During a break in having foundation slapped on my face I looked over at the guy who was being fussed over and it was Nicholas Lyndhurst (Rodney Trotter). He was playing four different roles in the commercial, the mother, the father, and the son and daughter and was about to do a scene playing the mother He turned to me and cracked a joke about whether or not his lipstick complimented the rouge on his face. I was momentarily star struck when I laughed and said, "It suits you." I couldn't believe it; there I was in Pinewood studios having my make-up done with Nicholas Lyndhurst. We all swapped banter for the next 15 minutes or so which put me at ease. I was trying to be cool, calm, and collective but inside I was buzzing with excitement. Nicholas went off to shoot his scenes, the other walk-ons and I sat around the studio drinking coffee and eating the complimentary food whilst waiting to go on set. Just when I thought things couldn't get any better than the makeup scenario it did, it got a hundred times better when I was chosen by the director to do a scene with just Nicholas and myself. While waiting back stage for the director to shout action the pair of us exchanged more banter and jokes. I was surprised to discover that I was slightly taller than him since playing Rodney next to David Jason's Del-boy always made him look very tall. We did a few takes before the other eight or nine members of the cast came on set for the final scene which involved all of us dancing around the living room coffee table. I left Pinewood studios that day feeling on top of the world and couldn't wait to get home to tell everyone about my day. When the advert eventually aired on television around Christmas time I was treated like a star in my local boozer. People were phoning me every day to tell me they had just seen me on Television, it was a great feeling. At one stage I was in 3 different adverts at the same time on all the commercial channels.

There was this one time when I went up the west end to audition for the main role in a Nissan commercial. My agent told me the job paid £300 if I was to get the part. It also had a contract buy out fee of £2200 if they used my scenes. I wasn't really expecting to get the part and to be honest it was a hassle grafting half way across London for another knockback but I went anyway. I was dressed in dark blue jeans with a matching denim jacket and had my hair in a quiff that day. In the audition room there was about three or four blokes and a couple of women. The camera man asked me to state my name, age and name of agency to the camera and do the customary profile shots before starting the audition. I had to sit in a chair and pretend to be driving a car down a long desert road and occasionally change the station over on the car radio. That was it, the whole audition had gone on for about 30 seconds when one of the guys said,

"excellent, that's exactly what we want," and the rest of them agreed. I thanked them and left, still under no delusions that I had got the part since that's what they always said at auditions. They were just being polite and would probably say the same thing to the next 50 applicants. Ten minutes after leaving I received a phone call from my agent congratulating me and informing me that I had won the part which was very odd since it usually took a few days before you'd hear anything. I was delighted, it was going to be my first ever feature role. I had done plenty of walk-ons in the past but never a feature. On the day of the shoot I was picked up from my house in an executive Mercedes and chauffer driven to the film set which was situated in an RAF military base in Bedfordshire. I was given a Winnebago to doss about in until they were ready to film my scene which was going to be a night shoot. When darkness fell a makeup artist and the wardrobe girl came and got me dolled up just before I was taken to the Nissan Truck. My scenes took just 25 minutes to film and before I knew it I was being Chauffer driven back home again. A month later I received a check for £2500 and that was the sweetest two and a half grand I've ever made in my life.

Another good day was when I was cast as a servant in two short scenes next to Ray Winston and Sean Bean in a film called King Henry the Eighth which was being shot at Arundel Castle. Obviously it was a costume drama and it was great dressing up in sixteenth century Tudor clobber. My scenes were shot at night in front of a raging fire and a huge banquet in the castle grounds. I was serving red wine to King Henry (Ray Winstone) and Robert Aske (Sean Bean) as they roared with laughter when recounting some of their many battle stories while trying to impress a group of castle cronies and various noblemen. I have always been fascinated with this period in history so it was mind blowing to be in such a realistic setting. With everybody dressed in authentic costumes and acting out scenes within the walls of a real castle I almost felt like I had travelled back in time.

CHAPTER V

INSIDE
THE BLOODY PETER

T HE NEXT MORNING at the crack of dawn Terry and I were woken by a screw telling us to slop out and be ready to leave in ten minutes. Slopping out meant taking your buckets of shit and piss to the slop out area where you would empty them into a large sink like structure with a big hole, jets of water would flush the contents away, and then you would rinse the bucket out, return it to your cell and come back with your tooth brush to clean your teeth in the basins right next to the slop out units. Not the best way to start your day granted, but believe me by morning you would have done anything to get the stench of shit and piss (with a tinge of blood in Terry's case) out of your cell. Ten minutes later we were cuffed and taken to the processing area where they gave us back our belongings and civilian clobber. After changing clothes Terry and I were about to be taken to separate holding rooms to wait for our relative sweatboxes to ferry us to our new destinations.

"Laters Rick, I'll probably see you at Ford in a few months."

"Yeah, hopefully, and thanks Tel, you've been a life saver mate,"

"No probs bruv." We shook hands and were then led off along opposite corridors. That day nineteen years ago was the last time I ever saw Terry, and still haven't seen him since, it wasn't until my release when I had time to reflect that I realised just how much that week or so I spent with him had set me up with the mental tools I was going to need for the following five months.

A few hours later after another sweatbox tour through the snow filled streets of south east London, I ended up going through the usual induction process at Wanno, and after the "Yes sir no sir three bags full sir" I was taken to my new wing, I breathed a sigh of relief when the kanga led me along a landing on the two's towards my new Peter. There wasn't a fourth floor so Fraggle Rock had its own wing somewhere else in the prison. Although much the same design as Brixton, Wanno was a lot older and resembled the prison from the television sit com Porridge. It was built and used by the early Victorians, and apart from a lick of paint here and there it hadn't changed much. On first impressions Inmates appeared to be less tense than the ones in my last dwelling, Brixton felt like a pressure cooker ready to explode, but here at Wanno I heard laughter and the Hum of relaxed chatting as prisoners who had sweeping jobs went about their business. It wouldn't be long before my second impression would kick in, the screw opened the last door at the end of the wing it was a single cell with one bed. Still holding my bedclothes and plastic cutlery I walked in, the door slammed shut behind me, the sound of the keys locking the door had a profound effect on my psyche, again it was the realisation that someone else was in control of my life and I was powerless to do anything about it. I was about to put my bundle on the bed when I noticed it was soaked in blood right through to the bottom of the mattress, the surrounding walls were also covered in blood and a puddle of it had formed on the floor. The small window was about six feet up and had been smashed with trickles of dried blood coating the remaining shards. On the outer part of the window ledge were the stereotype prison bars and the ledge was covered in snow and had three pronged pigeon footsteps in it. A snowy chill was blowing through the broken window which offered a view of another two or three prison blocks with hundreds of iron barred windows and acres of barbed wire stretching across the highest brick walls I'd ever seen. There was absolutely no civilian landscape in sight which added to the soul destroying feeling of being institutionalised. The slop out bucket still had shit and piss in it, my heart began to sink, this was the lowest I'd ever felt in my whole life. I found a clean piece of floor near the door and sat down crossing my legs to prop up my bundle of sheets trying to keep them clean. I lit up a fag and began telling myself to keep it together. About five fags and an hour later I got up and decided to jog on the spot to keep warm and take my mind off what looked like the crime scene from a Jack the Ripper murder. I heard some activity on my landing which was heading in my direction and before long my cell door was unlocked.

"Exercise," said the screw with a harsh Geordie accent.

"Guvnor, my peter is covered in Claret, the bed is soaked and it's snowing in there," I said trying to catch him up as he marched back along the wing at pace. But my plea's fell on deaf ears; he weren't having any of it. I didn't pursue my complaint since I didn't want the other inmates to think I was wilting, so after calling him a prick under my breathe I joined the other inmates on the two's and headed off to get some exercise. The usual practice was walking around the yard for an hour but due to the snow and ice outside we were given indoor exercise instead. We must have gone through five or six locked iron gates before arriving at the gym. Given the choice of weight training or basketball, I opted for the latter since I used to play for a local team in Peckham and was pretty good at it. This proved to be a good move because my competence earned me the respect of most of my new team. After scoring at least 6 baskets and setting up others to score I had learned most of my team mate's names and they knew mine. During a rest period I got chatting to a group of blokes from my landing and soon built up a good rapport with them. Three of them were prison freshmen like myself and the other four had been here a lot longer.

"I noticed that you were given the end Peter," said one of the four old hats.

His name was Sean, he was slightly taller than me with long hair tied in a ponytail and looked about 30 years old, he was doing a 3 stretch for a string of warehouse burglaries.

"Yeah cell number 34, what happened in there, there's fucking Claret everywhere? I asked.

"Two days ago some poor Cunt who couldn't hack it turned Fraggle and cut his own throat with glass after smashing the window," explained Sean. "Why, have they still not cleaned it up yet? He asked

"I'm not being funny mate, but it looks like a fucking scene from the Texas chainsaw massacre in there," I moaned.

One of the other blokes called John piped up and declared,

"Well I heard whispers that the kid owed Mad Angus for a lump of gear and got carved up when he refused to pay,"

"Who the fuck is Mad Angus? I asked, already disturbed by the mere name of the guy.

"He lives on the three's and he's a couple of pork pies short of a picnic if you know what I mean, do what we do and give him a wide birth," said Sean doing a cuckoo impression.

"So did the poor geezer die then," I asked.

"Well let's just say he didn't look too healthy as they stretchered him out," Sean said as he moved his index finger from one side of his neck to the other.

"Yeah, he's definitely wearing a toe tag." Added John.

It did sound a bit odd that someone might cut their own throat and even though Mad Max's involvement was just a rumour it wasn't difficult to make the decision to avoid him at all costs. Sean suggested that as soon as we get back on the wing I should go to the wing office and put in a cell change request. So after exercise was over I took his advice and did just that. Everything you had to ask for involved filling out a request form, I wouldn't be surprised if they had a request form for taking a shit. While at the wing office I took the opportunity to fill out an application for re-allocation to a D category prison (a.k.a Open Nick).

"Get a fucking move on, it's lock down time," growled the Geordie kanga as he poked his head around the office door. By now the other inmates were already locked up and I saw my chance to appeal to his softer side as he led me along the landing towards my blood stained Peter.

"Guvnor, I can't make my bed, it's covered in blood . . ."

"Stop whinging, "you're here to be punished," he interrupted.

I was wrong, he didn't have a softer side and yet again he copped a deaf'un to my pleas.

Back in my cell I decided I would make the best of a bad job and made good the bottom end of the mattress with the two bed sheets which would give me a clean space to sit down, and maybe even big enough to curl into a foetus position when it was time for bed. One of the more charitable screws gave me the chance to slop out my bucket just after dinner. I remembered Terry telling me to always pick an orange from the fruit basket when collecting my food because if you put the peel in the slop bucket it would cancel out the acidic smell of piss, and to my delight this little trick worked a treat. If you were caught short and needed to take an un-scheduled dump the remedy was to shit on a newspaper, wrap it up into a parcel and drop it out of the window without getting seen by any patrolling screws in the yard. Anyone getting caught dropping shit parcels would be made to clean up all the other shit bombs that lay strewn across the gutter of the yard. There would be at least 150 bombs on any given day so believe me when I say not getting caught was imperative. All prisoners were issued with a shaving mirror about the size of a deck of cards which came in handy when checking for patrolling guards, anyway I hadn't eaten anything substantial over the last 48 hours and was constipated, so taking a dump was at the bottom of my things to do list.

Later that evening as darkness fell the snow blizzard outside was gaining strength and it was literally snowing in my Peter. Only half of the dull light bulb was working with a continuous blink like a disco strobe light. I was shivering under my loosely knitted flimsy green blanket so I tried to block the hole in the window with a two-week-old copy of the financial times that Sean had given me earlier. This worked for about ten minutes since the paper was getting damper by the second and could no longer withstand the force of the icy wind and snow. The sound of prisoners screaming, banging and shouting grew louder and louder and was beginning to piss me off because I was trying my hardest to hear the sound of Blakey's or jangling keys on my landing. I wanted to try and get the attention of one of the night shift Kanga's hoping they would be a little more humanitarian to my plight. I noticed there was a red button on the wall next to the door, initially I thought it was a light switch. It had press once written underneath it so I pressed it once for about five seconds but the cell light stayed on, what was I thinking? The screws controlled the lights just like they controlled everything else. I heard the metal ping of Blakey's walking along the two's getting closer and closer, the 6 inch square sliding peep hole on my door slid open with a bang. All of the prison fixtures and fittings seem to be made from iron so due to the acoustics created by the size and shape of the wing, any interaction with locks and bolts etc seem to echo for an eternity.

It was the fucking Geordie prick, he looked through the square gap and barked,

"What's wrong, why are you ringing the fucking bell, that's for emergencies only."

Hardened by the events of the last two days I was beginning to get the right hump and had dropped the little boy lost routine.

"My fucking bed is covered in fucking blood, the fucking walls and floor are covered in blood, there's fucking glass everywhere, and there's enough snow in here to house a family of fucking polar bears, now I'd call that a fucking emergency wouldn't you?

I snarled screwing up my face.

"Get ya fucking head down and stop fucking whining you soft southern bastard," he said in a whispered growl. At this point out of sheer desperation I'd lost the plot, all elements of logic and common sense had deserted me when I furiously replied,

"Bollocks you fucking northern Cunt, are you some sort of Prick or what?"

"You fucking talk to me like that again and you'll be up in front of the wing governor, do you understand, he said as he slammed shut the sliding peep hole pushing the bolt back down.

"Take me to the fucking governor, "I said banging the door. "Take me to the fucking governor, go on! I shouted. I'd already crossed the line so thought what the hell, even the block was sure to have a better cell than this. I fucking hated him and at that moment I was determined to look him up when I got out and kick his fucking head in. I even confirmed this fact during my angry outburst, which wasn't the most intelligent thing to do.

I heard him exit the squeaky iron gate at the end of the landing (what is it with prisons and squeaky gates?) and had a feeling he would be back with re-enforcements to escort me to the Governor, but he never did come back. I was pumped and it took at least half hour of pacing up and down in the two square feet of clean floor before I calmed down. Whilst sitting back on the corner of my bed I saw a book that I hadn't noticed before which was laying down on the otherwise empty bookshelf. Great I thought, I could get lost in this book which would take my mind of the fact that there were probably Eskimo's in Antarctica who were warmer than me. I grabbed the book then sighed deflated as I read the ironic title, Steven Kings Misery. After chucking the book at my cell door in despair I curled up as small as I could and pulled the blanket over my head in an attempt to drown out the screams coming from other prisoners who were presumably in Fraggle Rock. I rolled up a fag just before the cell's flickering light went out and I spent the next hour wondering how Terry was getting on in Cockroach alley. I wished he was here now, he wouldn't have let this happen, he would have made sure we had it cushtie. But like I said previously Terry wasn't gonna be there to wipe my arse and I would have to adapt and grow up pretty quick. It was a case of sink or swim and I was now treading water. I was exhausted after having an eventful and emotional day so not long after stubbing out my roll up I curled up like a dog in a basket and dropped straight off to sleep.

CHAPTER VI

PETER 23

THE FOLLOWING MORNING I was woken up by the Geordie kanga, (did he ever go home?)

"You're going to a new cell, leave all this shit here I've got you some fresh sheets and a new blanket, just bring your cutlery," he said with a softer tone to his voice.

Was this the same hard-nosed git from last night or did he have a twin brother? I asked myself. After grabbing my cup, plate, knife and fork I followed him down the landing, about half way along he opened door number 23.

"There you go, plonk ya stuff down on the bed, then go and get yourself a cuppa tea," he said kindly.

I couldn't believe it my new Peter was like the Ritz, it had a shinny chess board floor, freshly painted walls, a nearly new mattress, new Pillow, a square bundle of crisp new sheets and blanket, not a speck of dust anywhere, and to top it all the Geordie screw had turned into mother Teresa overnight. I paused and gave him a confused look, he stepped in the cell and closed the door then quietly said,

"Listen when you walked in here yesterday," you looked like a rabbit caught in the headlights, I've seen youngsters with that same look in their eye fall foul to some of the hard cases in here and were given such a hard time they were almost suicidal, that's why you got both barrels last night, then when you called me a northern Cunt I saw the change in your eyes, you were sticking up for yourself which made me realised that my job was done."

I smiled shaking my head, like the penny had just dropped.

"Now do yourself a favour, keep your head down, keep your nose clean and you'll be shipped off to D Cat before you know it, now go and get your tea, I'll be letting you back out for breakfast in an hour."

"Thanks Guvnor," I said as I took my cup down to the boiling hot tea urn. There was a full bowl of sugar and a fresh jug of milk, I got back to my new cell and lit up a fag in celebration and sat on my new chair drinking my sweet cup of Rosie. The Geordie came back to lock me in chucking me his newspaper as he closed the door. I nearly pinched myself to make sure I wasn't dreaming and would wake up any minute in the blood stained Igloo at the end of the landing.

From that point on I'd turned a corner, over the course of the week I had settled in to the prison regime and made more friends, and as predicted by Terry I bumped into a couple of Peckham bods. It wasn't long before I was swapping goods with my neighbours using my Sling. A Sling was a long Piece of string with a sock or makeshift little bag tied to one end, with battery's to weigh it down. For example if my neighbour two or three cells along wanted some Rizzla, or backy, I would put them in the sock, then using my shaving mirror to see his arm hanging out of his window, I would swing my sling back and forth with my arm stretched through the iron bars until building up enough momentum to reach my neighbour. He in turn would be looking through his mirror enabling him to see when the sling was coming making it easier for him to catch. He would empty the sock and re-load it with whatever he was giving me, i.e. half a packet of biscuits, matches etc. Depending on how far away the swap would be, determined the length of string and amount of battery's required to reach the destination whether above, below or along the wing. My Sling was about 25 ft long, and during lock up periods, (about 22 and a half hours out of 24) there was plenty of Sling activity going on, you had to time it right so as not to get tangled with another. There was an art to slinging, and obviously the longer your sentence the better at it you became, not only did you have to reach your target you also had to avoid the Pirates. Pirates were other inmates who would grab your sling and rob the contents, these were mainly drug addicts or prisoners that you just didn't accuse.

THE BUTTERED BUN

From the day I moved into Peter 23, every time I'd get back with my lunch a bloke sporting a long ginger matted beard would stop outside my open cell door and in a broad Scottish accent would say,

"Juwanmadunarfrabatobun," I didn't understand a single word and to make matters worse he was about nine or ten teeth short of a full set.

"Run that by me again" I asked.

"Ah said Juwanmadunarfrabatobun"

Still not understanding a word he had said and now lacking the patience to even try, I replied, "No thanks mate," I gathered he was offering me something in return for something else but due to the fact that he looked like the type of guy who would benefit from a few grand's worth of Psychotherapy, I thought it best not to try and find out what he wanted. But after about 10 repetitive days of Juwanmadunarfrabatobun Ginger beard was beginning to piss me off. So on the next day when he stopped at my door I was waiting for him and just before he got the chance to open his toothless gob I said,

"Look mate, have a fucking day off will ya, I don't understand a word you are saying, I aint got a buttered bun so stop fucking asking me every day." He didn't move and just stood there open mouthed with his dinner tray held in front of him so I shut the door in his face. Later on when let out for exercise I told my pal Andy from cell 22 about this feller,

"Yeah he stops at my door too, I think he stops at everyone's door and asks the same thing,"

"Do you know what he's saying? I asked him.

"Yeah," he said laughing, He's saying, "Do you want my dinner for a bit of burn," (meaning tobacco). "So he wants me to give him some of my backy for his dinner," I asked. "That's right," Andy said still chuckling.

"Has he lost the plot, why would I want to eat more of that shit and pay him for it with my ration of backy? I said as we laughed and carried on walking round the yard.

I got on really well with Andy, He was a muscle bound martial arts Instructor, and was 7 months into an 18 month stretch for GBH after the attempted murder charges were dropped. He lived just up the road from me in Camberwell, so we arranged to meet up for a drink on the out. He got a knock back on his first 6-month parole hearing. But was confident the 12 month hearing would give him his freedom, so both our e.t.r dates (earliest time of release) would be in June. Andy wasn't the sharpest tool in the box, let's just say he has never been known to use a word that might send you running for the dictionary, but he was a funny guy and always had me in stitches.

The circle of people I was moving around with were made up of Murderers, Robbers, and other heavy duty people who had reputations of violence, including a couple of fellers from Peckham who were doing bird for armed robbery. This served me in good stead when I found out I'd slammed my door in the face of Mad Angus's cousin. Mad Angus wasn't a big bloke, he was about my mark, he had the same long ginger beard as his cousin, and looked about 40 years old, but due to the fact he was a fully paid up member of the razor blade brigade and his first name was Mad, Slamming my door in his cousins face was not the healthiest thing to do. Even though at this stage I had some hard-hitting yardies and the Richardson's tribute band watching my back, I wasn't about to end up in a blind spot alone with ZZ Top, so I planned my every move carefully.

I was now three weeks into my sentence and had already adapted well into prison life after the initial shock of losing my liberty, but being locked up in a tiny cell for such long periods of time was taking its toll on my sanity. The feelings of isolation and disconnection from civilisation affected the way you would think. Living in a different world changed you into a different person, you became part of the institution, part of the prison and part of the walls of your cell, it's hard to explain, you could only understand if you had been there yourself. Things that were important to you on the outside had no relevance on the inside. So when my mother and brother turned up for my first visit they were the first piece of normality I had experienced for 3 weeks and as much as I tried I couldn't hold back the tears when my mum asked in her gentle caring voice, "Are you ok darling," Those four words broke down every mental wall I had built up, all that hard exterior I had learned to show since my episode in the blood bath was now flowing out of my eyes like a tap. Although not actually crying I was still trying not to show any weakness to the other inmates in the visiting hall, so quickly dried my eyes and took a minute to compose myself before continuing the conversation with my family. After the 50-minute visit I was searched and led back to my Peter. It was nice to see my nearest and dearest but tasting that slight bit of normality made my cell look even smaller when the door was locked behind me.

The following morning I got my first lot of mail from the outside, an ex girlfriend had sent me in a radio which made my cell feel more homely. There was a letter from my mother and brother and one or two from friends, reading them cheered me right up and I read them over and over again, Letters played a major part in keeping you sane while doing bird. It gave you something to look forward to when waking up in the mornings.

At lunch time our cell doors were unlocked and each landing would have to wait until the floor below them had finished getting their grub before being allowed down to get your own, so we'd all be lolling about just outside our cells for 10 minutes or so whilst watching all the commotion below us. One day a bunch of us were leaning over the railing and chatting while waiting for our turn to raid the bay marines, my immediate two neighbours to my right and my immediate two neighbours to my left and I had our own little clique and usually moved about together, I couldn't help noticing there was something familiar with the situation and for some reason I mentally projected myself to the landing directly opposite and looked back towards our group. All of a sudden I was overwhelmed with a rush of de ja vous but this time no vision because it wasn't a vision, it was real life, it was five blokes leaning over a railing with a landing just above their heads (the 3's) and due to a couple of spent light bulbs our section was dimly lit. I was the man in the middle, the face that I felt a very strong connection with but could never quite work out who he was due to the blur on zooming in. Aghast I started to walk backwards into my cell which was directly behind me, I was trying desperately to take it all in and make sense of it. With my jaw still a couple of inches short of hitting the floor I sat on the bed in a daze, what I had just seen in real life was the exact same picture of my vision word for word. I became aware that I was staring at my calendar and checked the date it was February 20th 1991, precisely a year after I had a fit in Maria's bedroom. I was numb for the whole day just trying to get my head around it, had I predicted my future? Had something or someone been trying to warn me that this was where I would end up?

Back in 1986 whilst asleep in bed with Lorraine I dreamt that the caretaker of my primary school (Mr Boyce) had just told me that Deb had been killed in the war which was taking place there and then in the school playground, I was woken up by the phone ringing at about 11.30 pm. It was my mother, she was calling to let me know that Deb had just been found dead in his flat. Now that freaked me out but it was nothing compared to finding out I had predicted my own future down to the last detail. The thing about Prison though, was that things happened and situations changed on a daily basis so you would never really dwell on one particular issue for too long.

BACK TO REALITY

I found out that Mad Angus had no beef with me when I mistakenly ended up alone with him in the washroom whilst washing my hands. He walked straight past me to the next sink and started brushing his teeth whilst humming a tune between spitting out the paste. He had ample opportunity to make a move on me, but whether or not he was in the dark about my episode with his cousin, or he was worried about the company that I kept was anyone's guess, after all shutting my door on his cousin wasn't exactly crime of the month. That evening around the time when the tea round usually came along the two's, I got my plastic cup ready for filling as the screw unlocked my door. It was the Geordie, "After your tea get your stuff ready for the morning, you're being shipped out first thing," he said handing me a small prison issue transparent plastic bag.

"Where am I going Guvnor? I asked as the inmate filled my cup from the tea urn

"Butlins, you lucky bastard," he grinned.

"What do you mean, Ford? I asked excitedly

"No Stanford hill open nick on the Isle of Sheppey, I'll be back in the morning at 6.am." he said as he closed my door. Sitting there drinking my tea and smoking a stick thin roll up, I had a mishmash of emotions, on the one hand I was excited about going to this place I'd heard so many good things about, on the other hand I had settled in at Wanno. I had made friends and knew where I stood so going somewhere new would mean starting all over again. That night I wrote a few good-bye and good luck notes for various different friends that I had made during my stay at Wanno and left them with Andy to deliver. I hardly slept a wink that night, with a mixture of excitement and dread my brain was working over time, it was the not knowing that caused the trepidation. By 2.am after nervously smoking my way through 10 roll ups I eventually fell asleep. As before I woke every hour on the hour tossing and turning until dark inevitably changed to light. It was my last night in bang up and my last night in Peter 23, within the few weeks I'd spent there I knew every brick, every nook and cranny of my cell right down to the last detail.

CHAPTER VII

LEADER OF THE B WING FIRM

A T 6 AM on the dot I was taken down to the processing area and went through the usual scenario of changing clothes etc before joining a group of other inmates who were also going to the Island. This time though we were hand cuffed in two's and then loaded on to a standard run of the mill coach. At first it was strange to see civilisation again after being locked in a cell for the last three weeks, it felt like I was being released but the journey to the Isle of Sheppey would take us through the out skirts of my old manor, so driving past places that were close to my home, and knowing I couldn't ring the bell and get off the bus, reminded me I was a prisoner with at least 4 months left to serve.

It was sunny and quite warm for February, the snowy streets had begun to thaw, gardens and parks had the remnants of melting snowmen dotted around. I was handcuffed to an Irish bloke who was about 50 odd, he looked like he'd just been picked up from a park bench and had all the signs of a homeless alcoholic. He had two fingers missing on one hand, a broken nose, scars all over his face, and a Nicotine stained grey moustache to match his remaining fingers. Every time we drove past a pub he would tell me how he used to drink there, and had a story to tell for each venue. When he wasn't boring me with his life story of intoxication, he seemed to be having a conversation with himself, so I was relieved when we pulled into the gates of H.M.P Stanford Hill.

Stanford Hill was nothing like the high security bang ups in London, it had wide open green spaces, a dairy farm with at least 200 cows grazing in the fields, a pig farm, a Church, a library, a gym, an Indoor swimming pool, a football pitch, and two new red brick buildings A wing and B wing. On first impressions it appeared to be like an on campus college or university. There were no walls or barbed wire or patrolling guards with dogs, no bars on windows or shit parcels in the gutters. Inmates were walking about with no sign of handcuffs or being shadowed by a screw, there were prisoners laughing and chatting while mowing the lawns and tending to the flowers, I was beginning to understand what Terry meant when he said, "It's Like an 'olliday camp."

As we drove towards the processing unit I recognised at least three blokes from Peckham who were holding rakes, brooms and grass clippers. They were part of the garden party who were responsible for looking after the lawns, trees and flowers in the prison grounds. There were plenty of other inmates who although trying to appear nonchalant, were purposefully gravitating towards our coach hoping to see familiar faces. One of the screws began un-cuffing us just before we got off the coach. Within seconds of stepping on to the tarmac and stretching my legs I heard a familiar Cockney voice.

"Oi, what the Fuck are you doing here?

It was Ed, I had known Ed from the age of 11, when he was 16 and lived next door to a couple of my mates on the Cossal Estate in Peckham. I wasn't that surprised to see him in prison, since from the early 80's he had rubbed shoulders with Peckham's underworld, and was always in the company of hardened criminals. In those days I was always climbing on roofs, Lighting fires, or breaking into the caretaker's office on the estate, and my name was always bought up at the tenant's association meetings in the Cossal club hall. Ed would occasionally tip me off about their plans to put a stop to my rogue activities, but at the same time telling me to behave my fucking self. I respected him for the tip off, but pot calling the kettle black came to mind when telling me to behave. As I got older I began frequenting the local pubs, the Star of India to name one. It was the liveliest boozer in the area and was always buzzing, the music was Pucka and people were always dancing. It was very comfortable with sofas and armchairs positioned around an open fire in the colder months. The best times were Christmas and New Year when everyone who knew anyone would be there. Even if you hadn't been there for ages it was the place to be during Christmas I've never known another pub with the same atmosphere. Ed would be at the centre of all goings on and would be flanked by the local names from the criminal brotherhood of southeast London. Being 5 years younger I hung with a younger crowd but would always acknowledge Ed and vice versa. One night that stands out in my memory is when I was sitting having a drink on the sofas with my girlfriend Lorraine, my brother John, and his girlfriend Janet. It was around about the time of the BROS hysteria, the DJ had just started playing "When Will I Be Famous," when in walks Mattie with two Brosettes on each arm. He was dressed in the stereotype Bros leather bomber jacket, the Bros ripped at the knees jeans with an American flag on them, his blonde hair slicked back, and sporting the Bros sunglasses. He was a dead ringer for Luke Goss and was milking it to the max. The Dj just happened to be his brother Dickie, so I'm sure he had planed his grand entrance beforehand since the timing was impeccable. He walked in like a star and everyone started cheering and encouraging him on to the dance floor. It all started a few weeks before when a gang of us were having a drink in the Pyrotechnic arms just up the road from the Star, and someone pointed out that Mattie looked like Luke Goss who along with his twin brother Matt Goss and a guy called Craig Logan, made up the pop group Bros. So he decided to cash in on his newfound stardom and went out to buy the clobber. Well it worked because I'm sure the four pretty Brosettes hanging off him were convinced he was the real thing, and he'd sometimes purposely walk past Matt & Luke's house in commercial way Peckham and get chased up the road by a mob of screaming girls. (Brosettes).

THE RAILWAY TAVERN

Everyone was gutted when the Star got shut down, and then later demolished. We always had the Railway Tavern to fall back on which eventually became our new Star of India.

A couple of years after being released from prison I started dating Mattie's sister Louisa and before long moved in to her family home with my dog Ben. Her house was opposite the pub so naturally we spent quite a bit of time in there. I was the captain of the pub pool team and we won every competition and trophy in site, we even made the sports pages of the south London press newspaper with a photo of the team surrounded by our trophies. One of the funniest games we used to play was something we called The Bottle game. Three or four of us would start playing and before long everyone else would get involved. Each player would stand behind a designated chalk line with an empty beer bottle in both hands. Using the bottles as support you would have to stretch out as far as you could without touching the floor with any part of your body, then place one of the bottles as far forward as you could manage before making your way back to a standing position using the remaining bottle. Everyone would scream with laughter when a player collapsed flat on his or her face. Another mate of mine Bradley was a lot shorter than me and the other players but he would somehow always pinch a couple of inches to edge his bottle in front of mine. After an hour of giggling our way through this game we'd have to stop since the bottles really took it out on your hands, we would end up with deep round bottle neck marks indented into our palms. The Railway Tavern was full of characters, and also had a large gay population, which made for a colourful atmosphere, and lots of banter. We all got on really well and there were no prejudices, but like any boozer there was always the occasional fall out and the pub had its fair share of trouble from time to time. In the mid to late 90's the cocaine era kicked in and it got to a stage when it would be difficult to find somebody in there who wasn't high on cocaine or stoned on wacky backy. The landlord Alf, was a diamond 99% of the time and also used to shovel a shit load of Charlie up his hooter which made it easier for everyone else to do it while on the premises. In fact Alf allocated one of the many rooms in the beer cellar particularly for the purpose of doing a few lines of coke and gave access to a privileged few of us. His logic was that if he kept us all hidden and out of sight, the other punters wouldn't catch anyone doing it in the toilets or anywhere else within the boozer. On the other hand it must have looked a bit suspect when half of the pub would just disappear and then re-appear half an hour later. In staggered groups of two or three and making sure we weren't seen we would go through the door marked private that led from the pool bar into the area behind the scenes where you could either go upstairs to the living quarters or down stairs to the cellar. Being in a cellar meant that our room had very low ceilings although it was just high enough to stand up straight unless you were a double for Peter crouch. The decor had no frills, it had damp brick walls, cob webs all over the place and smelt musky like a pile of dead rats but that was all part of its attraction. It wasn't long before we had make shift seats and tables and a few mirrors dotted about here and there, at times there could be anything up to ten of us drinking and of course chatting (mainly bullshit) down in our little lair. It soon became harder and harder to resurface back up into the bar since all the fun was taking place in our secret drugs den where people could drink, smoke dope and sniff cocaine at will, it was perfect. We'd keep Alf sweet by chopping up a few big old tram lines of Charlie for him to Hoover up his beak every 15 minutes or so when he'd pop down to check on us. He used to make sure we'd make an appearance upstairs periodically so as not to arouse too much suspicion, it would only take one miserable nosey bastard to clock on to our activities and we could all be on for a police raid which would result in Alf loosing the pub and us losing our underground club. Only trusted regulars were allowed in to our club and each one of us would have to be in Alf's immediate circle of friends and confidants unless they'd come highly recommended by one of us. I was well in with Alf since I was the captain of the pool team and he loved playing pool, like I said the Railway Tavern pool team had a fearsome reputation and were widely respected in the south east London pool circuit. We had countless trophies from our many victories over the years, so when Alf took over the running of the pub he also inherited the best pool team on the south side of the river Thames which pleased him no end. Our regular get-togethers in the pub cellar were rather like a freemasons meeting for the common man, only the secret handshakes were replaced with a nod and a wink and we never wore dodgy costumes, but we did help each other out. In our midst were Painters & decorators, plumbers, builders, van drivers, Cocaine dealers, Cannabis dealers and thieves you name it. There were stolen goods passing hands all the time and if one of us wanted something in particular there would always be someone else who knew were to get it. We were all pretty tight and most of us could rely on one another should there be a punch up on the cards. Talking of cards, Poker was also a key factor within our fold so you can imagine the scene, Beer, Poker, mirrors full razor blades, rolled up bank notes and lottery tickets full of nose candy, ashtrays full of spliffs, lots of laughter and plenty of people talking bullshit. It sounds like a very macho environment doesn't it, well that couldn't be further from the truth since half of our club were women. The women were the worst, they could snort coke at twice the speed of any bloke and could chat the hind legs off a fucking donkey. As usual all good things have to come to an end and it all went pear shaped after Alf suffered a severe stroke losing the use of the left side of his body. So it was a double blow seeing as he was no longer able to play pool, drink beer, smoke or take cocaine, meaning that it was no longer to his advantage to allow us to keep the Basement club running and our outfit was soon closed down. On top of that we lost a very good player from out pool team. Eventually just like the Star of India the Railway Tavern fell foul to property developers in 2003 and was to be demolished to make way for new homes. Decades of the local community's history, the pool team and our exclusive basement club was reduced to rubble along with the pub that had once sold ale and entertainment to the Victorians. Today in place of the once historic building is an ugly block of flats that resembles something my 8 year old son had once made from his Lego set. Luckily over the many years frequenting the pub I took plenty of video footage of various party's and charity do's that took place there, I also took some random footage of me and my pals playing pool or pretending to be filming a reality show and I am so glad I did since it was a special place for lots of us and holds fond memories from when we were young teenagers.

INSIDE

Like I explained earlier, whilst going through my teens I often ended up on the wrong side of the law, but on a much lower scale than Ed. Anyway hearing his familiar voice as I stretched my legs from the long coach journey immediately put me at ease, the fact of knowing someone from your manor was bonus enough, let alone someone who would definitely have had his fingers in all the pie's, and it wasn't long before this was proven to be true.

"Hello Ed, fancy bumping into you," I said smiling as I shook his hand.

At this point the screws began hurrying us along to the Processing room, so walking beside me for about ten yards Ed put his arm around my shoulder and under his breath said,

"Try and get on B wing there's loads of us from the manor in there",

"Ok B wing, so who else is here then? I asked.

He reeled of a few names including a member of his family, then pointing to a large hut like structure he said,

"See that hut, that's the stores where you will go to get your clothes after they've allocated you to a wing, give me a shout before you go in there."

After giving me a nudge and a wink he peeled off from the line and went back to raking the lawn. I re-joined the rest of the group and we were led into a small building for processing.

"Welcome to Butlins! Said a screw sitting behind the desk as I was shown into the allocation office.

"You will find this is a much more liberated regime than the prison you've just come from, but don't make the mistake of thinking we won't come down on you with the same severity if you step out of line, if you get kicked out of here for misbehaving you'll be getting a one way ticket to Camp Hill," he said as he gave me a kit change slip and a key with an (A19) tag, Camp Hill was notorious for violent offenders and madmen, no one had a good word to say about it.

"Off you go," said the screw.

I looked at him with confusion, "What happens now then Guvnor?

"Now you go and find your new cell in A wing then get your prison uniform from stores, then find yourself something to do for a couple of hours before lunch."

"What, no hand cuffs, no escort, just find my cell? I asked with a giggle.

"That's right, unless you prefer the cuffs," he quipped.

I didn't, and made a hasty exit from the office after collecting my property. When I got out side it actually felt like I'd been freed, I could go in any direction within the boundaries at my own pace, and without a screw escort. I had just come from a claustrophobic environment which had its own stereotypical bang up stench that I can only describe as a mixture of sweat and boiled cabbage, and now here I was breathing in sea side air coupled with the aroma of the freshly cut grass. I began ambling towards (A) wing taking in my surroundings still not quite believing I was still in prison. Other inmates were busy working or walking back to their various jobs after having their tea break, which is what I assume Ed was doing since he was no longer with the garden party. New inmates had to go through a week of inductions before being allocated a job. This gave you plenty of time to settle in and get used to the new regime. After a few minutes of walking about I arrived at my new wing, I was a bit gutted not to be given (B) wing, (another building about 100 yards away) but that all changed when I later saw the difference between the two. I walked through the door and found myself in a grand hall with a wing to the left and right, there were signs indicating the number directions and I found out my new cell was in the right hand wing on the 3's (top floor). The whole place was clean, bright, and buzzing with activity. There was a relaxed ambience about the place as I ascended the wide staircase; each floor had a large reception hall between wings. The first floor hall had two full size snooker tables and a TV room. The second floor hall had two table tennis tables and a TV room; I walked along the landing to number 19 and opened the door with my new key. It was the same layout and size as the Wanno cells, only it seemed more like a room than a Peter since it had a small MFI type wardrobe and desk, and no bars behind the normal looking window that had grassy hills and fields for a view. The bed and bed linen were pretty much the same as those in bang up.

Having a key to the door was gratifying enough let alone having a constantly boiling hot water urn just 5 yards from my Peter, it was situated in an alcove next to the washrooms by the entrance to my landing. I took my new blue plastic cup and a tea bag from my ration pack that was given to me when collecting my property and made my way to the urn, as I passed cell 18 next door, a feller about my age came out and introduced himself as Paul, he was to become a good friend of mine during my stay. Joining me for a cup of tea he gave me a quick rundown of the landing politics on the 3's and the rest of the prison in general before rushing off back to work on the farm. After another tea and a fag I wanted to take advantage of my newly obtained semi-freedom, and took my kit change slip with me to find Ed. I was curious to see what (B) wing was all about so went over there to look for him, It was a carbon copy of (A) wing apart from the Shabby décor, and the ropey fixtures and fittings looked like they'd seen better days.

I guessed Ed had just taken a quick shower when I spotted him coming down the staircase with a white towel wrapped around his neck and shoulders looking like a dead ringer for Roger Daltrey's Mcvicar, he was strutting around like he owned the place, I soon found out that he practically did. If you've seen the old classic film called Scum where Ray Winstone played the role of Carling then you would know what I'm talking about when I say this geezer was the fucking Daddy.

"You got ya slip," he asked me as we walked out together,

"Yeah, Here it is,"

"What does it say Rick," he asked.

"Prisoner W0290, on presenting this kit change slip at the stores you will be provided with, 2 towels, 1 Pair of prison issue jeans, 2 prison issue shirts, 1 pair of shoes, 2 pairs of socks, 1 jumper, 2 vests and 2 pairs of under pants. You will be required to wash your own clothes when needed blah blah,"

"Take no notice of all that bollocks, follow me." He said leading me over to the stores. The normal procedure was that you'd be issued with second hand prison clothes to the nearest fit, so if they didn't have your exact size you'd have to suffer whatever you were given. This could prove to be very uncomfortable when getting second hand shoes or boots especially if you worked on one of the prisons farms. Ed stopped briefly to chat to a bloke just outside the door. The stores hut had distinctive military feel to it resembling a makeshift air raid shelter. It was dark inside with a very low ceiling and most of the hut seemed to be built with corrugated iron. Inside there were two inmates working behind the jump. I gave them my slip and they began gathering my worn out tatty clobber instructing me to try them on. I was just putting on a moth bitten shirt when Ed walked in and said to the lads.

"Take all that lot back, this is my pal Rikki, I want you to kit him out with 4 new shirts, 5 pairs of socks, 4 new pairs of jeans, 5 new pairs of pants, what's ya shoe size Rick?

"Size 10,"

"And a new pair of size 10 boots, oh yeah, chuck in 4 towels as well, and if you see him in here again give him what he needs,"

"Yeah, Sweet as a nut Ed," said the two fellers as they started to rip open the plastic covers from my brand new clobber. The shirts along with the trousers and boots were a perfect fit.

"Don't let any Kanga's see you taking this lot on the wing, and for fuck sake don't let anyone on your landing know you've got all this new gear, you can't trust half of these Cunts."

"Nice one Ed you're a fucking diamond mate," I said as I finished packing my new clobber into a black sack.

I shook hands with the hut workers, "Cheers lads,"

"No probs bruv, sweet mate," they replied.

"I've got a bit of business to take care of Rick so come and find me in the lunch hall at one o'clock, you can sit at our table," whispered Ed before walking off to join his work party on the gardens. I managed to get back to my Peter without raising any suspicions about my over loaded bin liner, I hung some of the clothes in my wardrobe and hid a pair of jeans and two shirts under the mattress. Looking back I realise that if I was to have had my cell searched, the Kanga's would have looked under the mattress straight away, so there was no real need to hide them.

There was a seating area downstairs on the one's (ground floor)where some of the other lads from my induction group had gathered, so I made myself a coffee and went down to join them. We went through the list of jobs available while getting to know each other better. The highest paid jobs were the tedious ones for example, Components workshop meant sitting at a table putting industrial components together all day, I'd sooner stick pins in my eyes, or working in the Mill, this involved moving sacks of grain around in a dark and dusty shed and having to wear a dust mask all day, Fuck that for a laugh. I hate being confined and cooped up indoors so decided I was going to apply for the garden party, or the dairy farm, the money wasn't bad and at least I would be out in the open. The next hour or so dragged on a bit and I was Hank Marvin so when the lunch bell rang at 1. Pm I couldn't get over there fast enough. Whilst queuing for my lunch I spotted Ed and his some of his firm occupying a couple of tables. The dinner hall was massive, it reminded me of a large building site canteen and was already near full capacity. It was alive with the noise of chitchat, laughter, arguments, and food being scraped off the plates into the bins. I made my way over to Ed's table with my tray of food; he pulled out the empty chair from the space on the table that he'd saved for me.

"Everything alright Rick? He asked as I sat down.

"Yeah mate I just walked straight up to my Peter with the bag and no one batted an eye lid."

"You've had a right result, all that new gear only came in yesterday,"

"Yeah thanks for that Ed, that other old gear they were handing me was well ropey."

I recognised a couple of faces from our manor and we acknowledged each other with a nod and a wink. There were about seven members of Ed's firm including his brother Mark, and they were all dressed in new sharp looking prison attire. I sensed an air of dodgy tension around the group and noticed Ed's knuckles were bleeding and he was sporting a deep scratch on his neck. One or two of the others also had some battle scars. I soon found out that the business Ed had gone to take care of earlier had nothing to do with buying and selling when I asked.

"What happened to your Gregory?

"See them Darkies over there? He said nodding his head in the direction of a table full of black feller's who were looking battered and bruised.

"Yeah, I see them,"

"Well a few of them cornered a couple of pals of mine in the gym toilets, then they bashed them up before half inching their backy and a quarter of puff that they had been holding for me."

Ed never kept anything except a small bit of Percy on him or in his Peter and would always have someone else carry and deal his gear.

"They took fucking liberties and had it coming to them, so about half hour ago when everyone was on the wing getting ready for lunch, me and this lot got tooled up with a P nine in a sock each, then we raided their Peter's and done the black Cunts good and proper." A P9 was a lumpy old industrial battery about the size of a large bar of soap, so putting them in a sock and whacking it around someone's head was going to up the odds on you coming out on top and your opponent getting the message loud and clear.

"We ended up raiding four Peters and battered everyone of them cunts on that table, so they won't be taking any more liberties."

"Business as usual then," I smirked, provoking the odd knowing chuckle from around the table.

"Pity you never got on (B) wing Rick, we're running things in there, and you would have been well sorted."

"I did ask the Kanga for (B) wing, but he said you can't pick and choose where you want to go, you get allocated a wing and Peter and that's it,"

By now Ed and the lads had finished eating and began peeling off towards the bins to scrape and wash their plates and stuff,

"I'll catch you up later Rick, and if anyone gives you any grief give me a shout," said Ed as he got up and left.

"Laters Ed." I said sitting at the now empty table on me jack Jones.

At this point the battered and bruised Jackson 5 were giving me Daggers as I tucked into my apple crumble and custard, which left me feeling slightly worried. Would they Plot their revenge on E's firm, and if so would I be in the firing line, or did they taste enough P9's to just keep their heads down? Under normal circumstances in and around our manor back home, I would have gone with the latter, but this was prison, and politics were a different kettle of fish in here. Well the short answer is no, there were no plans for revenge, they probably didn't fancy eating any more battery's.

Over the course of the week I didn't really see much of Ed, since my daily programme of inductions kept me busy in another area of the prison, and I found out that my lunch and dinner times were supposed to be half hour later than his. Basically the workers got to have their dinner earlier than the non-workers. Still, every couple of days he would come and find me on my wing to see how I was getting on and would ask if I needed anything. I was doing fine and getting my own little perks here and there, but it was good to know he was there just in case something came up that I couldn't handle. Even to this day I have nothing but respect for the way he looked out for me in Prison.

CHAPTER VIII

MAD MAX IS
JEKYLL & HYDE

TWO WEEKS IN to my Bird at Stanford Hill I had built up a good relationship with my neighbour Paul and got a job on the Dairy farm on his advice, Paul was an inch or two shorter than me and had dark curly hair. He was about 21 years old and we had similar athletic builds, every now and then we would playfully throw punches at each other in a mock boxing match, occasionally we got carried away and the punches became less playful but we knew where to draw the line and never fell out over it. I think it was just us taking the opportunity to off load some pent up frustration. I was also very friendly with a Cartoonist called Jim who lived in cell 17, being an artist myself gave us plenty to talk about. It wasn't long before I established my supremacy playing table tennis, and would be on the table for most of the evening since the order of play was winner stays on. My nemesis was a feller who was called Phil who lived on the landing opposite mine on the three's. There was nothing between us in ability and we had some major rallies that even the waiting queue would enjoy watching. Phil who Paul and I referred to as KD (keep dog) was a funny character; he was about my height 5'11", slim build, dark brown hair and was a couple of years older than me. His main passion in life was keeping dog, I mean this bloke never relaxed, the door to his Peter was always open, and the split second a Kanga entered our wing he would stick his head out of the door and holler out, ON THE THREE'S, he even covered the one's and two's. He was as reliable as clockwork, and hated it if someone beat him to it; a surprise ambush from the Kanga's was nigh on impossible with this guy around. So my neighbour Paul and I would purposely wait until we saw a kanga approaching our wing so we could holler out, "ON THE THREE'S just to wind KD up, it was worth it just to see the vacant look on his face after realising he had missed an opportunity to keep dog.

Everyone from my manor lived in B wing, but I was quite happy where I was after having made plenty of friends in a short space of time. There were a couple of Northerners from the two's who were tickled by the fact that I came from Delboy's neck of the woods, so they started calling me "Peckham" for a laugh. It wasn't long before my new nick name stuck and from then on I was known as 'Peckham' by most people on A wing.

From 9.pm we were confined to our landing but were free to socialise until 10.pm, after which we would have to stay in our Peter's unless gagging for a shit or piss. I started drawing portraits for my fellow inmates, mainly of their wives and children, and would earn extra backy, food or phone cards, which was the main currency in the nick. So I had plenty to keep me occupied after ten o'clock. While drawing I would listen to Caesar the geezer on Invictor fm, he had a wind up show that would have me in stitches. At this stage I had photos of my family and friends pinned on my notice board, plenty of fags and munchies, tea and coffee on tap, new lemon and peach smelling toilet tablets in a dish of water that filled the room with a fresh aroma, so my living conditions had notably improved since being in Wandsworth, but although much more comfortable than bang up it still had its low points. I was still under lock and key and had limited movement, It was prison, frustration and depression would still kick in, but that wouldn't last long due to the fact of being too busy to let it drag you down, anyway going to work on a diary farm every day was great fun even if it was hard graft at times. I've never tasted anything fresher and more thirst quenching than milk immediately after it had been pasteurised and chilled. This also had its perks as I would sneak a bottle of milk on to the wing and it was great currency around the tea urn. We were all at it, (my work team) there were a group of six of us who worked with the 272 Friesian cows. Our job description required us to feed them vitamins by filling the 150 meter long metal troth with oat type spherical biscuits. They would stand side by side on either end of the troth whilst eating, mooing and pooing. It wouldn't take long for the cows to polish off every last crumb, then we would lead them out to the fields to graze for the day. After doing so, it was our job to clear up the river of knee deep cow shit that they left behind while eating from the troth. Once we had finished pushing this river of shit out of the massive cow shed and into various big drain holes we would have to make their bed. This was done by spreading a fresh layer of hay on top of the old layer of hay which was matted with cow pat. We also took part in looking after the newborn calves, and making sure Del Boy (the farms only bull) was looked after. He had his own little shed and yard, he looked like he was wearing Del Boys sheepskin coat, hence the name. There was a gap in the wall just big enough for a person to pass through it by standing sideways, so a couple of the lads and I used to dare each other to stand inside his pen and wait for him to charge before escaping through the gap. Well one day when it was my turn again I was standing there eye to eye with this angry bull, I was 20ft away but due to the ferocity of old Del boy 20ft was still eye-to-eye in my opinion. You knew when he would charge because he would always scrape the floor with his hoof a couple of times before he bolted. At the point he began scraping his foot I turned to check my escape route to find the two other lads where giggling while propped up behind a 4 by 6 foot sheet of wood, and were blocking my escape. "You fucking wankers," I shouted. My heart skipped a beat as Del boy began to charge, I would have put Linford Christie to shame if you'd have seen how quick I got to the far wall which was low enough for me to scale at speed. This two tonne beast was eager to get revenge for all the teasing we had put him through by either crushing me or by goring me and throwing me skywards. I leapt up and just about got my legs out of the way in time. Del Boy was now shuffling in reverse so as not to crash into the wall. That was the last time I played dare Del boy, even though I swore to avenge my two giggling colleagues.

One of my work party was a Spanish Smack addict called Max, he was a dead ringer for the boxing legend Roberto Duran. He spoke good broken English with a Spanish accent and was in his mid to late twenties. He was a proper Jekyll and Hyde due to his smack habit, If he had his fix of heroin in the morning he would turn up for work whistling and singing and would happily work hard and was a team player, and great fun to be around. Along with the rest of our colleagues we'd often spend days in the fields gathering members of the herd who had strayed to the far corners of the farm, most of the time we would be jumping from one hay stack to another, or we'd just wander around the sun-drenched meadows chatting and telling funny stories. We cheered waving our arms in the air with pride when the groups of Tornado's returning from the first Iraq war would do a low level fly by spinning horizontally to show off. Most days on the farm resembled an episode from Last of the summer wine.

But if Max hadn't had his dose of smack he would be the most irritable, spiteful, lazy horrible bastard you could ever meet and during our 15-minute tea break he would often sit there and bitch about everyone and everything while continuously scratching his bearded chin, side burns and ears. On one of his bad days we'd regularly see him using a pitch fork to spear one of the massive rats who were co inhabitants with the cows. No one ever knew which max was going to turn up every day. So there was Paul who was doing 18 moons for burglary, Roy, doing life for multiple armed robbery, Trevor a.k.a. Pasty (he was from Cornwall), a 60 year old oddball who should have been on medication in Broadmoor, he was doing life for shooting dead his missus and her lover, there was Sean the leg, a.k.a Skippy whose right leg was about 6 inches shorter than the left, he was doing a three stretch for fraud, Max the smack head, and myself. One day Max had turned up for work in a bad mood because he was clucking for a heroin fix. We all watched him walk up to Daisy, (a cow that the rest of us had previously helped while giving birth) She had her head sticking out of the birthing shed door whilst allowing the new born calf to suckle at her udder. Max drew back his arm and punched her as hard as he could on the side of her face. That was the last straw, collectively we were already fed up with having to put up with his ever changing moods on a daily basis, so we all screamed at him." Oi, what did you fucking do that for? You spiteful cunt."

"Oh fuck off, he replied, we threw down our pitch forks in disgust and surrounded him. Roy, who was a big bloke, punched him in the face and growled, "How do you fucking like it," in his brummie accent, this led to the rest of us giving him a few kicks and punches too while calling him a fucking coward and an evil bastard. He rolled up on the floor into a foetus position covering his head with his hands. At this point we all stood back and noticed Trevor was gritting his teeth and had a crazed look in his eyes which were magnified by the 2 inch thick lenses in his national health glasses. He was the only one still holding his pitch fork which he pressed up against Max's neck and growled in his pirate accent, "if I ever catch you doing that again I'll ram this fucking thing through your sorry bastard head, do you understand? To which Max replied, "Ok, ok, I'm sorry, it won't happen again."

We eventually managed to get Trevor to back off and leave him be after convincing him that Max wasn't worth losing time for. After that day Max had lost the little bit of respect he had left within our group. He was shunned from any conversation we took part in, so inevitably he put in a request for a job change and got a job sweeping the wing.

CHAPTER IX

THE KING OF THE TABLE

TWO MONTHS HAD passed without incident; I had got to know lots of people and was quite popular and famed for being the man to beat on the table tennis tables since I was now more often than not getting the better of Phil (k.d). I noticed this middle aged man who would sit on the window ledge some distance from the tables and watch me beating player after player night after night. This went on for weeks he never said a word, he looked eager to play and I assumed he was either rubbish at the game or too shy to get involved. One day while chatting to a group of people whom he was with, he introduced himself as Alan before saying to me, "I see you love playing table tennis"

"Yeah, I'm the King" I replied with a confident cocky manner,

"You're good, but have many weaknesses" he explained.

By now the rest of the group had shown interest in our discussion, and not wanting to lose face I said with a cocky chuckle, "Oh yeah? Think you can take me on do you?

"I'll give you a game if you like" he said in his softly spoken voice.

"Ok let's have a quarter ounce of old Holborn on it then? I said giggling as I looked at the rest of the group as if to say, this geezer is mad he's going to get thrashed, to which they giggled back in agreement.

"Let's make it half an ounce" he retorted.

Still cocky and confident that I would send him back to his peter a broken man, and shy of half ounce of burn I said, "see you here at 8p.m then."

I have always been competitive and was pretty good at most sports; I love the buzz of winning something that I'm good at and hate losing. I've never been a gambler except on special occasions like the Derby or Grand National and have had the odd flutter when on a night out at Catford dog track with the lads. One night I was at the dog track with a few mates, Mattie, his brother Richard, and some other friends of ours who owned a couple of Grey Hounds. This particular night their quickest dog Nunhead Girl was in a cup race and the owners were confident she'd win. The bookies didn't agree so it was good odds at 5-1. Mattie and I joined our mates in putting a few quid on her. She was in Trap 4 and gagging to get out as the rabbit shot past. The race kicked off and 4 dog took the lead from the first bend, we were all shouting and cheering her on in amongst the crowd of other punters who all seemed to be echoing our over zealous screams of encouragement. Still in the lead at half a lap Mattie and I began to shout louder and louder excited at the prospect of winning a bully each. **"Come on 4 dog, go on 4 dog,"** we shouted as she came round the last bend a mile in front of the chasing pack. She Crossed the winning line and Mattie and I jumped in the air cuddling each other shouting YEEEESSSSS, the immediate crowd around us stop cheering to look over at us celebrating like England had just won the world cup, then Richard said, "there's still another lap to go you fucking dipsticks. The crowd turned their attention back on the race while the now red faced Mattie and I died with embarrassment. The excitement began to reach its peak again as Nunhead Girl kept her lead and romped home down the final straight and we went through the whole celebration routine again, only this time justified. We were the laughing stock down the pub for a few weeks but we took it in our stride since we also thought it was hysterical.

Word got around fast and by 8.pm there was quite a gathering around the main TT table. As I entered the hall the atmosphere was one of expectancy with my usual victims, who were muttering and chuckling to each other knowing this grey middle aged man already at his end of the table with bat in hand was going to lose embarrassingly to the King. There were some whoops and cheers of encouragement as I approached the table, although secretly the now 30 strong crowd were probably hoping that Alan would wipe the cocky grin off my face since they were getting blown of the table night after night. The game had started and before long I was running around like a Gazelle escaping from a pack of hungry lions whilst trying to return his shots as he stayed put at his end of the table. It was five nil to him by now and my serve. Ok I thought to myself, let's see if he can handle my famous spin serve followed by a slam shot which usually sent my opponents to the back of the waiting queue. At 10 nil I was beginning to worry since he returned everything I hit him with without moving from his spot, while I tried my best to get from one side of the hall to the other struggling to reach the ping-pong ball. The expectant chuckling from the audience had now changed to one of disbelief at 15 nil. I couldn't understand how easily Alan was beating ME, THE KING, with no effort at all while I was sweating buckets trying my hardest not to lose by a humiliating 21-nil. Losing my tobacco was nothing compared to the deflated feeling I had when looking at thirty or so faces with chins on the floor after not scoring a single point against this magician with a bat. My arse was well and truly kicked, so with my ego still on the floor I ambled off to my cell. KD came to the table trying to restore some pride since he was my second in command. Yet again 21 nil. After seeing the king and the prince losing a battle against this new table tennis Wizard, the rest of the crowd declined Alan's invitations for a game so he came to my peter to collect his winnings where he found me still in disbelief at my downfall. I invited him in and started to divide my ounce pouch of tobacco into two halves and handed him one half.

"Keep it," he said putting it back on my table,

"No, it's yours, you deserve it after playing like that," I said

"I don't gamble, he said, "I just wanted to prove a point.

"Well you certainly did that" I sighed.

He then let me in on his secret. "During the seventies I was the British Table Tennis Champion for five years on the trot,"

He went on to explain how alcoholism had halted his career and ruined his marriage etc,

"I'll teach you how to play proper table tennis if you like, you are good but you approach to the game is totally wrong."

From that point on I spent every evening on the other table with Alan while he taught me how to stand and how to get your opponent doing all the work by placing the ball instead of relying on spins and slams. He taught me a whole new aspect to the game and before long (about a month later) I was winning at least 3 games out of 7 against him. Anyway loosing that very first game 21-nil in front of the expectant crowd taught me a very good lesson in life, no matter how good you think you are there is always someone out there better than you, so don't get too cocky. Before long Alan had been released so I began taking on the Queue of blokes on the other table again; this time much more relaxed, dignified, less cock-sure, and became even harder to beat. This whole episode came to a climax when I beat B wings champion in an all out prison contest. Alan would have been proud of his new apprentice, he urged me to take it up seriously when I got out, and regrettably I never did. All though I loved table tennis and got to a good standard, Snooker was my real passion. It was in my veins, I had been playing snooker and pool from a young age, and my real dad and my grandad had it in their veins too. My dad ran a snooker club in a work mans club in Cricklewood. I remember when we were quite young he gave John and I our late Grandfathers Snooker cue, it was a two-piece cue, nicely weighted and smooth, and definitely improved my game. I still have it in my Garage, it's a bit bowed so I don't use it anymore I have a nice one that I bought from the famous cue maker John Parris over 10 years ago.

Half of the pool team. from left to right, Mattie, Paul, Me, Dickie, Lisa

Me at Kims wedding

Me aged 13 -14 & Boomer, my neighbours dog

Me and Dickie in the Clayton arms

Jamming session with me on the piano and Mattie on the drums

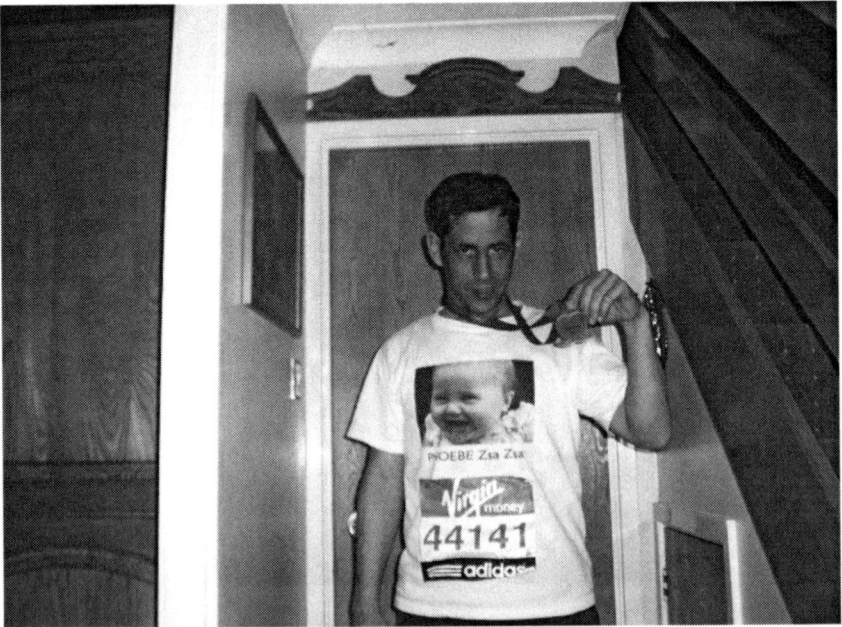

Me and Phoebe ran the london Marathon in 5.47 hours

Raul road, where I lived and grew up until aged 11

They Boysons, Me, with My cousin Lee and Brother John 2009

Tower block from where I threw the parking meter

CHAPTER X

NAME AND NUMBER TO THE GOVERNOR

ONE DAY WHILST at work on the dairy farm I had just filled up my plastic bottle of milk and plugged it away in my hiding place ready for smuggling back on the wing, when a gang of four prisoners from veg prep came down to fill up some bottles from the milk pasteurising unit. I got my blue plastic cup and filled it with milk and started drinking it as the gang were about to leave with their booty. Out of nowhere appeared three Kanga's, two were prison screws and the other was what we called a Civvie screw. He was the Pig farm manager (the opposite number to our dairy manager) He had always had it in for me after a failed prosecution attempt when on a previous occasion he thought he'd caught me stealing milk. They arrested all five of us and we were given a charge sheet, which read,

> *You have been charged with the un-authorised possession of prison property*
> *(milk) and must take this charge sheet with you to the governor's office in*
> *the block at 8.30 am.*

This would be my second visit to the block for the same offence, but I wasn't too worried since I had been in my place of work, and the Dairy manager always allowed his work team one cup of milk per day. The block was like a Police station, the cells were cold and glum and had a cardboard chair and table next to a concrete slab extruding from the wall with a blue plastic mattress. Prisoners were allowed to write their defence story on the back of the charge sheet which would be given to the governor 10 minutes before being hauled up in front of him and the prosecuting screws. I wrote the following.

> *I believe this charge is unjustified due to the fact I happen to work in the Dairy and was merely drinking my allotted daily cup of milk after a hard mornings work removing rivers of cow excrement from the barn.*

After fifteen minutes or so two Kanga's took me into the hearing where the judge and jury were sitting around an oval table. The pig farmer was sitting there with a look on his face that said, I've got you now you little toe rag. The Dairy screw was also present since he was in charge of the cow farm. One of the two screws either side of me who were looking straight at me shouted, **"Name and number to the governor"**

"Atkinson W0290 Sir," I shouted back whilst standing to attention.

"Prisoner W0290 you are charged with the theft of prison property how do you plead"

"Not guilty sir."

"We will now hear evidence from the arresting officers," said the governor who looked and sounded like a bumbling Mr Rigsby when trying to get into miss Jones's knickers. The pig screw began by explaining how he caught me with 4 other inmates filling plastic bottles from the milk unit witnessed by the two accompanying officers.

"Do you have any questions or anything to say in your defence? Said Mr Rigsby. (They obviously hadn't read the back of my charge sheet I thought.)

"Yes Governor, I would like to ask the two accompanying officers exactly what it was that they had witnessed me doing? I said whilst staring the pig screw straight in the eye.

One of the screws whipped out his little black notebook, took about 15 seconds to read over his notes and said, "On arrival to this particular area of the farm we found Prisoner one, two, three and four in possession of 4 plastic bottles filled with milk that had been taken un-lawfully from the pasteuriser unit, and prisoner W0290 was standing to the side drinking milk from a blue plastic cup sir," he said looking directly at Mr Rigsby.

"So you never actually found me in possession of any other milk apart from that which was in my cup? I asked.

Mr Rigsby nodded to the screw as if to say answer the question. After checking his notebook briefly he said "No, just the blue plastic cup."

"Well I'd like to say in my defence that as a dairy worker I have permission from the Dairy manager to take and drink one cup of milk per day, and when the officers arrived I was merely having my quota of daily milk." I said looking at the milk manager hoping he was going to back me up.

I was using my best official court language that I had learned over my many appearances in front of a magistrate for driving offences. The milk screw was actually quite easy going and more laid back than the pig screw, and I had always got on well with him.

"Is this correct? Said Rigsby to my boss.

"Yes sir, I have always given my work party permission to drink one cup of milk per day." The pig screw's face was a picture of anguish and shame, and then his cheeks went bright red like they were filled with venom as my eyes, now filled with imminent victory were fixed on his.

"Take the prisoner back to the holding cell while I make a decision on this case," said the governor to the two screws who had brought me in. An hour had passed before I was led back to face Rigsby for his decision. The other four prisoners had already been punished with a loss of remission totalling 30 days each for their crimes.

"Prisoner W0290, after hearing evidence from both sides I have come to the conclusion that no offence has been committed by yourself on this occasion, but let me remind you this is the second time you have been up before me on the same charges, and even though you have twice proven your innocence, you may not be so lucky next time, If I find you before me again no matter what the circumstances I will have no choice but to sentence you to 30 days loss of remission (a month on top of my original sentence) do you understand?

"Yes sir," I answered in an obedient manner, I glanced over at the pig screw who was now giving me a Charles Bronson type vengeful glare, even though he was a ringer for a plumper version of Stan Laurel.

"To avoid any more milk incidences I have advised your Dairy manager to put you in for a job exchange for either Veg-Prep or Catering duties in the kitchens, Said Mr Rigsby. Before long I was led back out into the main population. Whilst walking towards my wing I was gagging for a fag and found my charge sheet still in my coat pocket with my tobacco pouch. I'd stopped to light up a fag when I heard fast paced footsteps behind me, the pig screw had caught me up and tapped me on the shoulder, I turned to face him as he said, "you will fuck up again Atkinson, and when you do I'll be there to see you get what you deserve you cocky bastard."

"If you say so guv," I said blowing smoke hoops in his general direction followed by a wink. This pissed him off even more and he stormed off back to his pig shit farm.

After lunch I found myself with some free time on my hands since I had been banned from going anywhere near the Dairy, and I wasn't due to start my new job at veg-prep until the morning. I went to my peter and made a cup of coffee and made my way down to join a couple of pal's hanging around on the ones. My co-defendants were also knocking about and one of them who was called Brian piped up and said,

"Oi Peckham, how many days did you lose?

"None," I answered. There was a collective sharp intake of amazed breath.

"Fucking hell, how did you get away with that? He asked.

Before I had a chance to explain myself, one of my so-called pals named Robert popped his head out of his peter and said with a chuckle, "he probably grassed you all up."

Robert was a tall skinny bloke with receding blond wispy hair and was doing a three stretch for aggravated burglary, but pal or no pal he had just crossed a serious line. Even in jest, aiming the word grass at a man in prison could put him in grave danger. The atmosphere had changed in a split second, chitchat within earshot had turned to hush, you could hear a pin drop. I had to act fast to avoid any Chinese whispers and a possible conspiracy. All eyes were now on me, my stance changed from one of a relaxed posture to one of attack.

"What the fuck did you just say you fucking long streak of piss? I growled as I walked towards him.

"I was only Joking Rick," he said still trying to laugh it off. I grabbed him by the throat and pinned him up against the wall.

"Don't call me a fucking grass you stupid lanky cunt, I don't give a fuck if you were only joking." I snarled still gripping his throat, "Some people might not see the funny side, do you fucking hear me?

"Yes," he squeaked from his now traumatized voice box, "calm down for fuck sake Rick I never meant it like that".

"I don't care how you fucking meant it, you don't say things like that in here, and it's got fuck all to do with you anyway" I let go of his throat and gave him a firm but amicable slap around the face before I walked back over to Brian. I took out my charge sheet and started to read from the defence section.

I believe this charge is unjustified due to the fact I happen to work in the Dairy and was merely drinking my allowed daily cup of milk after a hard mornings work, etc.

"That's why I got away with it, they had nothing on me since I was well within my rights to be drinking the milk."

"Sweet mate, we know you wouldn't grass us up," said Brian as one of the other milk thieves glanced over my charge sheet whilst agreeing with him.

"Yeah but that silly cunt could get me carved up with his stupid sense of humour." At that point I didn't want to protest too much and decided I'd done enough to nip it in the bud there and then. At the same time I didn't want to walk away and leave them all to gossip amongst themselves, so I hung around and carried on like nothing had happened. Robert was trying his best to make it up to me after being told by one or two of our pals that he was fucking out of order. He invited me in to his peter to share a big fat Joint with him and a couple of other mates while we played cards. By lock up time the whole "Grass" episode was dead and buried, I returned to my peter on the threes stoned and ready for a good night's kip.

CHAPTER XI

THE FIVE LITRE CREEPER

A COUPLE OF weeks had gone by and me and the rest of the prisoners on my landing were relegated to using coffee mate as a milk source since I had been the only reliable fresh milk provider. Paul 18 still worked in the Dairy but would keep his bottle to himself. Most of my perks had dried up, I'd run out of my fellow inmate's families to draw and no longer had currency around the tea urn. I found myself in debt to the wing's puff dealer Bob after bailing a couple of £5.00 draws from him. I usually paid him with phone cards but had used them up on a deal the week before. Paul and I would take it in turns to supply the puff for our nightly game of cards in his peter. But this particular week we had no more strings to pull. It was Monday, we'd just eaten lunch and we were clucking for a spliff. I went to see the dealer who was around fifty yrs old and spoke like Bob Hoskins's character in the Long Good Friday. Somehow he always seemed to be half pissed, which was probably down to the fact that he was getting a regular supply of Vodka from a couple of lags known as runners. The runners would sneak out to the offy in Eastchurch village in the early evening to buy booze for the more affluent prisoners (dealers), and they would be paid handsomely for their troubles, since getting caught would mean getting shipped out to an A cat prison. Anyway when someone was as loaded as Bob there was no need to go down the prison Hooch route, since it tasted foul and you could never be sure of its ingredients. I knocked on his door (no: 26) and went in, he was counting phone cards from a stack of about 30, tied with an elastic band. He looked up over the rim of his thick sixties style glasses and said, "Have you come to settle up?

"No not yet, I promised you by Friday remember? I explained in my best trustworthy voice, but sensibly he trusted no one,

"You owe me a cockle so that's two cards, how are you gonna get two phone cards by Friday? You don't get your private spends 'till next week."

"My brother is coming on a visit this Friday and is going to slip me a twenty pound note," I told him reassuringly. "Tell you what Bob if you can give me a fiver's worth tonight I'll give you the score, so you'll be getting an extra fiver for the inconvenience.

"I've got a better Idea," he said grabbing his plastic cup full of coffee mate," I'm sick off drinking tea with this powdered shit, so if you can get me two bottles of milk I'll wipe the slate clean and you'll only owe me a card for today's bit of puff, how does that sound?

"It's a bit hot Bob, the fucking pig screw has got it right in for me and is dying to get his revenge, If he catches me even taking one step on the farm the fucking old bastard will have me shipped out on the next boat to Camp Hill."

"Take it or leave it Rick, 'cos that's the only hope you've got of getting any puff out of me before you pay what you owe."

"I'll see what I can do," I told him as I walked back down the landing to have a word with my partner in crime. After going over the details with Paul, he agreed that although very risky this was our only hope of getting stoned tonight.

As a teenager I had plenty of practice with entering buildings and evading capture, like Jones & Higgins for example, I'd also spent a fair bit of time up on the railway lines constantly looking for new adventure and easy ways of gaining access to various shops and small factories. In fact I was spending so much time up on the railway it got to a point where I was neglecting my girlfriend Sian, who could only tempt me into coming down with the promise of a bunk up. At 14/15 yrs old a leg over would outweigh any other priorities.

Paul 18 had been convicted for a string of burglaries called Creepers; they were given this name because the burglar would break and enter into a property regardless if the occupants were in or out, so would creep around as quietly as possible. You'd think you would have to be a bit of a creep to do something like that, but Paul was a speed freak and would inject himself with a gram of speed before setting off on a job. So we both had the necessary qualifications to pull this off. The plan was that I would meet him at the back entrance to the Dairy 10 minutes after he and his work party had locked up for the day at 4.30pm. This would give us about 20 minutes to get in and out of the building before the usual lorry would turn up to ferry the milk off to various other prisons on and off the island. The milk was put into 5 litre plastic transparent bags that were sealed at the top like the nozzle of a balloon. Then packed in to boxes, these boxes would then be loaded on to the lorry by the driver and his co-pilot who had their own key to the building. I had told Paul to make sure he knew the exact whereabouts of the pig screw before I came anywhere near the farm. So by 4.45p.m after a quick scout around Paul met me at the gate behind the Dairy.

"Where's the Pig screw? I asked him.

"Don't worry he's right over the other side of the farm," he said reassuringly. So in I went, there was no turning back now, it was all or nothing. We climbed up and on to a storage hut roof, which was attached to the milking building.

"Wait here and get ready to catch the bottles when I pass them out," said Paul as he disappeared through a window taking three empty plastic Lucozade bottles with him. After all burglary was his living, and I had only burgled shops/factories for the adventure and the adrenalin buzz. From my position I could see the narrow half a mile long dirt track that would be the lorry's route to the farm from the main road. I stayed low to make sure there was no chance of giving myself away to the pig screw or any other stragglers still knocking about on the farm. I looked around and began to panic when I noticed in the distance the milk lorry had just pulled on to the dirt track. Opening the window I called out to Paul in a loud whisper, "Hurry up the fucking lorry is coming." The lorry was half way along the track when Paul looked out of the window and said, "Grab this Rick," he was holding one of the five litre milk bags. I took it off him and he climbed back out of the window onto the hut roof. It turned out that Paul was having trouble opening the nozzle to one of the bags of milk so decided to just bring the whole bag by ripping the box open.

"How the fuck are we going to get this on the wing without being seen? It's fucking massive," I giggled.

"Let's get out of here, we'll cross that bridge when we come to it," he said as we climbed down off the roof taking care not to drop the bag. Five litres of milk is quite heavy and not easy to carry when escaping across a field. We managed to smuggle the milk on to the wing using my prison issue over coat while Paul went on slightly ahead to make sure there were no Kanga's en-route. We took the bag into one of the shower cubicles in the recess on our landing and filled up the 3 empty Lucozade bottles. This left us with about three litres left in the bag so we secured the nozzle put it inside a plastic carrier before hanging it out of the bathroom window. Most inmates had smelly trainers hanging in bags outside their cell windows so it just blended in with the others. I took the three bottles of milk along to Bob and gave him the 3rd bottle as a sweetener.

He smiled and handed me a fivers worth of puff saying, "that's on the house Rick, and we're all square now alright? "Nice one Bob," I said, eager to get back to my peter to celebrate with a nice joint and a milky cup of coffee. Three bottles of milk for 15 pounds worth of rocky, you might be thinking doesn't add up. Not in the real world but in here the fiver lumps of puff were no bigger than a fag butt. So when all is said and done we had risked getting our arses sent to Camp Hill for a fag butt worth of Rocky, But boy were we giggling that night? For the next couple of days or so prison life had got somewhat easier, the whole landing on the three's had milky coffees and teas, Paul and I were never short of biscuits and the odd spliff, the pig screw missed his chance to wipe that fucking smile off my face, and I was £20 quid up after a visit from my brother.

CHAPTER XII

OUT
DOWN THE OLD KENT ROAD

M^{Y BROTHER AND I} have always been close and he was my hero when we were teenagers cruising the south London streets in his Triumph Dolomite Sprint, most of John's mates drove Dolomites too and we always drove around in a gang of 4 or 5 cars. The last Saturday of every month was the Chelsea cruise where people would gather to show off their customised cars, the atmosphere was great and the motors were even better, so in a five car convoy we'd head down to Chelsea bridge to join all the other enthusiasts. Once there the Cruise route would take us over the bridge and left on to the Chelsea Embankment heading west to Albert bridge then back over to the south of the river turning left onto Prince of Wales drive which took us back to the starting point. John always had a top of the range car stereo system and we'd listen to Aint Nobody by Rufus and Chaka Khan, Encore by Cheryl Lynn and Magic touch by Rose Royce was another driving classic. The official cruise would end at 10.pm, which was also the start of the un-official cruise that would take us on a trip down the A4 to Heston services. Getting there was the main event since everyone would be racing each other along the six or seven mile stretch of dual carriageway. Although not the fastest car in the race, Johns Dolomite wasn't called a sprint for nothing and we held our own in plenty battles of speed. I learnt most of my bad driving habits from my brother like overtaking someone who was overtaking someone else, or just taking damn right liberties. If ever I needed help or was in trouble John was the only one I could trust to come up with the goods when needed. For example when everyone else left me in the shit one night, my brother beat the odds to be there for me.

In the mid to late nineties the Gin Palace up the Old Kent Road was the place to be on a Wednesday night, I usually went with my brother and some other "pals" but my brother had an early start on Thursday and couldn't make it this particular night. I went in there with five so-called mates, who when down our local pub would talk a good fight and carry on like they were Jack The Biscuit or Big Time Charlie Potatoes. Everything was going well, we'd been upstairs on the roulette table and had a giggle before coming back downstairs to the main bar. We spread out across the dance floor and I had been dancing in the same spot for about ten minute, when all of a sudden this bloke taps me on the shoulder. He was holding his mouth and said that I had knocked his bottle while he was drinking from it and chipped one of his front teeth. He was with a crowd of about four other blokes who had also been dancing next to me, anyway I explained to him that I was unaware that I'd even touched him so offered to buy him a drink. He accepted my apology and offer of a pint, and we shook hands and that was that. About twenty minutes later another three or four of this feller's mates bowled in, and it wasn't long before they had convinced Chipped tooth that I was out of order and needed sorting out. I could tell the atmosphere around them and me was getting tense and before long the leader of the bunch came over to tell me just how out of order I was for chipping his pal's tooth. No word of a lie, he was nigh on seven foot tall, but I used to stick up for his older brother when we were in junior school, although he never knew me I knew him, he was only about 18 but used to get away with being older due to his size, I had knocked out a couple of blokes with one punch in the past, so this kid no matter how big he was just didn't faze me, so when he leant over and told me to fuck off to the other end of the club in his best threatening voice, I looked at him in the eye and laughed.

"Fuck off mate, you're only a boy, do you think I'm worried about you," I said as I looked him up and down. "I aint going fucking nowhere, you fucking move," and he did, he backed down, I don't suppose he was used to shorter men standing up to him. I guessed he'd never been in a fight in his life, since his size was all he needed to put off any troublemakers. He probably went back to his gang with a story that he'd told me to fuck off and I shit myself. I could tell they were plotting my downfall for when the club shut. While all this took place I knew my so-called friends were aware that trouble was brewing, but still kept their distance. I went to each one to explain what had occurred, three or four of them said don't worry mate we'll back you up, and one of them Darren Thringe completely turned his back on me there and then. This bloke who had been my brothers best mate for year's when they were at school together, this bloke who used to spend hours at my house, and me at his when I briefly dated his sister, this bloke who down our local pub was the hard man of Peckham, Just turned his back and said I don't want to know, don't get me involved. Now I have never asked or expected any of my "mates" to back me up, I have always judged situations on how best I can handle it. To be honest I just wanted to have a chat with someone so as not to stand out on my own like a sore thumb. I never asked any of them to help me out, they just assumed I did. By the time the bouncers began ushering people out at closing time, everyone who I'd originally came in with were nowhere to be seen having snuck out half hour before. I could see the gang of lads waiting outside on the street, so I went to the pay phone at the end of the bar and phoned my brother who was asleep at our mother's house about two miles away. In the middle of explaining the situation to him the phone went dead. So I made my way to the back of the exiting crowd and finished off my pint of lager and mentally prepared myself for my surprise party outside the door. About three or four minutes later I was finally ushered on to the street and the first thing I saw was my brother John standing there in his joggers which he wore to bed, and an opened coat on his body, he must have leapt out of bed, grabbed a coat and jumped in the car without so much of a backwards glance, and he got to the club in three minutes. "Alright Rick, where are they, is it this lot here to my left? He asked as he put his arm around my shoulder. "Yeah that's them," I replied.

"There's my motor over there let's just go home," he said as we crossed the busy Old Kent Road. John explained how he'd seen my "pals" a mile and a half away walking home as he passed them on his way to meet me. I got to the pavement on the other side of the road, then urged on by his "mates," the bloke with the chipped tooth came bowling over towards me carrying a bottle and growled, "You chipped my fucking tooth you Cunt,"

"Yeah, and we sorted it out remember? I answered while slowly backing up to the iron grill of a shop. "Now do yourself a favour and fuck off back to your mates before you get hurt," I warned him. With that he tried to smash the bottle into my head, I dodged it and it exploded into the grill where my head had just been. This gave me time to draw back and lamp him one on the chin with my hardest follow through right hand punch. I called it The David Muller Punch, which I will explain later on in this book. He was out cold on the pavement doing star impressions for about five seconds, then he came to and got on to his hands and knees, I noticed John was grappling with one of the other feller's to my left, and the rest of the gang were making their way over the road in our direction. With my adrenalin now pumping and survival instincts kicking right in, my first thought was making sure old chipped tooth was no longer a threat in case I had to defend myself against any of his mates. So while on all fours and looking straight at me I kicked his head like I was taking a penalty knocking him right out of the game. Instead of coming to attack me, his mates grabbed chipped tooth's arms and pulled him away disappearing into the busy crowds of clubbers who were on their way home. I noticed two Old Bill making their way towards us while John was still holding this other guy in a headlock. At this stage I was standing still, and was calm and collected. The police then handcuffed the three of us. Calmly I tried to explain what had happened and kept insisting that my brother was only there to pick me up and was trying to stop the bloke he had been holding, from joining his brother in attacking me. Due to the fact John was still in his Pyjama's and wearing no clothes under his coat, they uncuffed him, but arrested me and chipped tooth's brother. Ridiculously I was charged with Affray and GBH, even though the person I was charged with causing harm to wasn't even in the picture, and never made any complaints or allegations of assault. The Police were going on what they thought they'd witnessed, which unfortunately for me was the Penalty I had taken with chipped tooth's head. By the time I was in the dock to face charges of Affray etc, the Old Bill had added arms and legs to their story, juicing it up somewhat to try and get a conviction. It was a farce; they each read their notes, which were word for word identical. They made up so much bull shit it was pathetic, it was my first taste of a fit up. All those times I'd listen to people complaining about the old bill fitting them up, I always thought they were probably exaggerating. Now I could see corruption in all its ugliness spewing out before my very own eyes. I wanted to shout out, You Fucking lying bastards, as one of the coppers reeled of a rehearsed script from his doctored notes that read something close to this.

"As we approached the area of the disturbance I noticed that the defendant Mr Atkinson was kneeling on a person and continuously reigning blows to and about the victims head, we had to drag Mr Atkinson kicking and screaming away from his victim, and he continued to kick out at my colleague and I. He began to lash out as we tried to place him in handcuffs, and made every effort to resist being arrested. Eventually we managed to cuff him and had to drag him once again kicking and screaming to the van." Anyway to cut a long story short they painted a picture to the court that I was a fucking violent lunatic. I noticed the jailer had come up from the pits and was rattling his bunch of keys in anticipation of another convict to lock up. Little did the old bill know, they were digging their own graves with all the lies they were spouting. My solicitor wasn't worth the cheap suit he was dressed in, he was a stand in for my usual brief and got to court 45 minutes late and had to apologise to the judge, he didn't have any of the case history and to top it all he was a yank. After the old bill finished their bit for the prosecution my co defendant (chipped tooth's brother) was now asked to give his version of events, let's remember the guy I hit was never questioned or came forward to make a statement. His brother was in the dock with me, and was charged with causing a disturbance. His solicitor obviously had a plan and gave him advice that would work out in all our favour. The magistrate asked him to explain why he was in a clinch with my brother during the disturbance, and this was his statement. "I was out having a drink with my brother and a group of our friends at the Gin Palace on the Old Kent Road. At some point during the evening a misunderstanding had happened between Mr Atkinson and my brother, which after a brief conversation was settled amicably by Mr Atkinson buying my brother a drink. By the end of the night my brother was quite drunk, he usually ends up causing trouble when intoxicated, since he can't handle his drink. Mr

Atkinson left the club a couple of minutes after we did, and was met by who I now know to be his brother and they made their way towards his car on the opposite side of the road. So when I noticed my brother pursuing Mr Atkinson in order to attack him I went over to try and stop him. By the time I had reached the other side of the road my brother had already lashed out at Mr Atkinson with an empty beer bottle. Somehow I ended up grappling with Mr Atkinson's brother who must have assumed I was there to join the attack and he held me in a headlock. The next thing I saw was my brother on the floor being dragged away by some members of our group. Two police constables then came along making their way through the now crowded pavement demanding to know what had just happened. At this point Mr Atkinson, his brother and I were all standing calmly trying to explain our version of events which resulted in the three of us being placed in handcuffs. Mr Atkinson was pleading with them to let his brother go explaining that he had only been there as a peace maker. The police did uncuff him, and then proceeded to arrest Mr Atkinson and myself since my protests of also being a peacemaker were ignored. We were then walked over to the police van and told to sit in the back on a bench before being taken to the police station at Woolworth road."

This guy's statement was a masterstroke, he put all the blame on his brother who had never been arrested or made any statements, and never made a complaint of being assaulted. So his testimony had exonerated me, exonerated him, and contradicted everything the lying, corrupt, and now red-faced old bill had read from their notebooks. The flabbergasted magistrate was now whispering with her cronies sitting either side of her. I was looking over at my co defendant and his solicitor in disbelief; I had originally thought he was going to blame me for knocking his brother out etc. But with reflection I realised it was the best thing he could have done since blaming me would have made his case less believable. So they were totally honest, I mean this guy wasn't in court as a witness trying to get his brother off, and whatever the outcome, chipped tooth was never going to be charged with anything. Without even taking the stand myself, the magistrate made a statement. "Based on what I have heard in court today I am ordering that this case be dismissed, however I urge both off you to behave in a manner that is in accordance with the law in the future etc etc. On my way from the dock Chipped tooth's mother approached me and asked me if I would forget the whole thing and make amends with her son by shaking his hand. I agreed, and on exiting court ten I noticed him sitting in the waiting area so I walked over to him offering my hand and said, "Your mother wants me to shake your hand, bygones be bygones and all that."

"Ok," he said looking puzzled.

"Oh, by the way there is a moral to this story, do you wanna know what it is? I asked.

"What's that then," he said still confused.

"Never send a boy to do a man's job," I left him to work it out as I joined my brother and walked out of court a relieved and free man. Looking back I should have asked the Magistrate what she was going to do about the blatant lies the old bill had spewed out in court, but I was just happy to get out of there, since at one point after the police had read their fabricated statements it looked like I was facing three or four years bird.

COOPERS

The Old Kent road was never short of drama since it was filled with pubs bars and night clubs which inevitably were filled with all kinds of characters. In the early nineties along with the Gin Palace a Club called Henry Coopers was one of our favourite haunts which was owned and run by a well known ex Middle weight boxer by the name of Teddy Haynes. In his 30 fight professional career he won 19 fights (15 by way of knockout) and lost 11. His face told the story of just how hard those fights were since he had no bridge left on his nose and his eyes were visibly showing signs of repetitive trauma. He was around 56 years old at the time my pals and I started frequenting the place on a regular basis which eventually ended up being Tuesdays Thursdays Fridays and Saturdays. Teddy was a minor celebrity and had his own corner of the club just to the left of the main entrance where he would meet and greet his circle of friends who were made up of mainly ex boxers and promoters. The club was on ground level and had a fair size dance floor with fitted tables and chairs along one wall situated either side of the DJ booth. The decor was dark and funky and highlighted with ultra violet lamps in strategic positions. I was spending so much time in Coopers that it wasn't long before Teddy was greeting me at the door and inviting me into his entourage for my first drink which he would always buy. We became quite friendly and when on occasions he took a group of his friends upstairs to the boxing gym to watch the latest good prospect training for his next fight, he would always include me too. I was never out of my depth since I used to be an amateur boxer myself and had always been a diehard boxing fan. It was a great feeling turning up at the club with some friends and having Teddy meet and greet me at the door as we walked in, it made you feel special and always impressed your friends. I think Teddy knew that, which was half the reason he did it, if he liked you he treated you well and if there was ever a private party or a lock in, I and who ever I had with me were always welcomed in. On a weekend it used to get so busy that you could barely move so it was nice to be able to escape to Teddy's corner every now and then where you had a bit of space. One particular night during a private party, stroke lock in at coopers I was sat at the bar having a drink and a laugh with a girl called Lisa and her sister Kelly. Lisa was my mate Mattie's girlfriend and this was probably the first time we had started getting on since we never liked each other from the start. She was showing off by telling me how Mattie was under the thumb and at home babysitting her daughter from a previous relationship. At this stage all three of us were quite tipsy and it was getting late, then one of the barmaids called Debbie came over and out of the blue asked

Lisa and Kelly if she could borrow me for 10 minutes. I barely knew Debbie since she was quite shy and we'd only ever exchanged polite niceties at the bar, I always found her quite attractive, she was a brunette with shoulder length curly hair, she had azure coloured eyes and was blessed with a great figure too but I wasn't losing sleep over her if you know what I mean. Being that it was an afterhours party the barmaids were allowed to join in the celebrations and have a drink too, so Debbie was also slightly worse for wear and now full of Dutch courage.

"You can buy him from us if you like," slurred Lisa before cackling with her sister Kelly in a sinister fashion.

"How much do you want for him? Demanded the now ever so sexy looking Debbie.

The sisters giggled and whispered their way through a five second private meeting before saying in unison, "Five fags will cover it, he's got to be worth that aint he?

"Two!!! Said Debbie with authority. I laughed at the fact she was bargaining with them.

"Two fags, is that all I'm worth, bloody charming aint it,"

"Three fags and you can have him," Demanded the cackling sisters.

"Sold," said Debbie as she flicked the three fags on to the bar, "don't worry I'll bring him back in one piece," she said as she grabbed my hand and lead me through a door into the other bar which was closed and in complete darkness.

"What's all this in aid of then? I asked her. I was amused yet still slightly confused at her intentions, but at the same time quite turned on by her sassy drink fuelled domination.

"I want you to Fuck me right here right now," she demanded.

"I'm up for that." I said enthusiastically. The only place in the bar where we wouldn't be seen was in a curtained off cubical made from long window panes surrounding the foot well of the other main entrance. So she pulled me in and immediately started to unbutton my trousers while we were passionately kissing. Our hands were everywhere frantically trying to undress and unzip each other's clothes, this was the most spontaneous sexual adventure I'd ever experienced. She had been wearing a low cut top and a denim mini skirt and looked sexier than ever. My trousers and boxer shorts and her sexy red frilly panties were now around our ankles but there was no room to lay, sit or kneel, so after freeing one of her legs I lifted her up above my waist and propped her up bum cheeks against the cold iron door with her feet pressed against the glass windows behind me. Then I slowly lowered her down onto my erection which was already standing to attention like never before. Debbie was wet and moist so it wasn't long before we had a good slippery rhythm going. She had a lovely pair of boobs with erect nipples which she was now demanding that I lick and suck, I obliged willingly causing her to thrust herself on me with added vigour. My already great night had turned into a fantastic night in the blink of an eye and I was enjoying every second of it now, which you would have guessed had you seen the massive smile on my face. I was so glad after about five minutes of lifting her up and down when she started to whimper, "I'm coming, I'm coming," Because I was ready to explode and hearing her say those two fantastic words was my key to let go and enjoy every inch of my orgasm. We paused for a while to catch our breath and regain our composure before getting dressed and doing our upmost to look like nothing naughty had gone on. Who was we trying to kid, the moment we walked back into the party Lisa and Kelly made the odd sarcastic remark like, "was he worth three fags? Apart from that both our faces were flustered and no matter how much I tried I could not get that silly grin of my face.

Debbie gave me her number and we did meet up again only this time it was outside of work and when we were both sober. The date just didn't live up to the excitement we had on that wild night so we kind of just left it at that and carried on being amicable when on opposite sides of the bar. So when I say the Old Kent road and all its watering holes were full of characters I'm not exaggerating. I know this sounds quite arrogant but I had deputy shag on hand in the Henry Coopers who I would always be able to take home should I fail to pull a new bit of skirt. Her Name was Michelle, she was married with a couple of kids and was a typical bored young house wife after marrying at a young age. She flirted round me from the day we met on the dance floor in the club. Michelle was one of a gang of girls who my mates and I were unloading our spiel on. We told them that we were low level tornado pilots and were on temporary leave from the Gulf war. They fell for our flannel hook line and sinker for the first couple of weeks but it wasn't long before they realised that we were Top bull shitters rather than Top Guns. Never the less Michelle had fallen for me big time, and at first I was into her too. We'd leave the club early to go back to my flat and have no holds barred sex before she'd get a cab back home to her down trodden husband. She was quite pretty and had a sexy body with long dark crinkle curled hair so physically Michelle was right up my street. But that was it, on any other level we were not compatible and besides that she was married with kids. I never once felt guilty about screwing some poor blokes wife, that was their problem not mine. If she hadn't of met me she would have been fucking someone else anyway, so she was using me just as much as I was using her. It got to a stage when I would pull other girls and leave Michelle behind, and if the following week I failed to pull a girl by the end of the night, she would gladly come home with me for drunken kinky sex. Michelle was so into me she would let me experiment with all kind of sexual games. Some games she liked and others she didn't, for example she loved it when I blind folded her and handcuffed her spread eagled to the bed before pleasuring her. However one drunken night I handcuffed Michelle's arms up above her head and attached them to my chin-up bar that happened to be fixed across the hall, then I slowly kissed her from top to bottom, back and front before having sex with her from behind whilst standing up. It was dark with only the moons rays as a source of illumination which came through my opened bedroom window and just about stretched into the hall. There was a nice breeze which made my curtains dance to the soft distant sound of jazz fm coming from my bedside radio which added to the already erotic ambience. Michelle shuddered and made cute little cooing noises which grew in volume the more I used and abused her. She was thoroughly enjoying every nibble on her neck and every stroke of her raised nipples that I made while slowly but purposefully penetrating her moist love entrance. It wasn't long before this evolved into thrusting and biting as we both began to climax ending in us panting and gasping for air. I went to the bedroom in search of the handcuff keys but being quite drunk had an effect on my memory and I couldn't find them. With all the fast paced climax to our sexual encounters in the hall and coupled with the fact I was heavily pissed I came over dizzy and collapsed on the bed into a drunken stupor leaving Michelle still handcuffed and half hanging from my chin up bar. I vaguely remember coming to every now and then and hearing Michelle angrily shouting at me to come and release her, but I was too far gone to even attempt to get out of bed so poor Michelle spent the next 3-4 hours with her arms above her head and having to stand on tip toes to stop her wrists from hurting. When I eventually came round she wasn't best pleased and i really had to go out of my way to win her back around. I did feel for her though, it was a very selfish thing for me to do. A few weeks later I was about to leave the club with a blonde girl I'd chatted up and in an attempt to get me to take her home instead, Michelle whispered in my ear, "you can handcuff me to your bar again if you like."

"What even after what happened last time, what if i fall asleep again and leave you up there? I asked.

"As long as you fuck me again when you wake up I don't mind." She whispered seductively. After that little performance she had just secured first place, so I told her to meet me at my car while I made my excuses to the blonde bird. This sort of thing went on for ages until Michelle's husband started following her about by turning up at whatever club she would be in and drive her home, so our little arrangement became less frequent over the next 6 months or so.

One of my group of pals who was also accepted into the Teddy Haynes precious circle of friends was a big bloke called Luis who was slightly over six foot and must have weighed about 17 stone. Every weekend without fail he would have too much to drink and always disappear about half hour before the rest of us left the club and you could bet your life we would find him curled up in a ball asleep in a church yard or lorry park. To the un-trained eye he resembled a bundle of old clothes but we were so used to finding him asleep in strange places that we knew what to look for. He was a nightmare and just refused to wake up. On the odd occasion we managed to get some sort of response from him he would just mumble and talk gibberish which would always end with Cunt or fuck, so we'd leave him there to sleep it off. One morning after falling asleep in a car park he even woke up to find tyre marks over his legs. Due to his inability to wake up when wasted Luis was a prime target for the makeup mob when at one of our party's. I have plenty of video footage of him with one eyebrow shaved off, two pairs of knickers on and around his head, bright red lipstick and rouge all over his face, a couple of fags sticking out of his nostrils and some sort of derogative statement written across his forehead in eye liner. He always saw the funny side and would take it in good heart even though it used to take months to grow his eyebrows back.

INSIDE
KRUGERS LESSON

I began frequenting the prison library more than usual after reading a couple of books that one of my neighbours had lent me, one titled Psychology of the mind, and the other was an S.A.S tactics book. I believe that reading these two particular books flicked a new switch in my brain that kick started an insatiable thirst for knowledge. I would read books on history, philosophy, hypnosis, meditation, body language, astronomy, psychology, and everything else I had been interested in but never bothered to look into. I think this could have been my brain telling me I needed to look deeper into myself, and study my own behaviour and actions. This turned me into an analyst and I would analyse everything to death, especially my own thoughts and actions. Why did I say that? What made me think this? How did I come to that conclusion? Analysing everything and everyone did serve me well later on in my twenties, when periodically I would have a brain melt down, and had a built in mental mechanism that would take me through a self-repairing process. I had the ability to recognise when the process was complete, it usually took a couple of months to fit all the pieces back together before I could understand why it had happened, but I always seemed to come out of it stronger and wiser. I realised quickly that cannabis played a big part in both processes for example the psychological breakdown and subsequent rebuilding, I think the answer is, you have to be very honest with yourself and be able to ask yourself questions, and look within, like if someone makes a criticism or points out one of your faults, don't be defensive, look within and find out if they could be right, and if you find an element of truth in what they have said, be conscious of it and put it right. I learned another one of life's little lessons when I met a guy called Andrew; he was one of the new monthly intakes. Like everyone else, when I first clapped eyes on him I had to take a sharp intake of breath. He was covered from head to toe in severe burns, sporting an obvious syrup, and had one or two fingers missing on both hands. I could tell people were avoiding him since they didn't know how to behave around him. I mean how do you start a conversation with someone like that. "Wow what happened to you? Or "that looks painful mate, does it hurt? It would have felt strange and slightly false pretending you weren't taken aback by his disfigurement when starting up a conversation with him. Well I broke the ice later that day when he was hanging around near the table tennis tables and I asked him if he fancied a game. He happily took up my invitation and it turned out he was pretty good, despite only having four fingers on his batting hand. We talked as we played not really counting the points, burns aside he talked and sounded like one of my own, I knew straight away that we were going to get along, and we did, he became a regular fixture of my circle of friends. I realised that when I first saw Andrew, I had him down as some sort of monster; I had judged the book before even reading the first page. After a week of getting to know him, I never saw this badly burned bloke anymore, I just saw Andy and his great personality had diluted his disfigurement to a point of invisibility. I learned a good lesson, and also learned a lot about myself through meeting him. Secretly when referring to Andy, people would call him Kruger, but he knew it was inevitable that somebody as badly disfigured as himself was going to be labelled for the rest of his life, so he was quite happy to go along with Kruger since taking the piss out of himself endeared him to people and took the sting out of their horrible remarks. To be honest he made Freddie Kruger look like Brad Pitt, but his personality and sense of humour outweighed his exterior appearance. He told me he had been a young boy of four years old when he got trapped in a house fire, so he had looked like that most of his life, I felt humbled and swore to myself never to complain about unimportant things, or feel hard done by when not getting my daily news paper for example. But like other human beings we all feel sorry for ourselves at some point sooner or later.

CHAPTER XIII

OUT
THE PEACH BOYS

YOU COULD SAY I needed teaching a lesson or two since I had been into all sorts of skulduggery throughout my youth, and was always trying to earn a few quid which would often get me in some kind of bother. From the age of twelve I was already forging five-pound notes using my school photocopier, a tube of Pritt stick paper glue, some colouring pencils, and a bit of artistic cleverness. After turning the tone settings right down I would photocopy both sides of a five-pound note and cut them out to correct size. I coloured them in with colouring pencils to the closest match possible, then I'd draw a black line in exactly the right place on the back of the Queens side before covering it with a thin layer of Pritt stick and joining the two sides. I ironed them on a warm setting and left them to dry for an hour. The finished product was very accurate but ever so slightly thicker than the real thing, but bank notes in those days were very basic making them harder to distinguish. Spending them was easy as long as I went to the right places, for example the short sited dinner lady on the till at the end of the dinner cue in my school. Another good place was a shabby little sweet shop just up the road from where I lived, it was situated under the railway bridge on Kirkwood road and was ran by a middle aged man and his elderly mother. The man was a couple of pork pies short of a picnic and definitely at the back of the cue when god was giving out logic. He would always be behind the till for the evening shift so if I needed a few bob I'd take my freshly made five pound note to his shop and would buy a can of coke for about 25p and walk out with the change. On one occasion after checking my fiver for the bold line through the middle by holding it up to the light, he murmured.

"You've got to be careful now days, there are lots of forgeries going around" and after depositing it in the till and handed me my change he showed me a forgery that his mother had found. It was one of my own from a few days ago, one of the corners had peeled apart where I had put too much glue. I'll be careful to make sure I don't get lumbered with one," I said with a smile as I left in a hurry. I also had a regular Saturday job down Rye Lane Peckham working for Eric and Eileen Horne and their son young Eric. They owned and ran about five fruit and veg stalls which were spread up and down the lane, so this meant the other stallholders had plenty of competition. Eileen aged about 50 at the time was the boss who was as hard as nails, she took shit from no one. Big Eric and his son young Eric had a reputation not to be messed with, so it felt great to be on their team. At first I was the runner, Eileen would say "could you run a box of apples down to Beverley, (Young Eric's Missus) then when you come back can you run this bag of potatoes up to Betty, (a middle aged women who worked on one of the veg stalls at the top of the Lane) so I spent most of the day running between the main shop and the other four stalls. When I turned fourteen I was given a small stall to run at the entrance of a tunnel that led to the back of rye lane shops, and I would off load the odd dodgy fiver to the dumbest looking person in the queue. Running the stall was short lived after a customer kicked up a stink about a forgery she'd received with her change, which I tried to pass of as a genuine mistake. Young Eric was six foot, blonde, blue eyed, fairly good looking with a rough edge to his appearance and always wore loads of Tom, he was about 24 yrs old and a great raconteur who thrived when in the middle of a captive audience, and like most people he would always add arms and legs to the story he was recounting just to add a bit more spice. His dad Big Eric was mid 50's, thicker set and a little more reserved than his son. He was never comfortable when Young Eric was holding court in a crowd of blokes. When I was about 13/14 yrs old I'd often go to The New Covent Garden Market with the two Eric's. Every fruit and veg or flower seller in London would come to buy stock and we'd all congregate in the market café where Young Eric would be the centre of attention because like I said he had a great way of reeling off a story that had you waiting on his every word. There were so many characters, 99 % of them were old school cockneys who had their own stories to tell, If you believed half the stories that went about you'd think they were once all members of the Richardson's or the Kray's Gang. Although some of it was probably true the main part was all bravado. My own claim to fame was that as a ten year old I' had been in Mickey Mcavoy's house when I was dating his niece, before the Mat Brinks gold bullion Robbery. But Young Eric was the king of the Jackanory's and he could handle himself too, I can vouch for that.

COME ON EILEEN

One Saturday morning down Rye lane there was Young Eric, my best mate Gary Harrington, Robert Brock (who ran a stall next to C&A opposite our main shop,) one or two other stall holders and myself. We were just going through our usual morning sing-song whilst setting out our fruit n veg shows. Most of the stall holders would have their radio's tuned into the same station, (radio one) so when Dexy's Midnight Runners would come on we'd all turn the volumes up and gather outside our shop to sing "Come on Eileen" to my boss who would blushingly tell us to turn it in whilst polishing the apples on the front show. When the song finished we'd disperse and go back to doing our jobs which in mine and Gary's case this particular morning was sweeping up the cabbage and cauliflower leaves that had been discarded by Eileen and Eric as they set out the show. The dustmen would come along in two lorries one from the east side of the lane and the other from the west doing one side a piece, we never had a good relationship with the dustmen since they always complained about the amount of rubbish they'd have to pick up from our five outlets and this fact never helped when they drove over one of the boxes of apples that we had left in the kerb.

"Are you fucking blind you stupid Cunt? Shouted Young Eric. With that the air brakes hissed to a stop and three dustmen Jumped out of the cab, one holding a butchers cleaver.

"Go and get Big Eric," whispered Eileen to Gary, "he's in the café," Gary slipped off round the cafe to find him, then Eileen instructed me to go into the back of the shop to get Justin. Justin was a meaty old baseball bat which she kept Justin case things got out of hand, which they often did with the amount of nutcases that frequented Rye Lane. At this point there was plenty of verbal going on as four or five dustman were now squaring up to Young Eric who just stood there as cool as you like. While on my way over to even up the odds a little bit by handing Justin to Eric, I noticed he had released his fag from his fingers allowing it to drop to the floor, a clear signal that Eric was ready to steam in. In a flash he head butted the one holding the meat cleaver taking him straight out of the game, then with a left and a right he felled the bigger one of the group, which put the shits up the other three who were now holding their arms up in the air hopping to negotiate their way out of trouble. But it was too late for that since Eric had the bit between his teeth and once he started no one could calm him down. Gary had found Big Eric who was now charging in after grabbing Justin from me. He whacked one of the remaining dustmen in the gut just hard enough to warn him off. Meanwhile Young Eric, after knocking down another bloke with a right-hander, was on top of him trying to bite his nose, the other dustman had had enough and all jumped back in their cabs. Big Eric grabbed hold of his son and pulled him into the shop shouting "That's enough!

No Old Bill were called, and that was the end of it. The dustman must have swapped shifts because a new lot came around next week and were much friendlier.

Over the years Gary and I became known as the Peach boys. While out and about at the pictures, or a party etc we would meet some girls for the first time and they would already know us as "those boys who shout "Peaches" down the lane." Along with Young Eric we'd sometimes pop into The Hope, a pub on Rye Lane which sat just next door to one of our stalls. As soon as we walked in the door a crowd of other market traders and locals would always shout out, "Here comes the Peach Boys," and after laughing through a verse of Everybody's Going Surfing, one of them would shout, "get them a couple of Shandy's. Our main Job description was to help Young Eric and his gorgeous wife Beverley to run the fruit stall situated outside McDonald's and during the summer the main money maker's were the peaches, melons, and tomatoes. Gary and I would work every day in the school holiday's, which meant we'd have more money than most kids our age.

"Holler out boys, Holler out," demanded Young Eric when the queue looked like dropping off. So Gary and I would begin reeling off our script at the top of our voices.

"E are girls six fa fifty pence ya peaches, come on you bargain hunters, 'ave a look about now." Then I'd show them the scoop from the weighing scales that was full of tomato's and shout, *"E are girls anywhere you like here today, two pand fa fordy pence ya rock 'ard salad tomaders,"* Then Gary would shout while pointing to me, *"Too late, too late, I hear you cry when the man with the bargains passes you by."* The punters loved all the patter and spiel, and you could hear us from either end of Rye lane, especially when other stallholders would start advertising their own wares by hollering out, we would turn up the volume even more, and then up the ante to seven peaches for fifty pence.

THE RUSSIAN HULK

The Horne family had a distinctive whistle that they used when trying to get each other's attention whilst on various stalls spread up and down the lane. It wasn't long before Gary and I adopted their whistle too which made sense since we were part of the team. One busy Saturday around lunch time Gary and I were left running the fruit stall which was set out on the left flank of McDonalds while young Eric had popped up to the main shop to get some change from Eileen. Beverly who would normally be working the fruit stall was looking after the veg stall on the other side of McDonalds because the usual girl had to take the afternoon off. The main shop was roughly 100 yards away on the same side of the road, it looked like a cave had been dug into the wall and was set underneath one of the two railway bridges that traversed the Lane leading to the Train station. I was working the main till on the right hand side of the stall, Gary had Eric's money bag tied around his waist while he pushed the peaches on the left of the stall. The money bag was a typical stall holders bag made out of denim with two zipped pockets in it, one for notes and the other for coins. Out of nowhere a feller appeared and started to act very shifty, he kept asking Gary how much money was in the bag. He spoke very broken English with what we described as a Russian accent, he was a fucking giant and stood at least 6ft 8 ins tall and filled every inch of his solid frame. He appeared to be drunk and unsteady on his feet as he made a couple of attempts to grab the money bag from Gary's waist. I realised this monster wasn't going to go away empty handed so I used the Horne whistle and got Young Eric's attention. Frantically I gestured with my hands for him to come quickly and on realising something was wrong Big Eric joined him and they hastily made their way down to us. I met them half way to explain what had happened and warned them that the bloke was a big fucker.

"I'll fucking kill the Cunt," growled Young Eric. "I don't give a fuck how big he is."

"No! Let me deal with this," said Big Eric while holding back his son who was now showing his teeth resembling a wild dog with its back up.

Big Eric walked over to the huge Russian while Young Eric led Gary around the back of the stall to the other side and took the money bag from him.

"Go away now mate, go on Fuck off now." Said Big Eric to the Russian.

The Russian who made Big Eric look like Ronnie Corbett just stood there and growled. With that Big Eric gave the feller a right hook to the abdominal area, now trust me plenty of hard men would have gone down after that right hook but this geezer didn't even flinch, instead he puffed his chest out and roared before up ending some of our fruit showcase. Seeing this Young Eric grabbed the end of a large wooden pallet from behind the stool and swung it round like a discus thrower and slammed it into the side of the Hulks head. The Hulk went down briefly before getting back up, he picked up the now discarded pallet and was about to throw it at Gary and me. After getting whacked by Big Eric and having a pallet slammed into his head I was beginning to think that nothing was going to stop this big old lump of a guy. Just then Young Eric appeared with a hammer that he had fetched from the van which was parked behind the stall. At this point Eileen was now on the scene after hearing all the commotion and began shouting "No Eric, no!

Young Eric flew at the hulk and hit him on the head two or three times with the hammer. The hulk went down and this time he stayed down, his eyes rolled back and he started to fit writhing about on the ground, then let out a moan before he stopped moving all together.

"You've Bloody killed him Eric, you've killed him, Whelped Eileen, "quick get out of here, take our car and go!" She pleaded.

I'm not sure if Eileen truly believed the Hulk had kicked the bucket or if she just wanted to get Eric away from the situation before he did end up killing him because the Hulk had started to show signs of life with a flicker of his eyes. As you can imagine a crowd of on-lookers had started to gather although cautiously keeping their distance, so there were plenty of witnesses. Just when we thought it was all over bar calling the ambulance the Hulk whose head was now covered in blood rolled over and jumped to his feet, (was nothing going to stop this guy?) again he roared and growled before running off down the road directly behind our stall. About 50 yards up the road he got into a Range Rover (well he was hardly gonna be driving a mini was he?) There were about five or six iron bollards strategically placed across the road which were supposed to keep the residential part of the road separate from the commercial end and seeing as he was parked in the residential part of the road, the hulk would have to turn his motor around and drive off in the opposite direction, or so we thought. After realising he had no route through, the Russian maniac got back out of the car and started to rip away at one of the bollards rocking it to and fro as he growled. He started kicking at the padlock that was securing the bollard to the ground and it wasn't long before the padlock buckled and gave way. The Hulk picked up the iron bollard and launched it in our direction before hurriedly getting back in his motor, this only served to anger Young Eric even more who at this stage was being restrained by his dad and one or two of the other stall holders who had come over to join the on-lookers. Hulk sat there for about a minute revving his engine as though readying himself for a charge, like you would see in the movies. We all stood there dumb struck in total and utter disbelief wondering what he was going to do next. It couldn't have been more obvious but since most of us were still in a state of shock having believed that we had just witnessed Young Eric killing this monster, you could have forgiven us for not registering. The Hulk floored it and sped towards us and the stall swerving from left to right, Eileen screamed "Eric !!!!" as the driver aimed the car at her son, who in true movie star style dove out of the way as the Hulk drove over the already up-ended part of the stall before screeching out on to Rye Lane and mounting the far pavement narrowly missing a load of shoppers. He disappeared out of sight after speeding away to the top end of Rye Lane. Needless to say we never saw the giant Russian again, maybe he went off to lick his wounds and had come to his senses after sobering up or taking his medicine, after all said and done he drove a top notch Range Rover and wasn't dressed like a typical wino or tramp.

Big Eric dealt with the old bill who true to form eventually turned up with urgency just when we no longer needed them. It wasn't long before they sped off in search of the crazed maniac leaving us to rebuild our fruit display and carry on as normal. The damage to the stall was superficial and was easily put right. This whole episode was like an early Christmas present for Young Eric since it guaranteed a captive audience in the cafe for ages and I loved being there to back up his story and I would add just as many arms and legs as he would, after all right or wrong he was my hero and I looked up to him. He was a local legend and I've never met another character like Young Eric, they just don't make 'em like they used to.

Eileen would give us our wages late afternoon on Saturday's always half hour before Erickson's the clothes shop closed which would give us enough time to buy new clobber for the weekend. There were racks of Fila and Sergio Tacchini tracksuits in all different colours hanging on pegs and Pier Cardin polo neck tops neatly folded on the many shelves. Cecil Gee coats and Lacoste sweat shirts were all the rage too. I really wanted the navy blue and white Fila track suit but they were £60.00 and back in the 1980's that was a lot of dough to fork out so I settled for a Gallino Jersey which only set me back a score. Eileen used to always pay us in one pound notes even if you were due £150.00, I didn't mind since it felt like I had more money than I actually did. Dressed in our new attire with a few bob in our pockets Gary and I would spend most Saturday and Sunday nights either at the Peckham Odeon Picture House, or walking around the west end with a few cans of Special Brew. We'd be looking for groups of girls who like us were just wandering around aimlessly looking for adventure, and believe me there were plenty of adventures around every corner up west. I stopped working for the Horne's when I was 14-15 after work dropped off and they had to close down a couple of their other stalls. They kept Garry on the payroll with a full time job since he was 16 and had left school. A couple of years later I used to love winding up the Horne's by standing half way between the main shop and the stalls that flanked McDonalds and then I'd do the family whistle and watch Eileen stick her head out looking for Young Eric or Beverley and vice versa. Once Eileen had sussed out it was me she'd crack a big warm smile and wag her finger at me. That particular whistle is now the Wilson family whistle and my mother and I use it when trying to locate each other or my children when in a supermarket or shopping centre or even just out and about.

So I had to look for other sources of income and soon found one after a couple of weeks. My brother John was one of the pie makers in Simple Simons Pie, Mash & Eel house just around the corner from Eileen's shop so I got myself a Saturday job clearing tables and helping out wherever needed. In total there were about nine people on the staff and on my first day I was keen to impress the boss, so I never bated an eyelid when the manager Steve Mac sent me out to Rye lane with a shopping list of items that he needed. Every member of staff was listening while with the straightest of faces Steve read out the list. "Right first go to Fads the decorating shop and ask for a left hand screwdriver, a tin of tartan paint and some sky hooks," then he handed me a metal pail and said, "on your way back take this to the fish mongers and ask for a bucket of steam." Whilst walking down the lane the only thing on my mind was, how will I get the bucket of steam back to the shop without losing any? Maybe they will give me a lid or something. In Fads I went straight to the lady behind the jump and read out the list. "Can I have a left hand screwdriver, a tin of tartan paint and some sky hooks please." She gave me a sympathetic smile before asking, "Have you come from the pie and mash shop darling?

"Yeah, how did you know that? I asked. She ruffled my hair as she explained how they have always sent new members of staff in with the same list. "You've been had sweetheart," she said giggling. Embarrassed and feeling slightly foolish I couldn't get out of the shop quick enough. On my way back I passed the fishmongers and realised how stupid I'd been to even think that they would sell steam, and the other items on the list were just as ridiculous. I walked back into work to find everyone in hysterics as they pointed at me whilst rolling about trying to catch their breath. I did find it funny too and joined in with the laughter. It was nearly as embarrassing as the time when I got mugged off by a balloon vender called Mick. He used to fly pitch next to Young Eric's fruit and veg stall with a bunch of about thirty or forty helium filled balloons and had sold all but one this day. He told me if I sold it for him I could keep the two pound, so there I was walking up and down Rye lane with this balloon shouting out, "E are two pound for the last balloon, who wants the last balloon for two pound.

The Pie & mash job only lasted a couple of months, I had been sent to work in the sister shop over in Lewisham since they were becoming very busy and were understaffed. It wasn't long before fell out with the manager for having too many fag breaks. I wasn't happy working there anyway since my main duties were cleaning and greasing the metal pie dishes. There were hundreds of the bloody things which kept me cooped up in a damp dimly lit corner of the kitchen for ages and when the greasing was finished I had to meticulously dig all of the eyes out of the hundreds of peeled potatoes. The kitchen was always hot, it was very small and had three industrial ovens chucking out heat as well as four large gas burners for boiling the spuds. All I ever wanted to do was escape into the fresh air, so I ended up going out into the back yard for a fag every half hour. The non smoking manager would constantly be on my case and would use his position of authority to make sure I did his share of work too, I couldn't move without him wanting to know where I was. What pissed me off was that he and the girls who worked behind the counter could sit in the restaurant and smoke and drink tea to their heart's content whenever custom had dropped off. The Boss would have sacked him in a heartbeat if he ever discovered just how much skiving the manager actually did.

CHAPTER XIV

ASSAULT ON SAINSBURY'S CAR PARK

WITH NO SATURDAY job Collecting 10'ps from discarded shopping trolleys in Sainsbury's car park Became a daily event for me and I would make enough dough for a packet of fags and a bite to eat. During the school holidays were the best times to earn, but I still made enough money after school in term time. However it wasn't as straight forward as it seemed, the car park attendants were pissed off at losing their perks to a young oik like me, and I found myself having to outwit them by being in the right place to capitalise on the laziness of the shoppers who couldn't be bothered to walk the 20 meters or so to get their 10 pence's back. The car park had around five levels including the upper open air parking bays, the busiest levels were one two and three, and my angle was to cover all three floors using the rarely used middle stairway, which enabled me to go up or down in a matter of seconds, it also provided me with 2 possible escape routes if it came on top. One route was over the edge of the first floor, which was a long drop but being around 14 yrs old I was agile and had grown up jumping from roofs, and high places and found it easy to scramble down the outside wall to make the drop less scary. The other escape route was through a side door, which was never locked and led to the delivery bay. Every now and then I would inevitably have a run in with the attendants, and this always turned physical since there was no way I was going to part with my fag money after 2 hours of work. One particular day the 10p's came thick and fast since strangely enough there seemed to be no attendants patrolling the car park, the money was rolling in I had amassed about £3.00 in about an hour. Now gagging for a fag I had decided to call it a day and was heading down the middle stairs on my way out to buy some snout, little did I know that one of the attendants was waiting for me on the bottom step next to the exit door. "Come 'ere," he growled, I ran back up the stairs to my first escape route (over the edge) to find the fat Turkish attendant and the skinny African attendant blocking my approach. I then headed for plan B the side door to the loading bay, with a flying kick I stormed through the door to be met by a 3rd attendant, a middle aged guy who I had previously had a set too with a couple of days earlier. It was a planned ambush, at this point the other two were already behind me and all 3 were trying to keep a hold of me as I was lashing out in a last ditched attempt to escape. After roughing me up with a few digs and slaps they riffled through my pockets and stung me for £3.00 in 10 pence's then frog marched me out of the premises shouting, "sling your hook and don't fucking come back or else."

This Pissed me right off so I swore I'd get my revenge while calling them all wankers and pricks. I made my way home still gagging for a snout.

Checking my pockets I discovered 20p that the wankers had missed so I went to my local offy to buy some singles. Embassy number five were the little short fags, they were five pence each so I bought four. I lit one up and sat on a wall smoking it while reflecting on the trolley scenario that had just taken place. There was no way I was going to let them get away with roughing me up, ok granted I was a larey fucker and relieved them of about ten quid a week in perks but I was only 14 and they took a diabolical liberty giving me a dig. If this happened in today's times all three of them would be up on charges for an assault on a minor, but things were different back then. I was never the type to get my old man to go round and have it out with them, for one: my old man at home happened to be my step dad Deb who could have kicked shit out of all of them, but would have probably told me off instead, and two: I always fought my own battles.

When I got home I hid the other 3 fags in between the hedge and the wall at the front of my neighbours house, it was a thick hedge and was great at concealing anything that I couldn't take in doors. I rang the bell of my house while trying to disguise the fact that my top was ripped and I had scratch marks on my neck as my mum greeted me at the door. I shared a room with my brother John who at this time was out and about with his pals so I had the bedroom to myself. Whilst sitting on the bed plotting my revenge on the wankers from the car park I remembered that John had a BSA Scorpion customized air gun hidden under his bed. I moved a few boxes and some bric a brac around and discovered the gun in an old Adidas school bag and to my delight there was a tin of mixed 2.2 calibre pellets with it, half were made of lead and half were metal. My revenge master plan then hit home, I would wait until it got dark, then take the gun to the car park and spend a few hours shooting all the wankers who had roughed me up. I knew that by 5.pm it would be totally dark, and they would all be working there until about 9 p.m. Mum called me down for my dinner so I stuffed the gun back under the bed and went down to eat.

It was Saturday and John wasn't due home 'till around 10.p.m, which made sneaking the gun out of the house a lot easier. Although by now a prolific shop burglar he always made sure he was in mum's good books and would have definitely put her in the picture unless I promised to wash and dry the dishes for him for a week. I ate my dinner whilst quietly and sadistically sniggering to myself at the thought of what was to come while terrorising the car park gang.

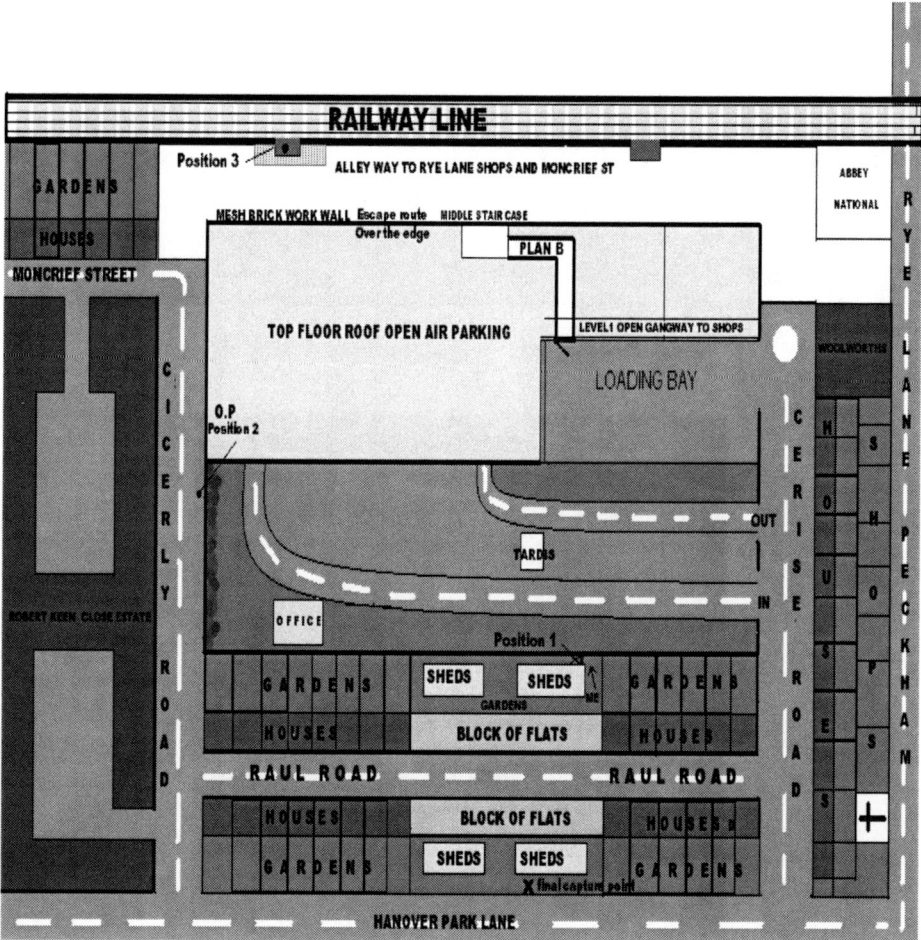

RAILWAY LINE

Position 3 — ALLEY WAY TO RYE LANE SHOPS AND MONCRIEF ST

GARDENS

HOUSES

MONCRIEF STREET

MESH BRICK WORK WALL Escape route MIDDLE STAIRCASE
Over the edge

PLAN B

ABBEY NATIONAL

TOP FLOOR ROOF OPEN AIR PARKING

LEVEL1 OPEN GANGWAY TO SHOPS

WOOLWORTHS

LOADING BAY

RYE LANE

O.P
Position 2

CICERLY

ROAD

ROBERT KEEN CLOSE ESTATE

OUT

IN

TARDIS

OFFICE

Position 1

GARDENS

SHEDS   SHEDS

GARDENS

SHEDS

HOUSES

BLOCK OF FLATS

HOUSES

RAUL ROAD

RAUL ROAD

HOUSES

BLOCK OF FLATS

HOUSES

GARDENS

SHEDS   SHEDS

X final capture point

GARDENS

CICERLY ROAD

ROAD

HANOVER PARK LANE

SUPER MARKET HOUSE

I was shooting from behind the fence on the left

over wall escape route, rear of carpark with meshed brickwork

Railway outpost

Tardis view from the exit

THE REVENGE PLOT

At fifteen sixteen John and his pal Stewpot used to burgle Woolworths every other weekend. I know how and where they had got in and out, but haven't got a clue how they kept getting away with it for as long as they did. It got to a stage where they would go in the store when it was open during the week and make a list of the stuff that they would take out when it was closed on a Sunday afternoon. One particular Sunday a friend and I were kicking a ball about not far from the gates of Woolworths back door delivery area. Out of nowhere and as brazen as you like, John and Stewpot came bounding over the wall carrying Woolworth shopping bags full to the brim with goods. Typical I wanted to know what they had nicked and whether I could have something. I got told to piss off and stop bringing attention to them, so I did after John promised to give me something later.

John was already well into driving cars and had secretly bought one from Exchange and Mart. It was a sporty Scimitar and he kept it parked a few streets away from the house so as not to get caught by mum. He fancied himself as a bit of a Mad Max and had a pair of black leather driving gloves and dark sunglasses. He would always go through the Mad Max ritual of methodically putting them on before driving off. So around 5.30.pm armed with the BSA scorpion, John's black leather gloves and enough bullets to start a small war I headed towards Sainsbury's car park. The car park shared a fence with the gardens of a block of flats situated on Raul road where I had once lived up 'till the age of 11, so I was very familiar with the layout and knew the area down to every blade of grass. In the back gardens there was a large block of sheds which lay parallel to the perimeter fence and stretched nearly the whole length of the gardens which also provided good cover from the residents. So all that lay between the car park attendants and me was a 6 ft wooden fence that had a few little gaps in it where the wood had decayed with age. Dressed in black I was invisible in the dark void between the sheds and fence. The whole garden area at the back of the flats was over grown with tree's and blackberry nettles. It was a damp cold night with a musky graveyard like stench in the air, and any of the local alley cats that were still out and about had already scrambled away on my approach to the back of the sheds. My position enabled me to have a clear aim at the yellow Tardis type cabin where the attendants would sit while collecting money and tickets from the incoming and outgoing shoppers. It was situated about 25 ft from the exit/entrance gate and was about the same distance away from my position behind the fence. The car park office was situated about 20 yards to the left of the Tardis and I could see through a small window that 3 of the attendants were in the office while the fat Turkish one was in the Tardis that had sliding Perspex windows on both sides and a front door that was missing its window.

My gun although powerful but not deadly made a short thud sound when firing a shot, so not really noticeable considering the constant engine sounds and hustle and bustle of the noise coming from the Sainsbury's loading bays. I decided to take out the fat Turk first since he was the one who gave me the slaps. I loaded my gun with a lead pellet for maximum effect but minimal damage. Luckily the sliding window was fully open to enable him to lean out to collect money or distribute tickets. I pointed the barrel through one of the larger gaps in the fence and peered through the telescopic lens. I was rushing with adrenalin at this point which made my hands a bit shaky. I remembered a scene from a movie where a guy was being taught how to be a sniper and was told to always shoot on the out breath, so I took some deep breaths to calm myself down then looked through the sight again. I looked at his face and feelings of you cocky bastard ran through my mind, he was wearing one of the standard issue car park aluminous overcoats so I decided I would shoot him in the arm. Now feeling much calmer I took a deep breath and aimed, as I exhaled I pulled the trigger and heard the slug hit his arm. He flinched and grabbed his arm while looking around the cabin trying to work out what had caused the pain. He was still unaware he had been shot and continued to rub his arm in completely bafflement. I reloaded and by now was buzzing with excitement and adrenalin, again I shot him in the same arm, this time he let out a loud **OUCH,** more in confused fear of what it was that was repeatedly hurting him rather than the stinging pain its self. Then I shot another slug at his back since he had to lean out of the far window to collect money from a car that was leaving. At this point I could see through the telescopic lens that he was terrified and he promptly abandoned the cabin and began to make his way to the office, which gave me time to reload and slug him in the arse causing him to yelp and jump in the air. By now I was pissing myself with muffled laughter and lit up a fag in celebration. Although not exactly a deadly weapon a B.S.A Scorpion was very powerful and lived up to its name by stinging like fucking hell should you get shot by one.

A few minutes later one of the other attendants (the middle aged guy) came out to investigate still unaware of what was really going on, he got in the cabin to sort out the queue of bibbing cars waiting to exit. This was too good to be true, as the last car in the exiting queue pulled away I shot the middle aged guy in the arm, he yelped and quickly shut all windows and started to call the others on his walkie talkie. I assumed he was telling them to stay in the office because it looked like he had picked up a slug from the floor and realised they were being shot at. I loaded the gun with another slug before re-positioning myself at the far right end of the gardens making sure I was still covered from behind by the sheds. From this position I just about managed to shoot a slug through the front door of the cabin where the window was missing. The pellet Ricocheted around the Tardis so on realising he was a sitting duck the attendant cowered down for a couple of seconds to gather his thoughts, then in a burst he stormed out of the cabin crouching down with his coat pulled over his head and bobbed and weaved his way over to the cover of the main office. Now fully aware they were under attack there was lots of frantic shouting and commotion coming from the office. At this stage I knew it wouldn't belong before they rumbled my position due to the fact that they were being slugged from one direction. So I packed my gun and ammo back into the bag and left the flats to take up another covert position on the other side of the car park.

It was now around 7.00 pm and Raul road was like a ghost town, it was dark and although it was getting noticeably colder the gallons of adrenalin pumping through my veins was keeping me warm. The adrenalin was also keeping me very focused on every eventuality and I was looking forward to the next phase of my operation. On exiting the flats I turned right along Raul road towards Cicely road, which led to the left flank of the car park. My plan was to confuse them as to my where abouts and send them in to a state of panic and disarray. The left flank of the car park had a tall metal grilled fence lined with bushes and small trees within the compound side of the car park, this provided me with enough cover to be able to see how they were reacting and observe there every move. I could see two of them scratching their heads and pointing roughly towards my last position behind the sheds. Not wanting to be seen getting up to no good by any residents on the other side of the road I resisted urge to shoot at them right there and then. I moved on heading to the extreme left hand corner of the main car park building to carry out my next plan. Along the back part of the building was a wide footpath that stretched about 300 meters all the way down to Rye lane leading to the main entrance of Sainsbury's. The rear car park wall was designed with sections of meshed brickwork each section was around 20ft long, and 10 ft high. When I say meshed it means every other brick was missing. The gaps were just big enough to get a Childs hand through so you could see into the basement level of the car park.

I shouted through the mesh in my deepest roughest voice,

"I'm up here you fucking wankers, come on then." The acoustics were like the whispering gallery at St Paul's, the echo would carry all through the interior car park. Again I shouted, "Oi fatty come up and get me, or are you a shiter? "you're all fucking shitters aint ya!!! They bought it; two of them began to run up the ramps to the upper levels. Directly behind me were a number of corrugated iron structures that I had previously climbed upon on a number of occasions to gain access to the railway line via a drainpipe. The railway line from Nunhead to Peckham and Queens road had been my playground for years, my mates and I were forever going up there pretending we were in the army and on a secret missions. We had several different camps which were usually disused workmen's huts randomly positioned along the sides of the 2 mile stretch of track between stations. The last 400 yards of track leading to the station ran parallel to back of the car park.

So up I went trying not to make too much noise on the creaky corrugated roof, then I shimmied up the drainpipe about another 15 ft to what I can only describe as an outlet in the top part of the wall. It was like an open metal cage petruding out and away from the train tracks so any rail workers could stand in there and keep out of danger when a train came along. This particular stretch of railway was like a viaduct with bricked up arches. My advantage was the fact that it was very dark up there and from this location I could see straight into level one and two of the back end of the interior car park. My position was parallel to my "over the edge" car park escape route and I could see both attendants. The middle aged bloke was on level two and was about 45 degrees to my right, the younger skinny African guy was on level one directly in front of me and giving hand signals to his colleagues who were at the front end of the car park outside the office.

Since the skinny African had not taken a hit yet I would take this opportunity to slug him while he was in my line of fire and facing the opposite way. I cocked the gun and loaded a metal pellet this time because he was at a longer distance, the heavier the bullet the more accurately it would travel due to its wind resistance. I was still slightly out of breath due to the quick ascent up the drainpipe and onto the caged outlet, but I wanted to fire at the African before he moved off, so without pausing for thought I aimed and shot at him. I knew I'd missed when I heard the bullet ping, it must have hit one of the many metal pipes that hung from the concrete ceiling. Realising he was under fire he ducked and scurried away almost on his hands and knees in shear panic towards a parked car. I was still in the lead as I was totally invisible up in my pitch-black lair. Now believing I was in the building and on the same floor as him the African began shouting into his radio in his broken English accent, "Level one, level one, he is on level one." The interior car park used to be quite well illuminated but due to vandalism had lost a few lights so was now dimly lit and in some parts quite dark in the shadows. This made it even more difficult to tell where I could be on anyone of first three levels. The Older guy made his way down to his colleague ducking all the way there and constantly rotating expecting a shot from any direction. I was in complete control and was buzzing. I was a 14 years old kid and I had them all in the palm of my hand, I felt like I was one of the snipers from the film Assault on precinct 13 which happened to be one of mine and my brother's favourite movies. Still assuming I was in the building they must have believed that they were safe behind the parked car and didn't realise I could pick them off whenever I wanted from my aerial position. At this stage of the game I would have been happy to call it a day and quit while I was ahead since two of the attendants had both been shot a few times and were in a state of complete panic, but the African had it coming since he was the one who scratched my neck and I couldn't leave without hurting him at least once.

I reloaded and was about to get ready to fire at the African still hiding behind the car when I heard the familiar sound of a train bibbing its horn about 150 yards away on its approach to Peckham Rye station. Knowing that the bright lights from its carriages could give away my position, I moved from the outpost and lay flat beside the wall out of view. The train roared past bibbing its horn again the ground rumbled and vibrated, as it thudded past me the whole area lit up like a torch. I stayed as still as I could to make sure no passengers spotted me, but due to the fact that I was dressed in black and the train was still travelling at speed, it made it easier for me to remain unnoticed. The train went by and pulled into the station about 350 yards in the other direction. Again in complete darkness I turned my attention back on to the matter in hand only to realise they had both disappeared from behind the car. Now I was even more determined to shoot the black guy before I called it a night, so I climbed down from my lair back on to the corrugated iron roof and sat down in the darkness of the shadows. With my head inside my coat I lit up my last fag and planned my next move. A few minutes later I was back on the ground and again I shouted "I'm up here," through the meshed brick wall before making my way back to the left flank in order to find out where they all were. I noticed the African was in the Tardis while one of his colleagues was watching his back from outside the office and the other two were running about on level one. Even in the darkness of the dimly lit level one the frantic puffs of breath exuding from their agape mouths were clearly visible. "That's it" I thought, I'll just go round to the right flank where the entrance/ exit is, position myself behind the brick column that supported the gates and shoot him from a more or less point blank distance through the missing Tardis window. I knew I had to get a move on since they were bound to have phoned the old bill by now, so I ran back along Raul road to the far right end and managed to get to the gate column without being seen. This time I loaded a lead bullet since I was going to be very close and didn't want to risk causing serious harm. It was impossible to miss the target as long as I aimed through the window. I shot at him and the slug hit his hand, this was evident by the way he screamed and started flicking his arm up and down in pain. Just as I was about to reload the older bloke spotted me from up on the first floor and bellowed out "There he is" while pointing at me and jumping up and down, "He's there by the gates, Duck! Get down" he screamed whilst gesturing with his arms," It's that little Fucker from earlier," he growled.

I turned and ran off back down Raul road and disappeared into the shadows of a small local housing estate where I rested for five minutes to catch my breath and recompose myself. As far as I was concerned I had done what I'd come to do, revenge was sweet and I jogged home with a satisfied feeling of accomplishment. I hid the bag with gun and bullets under my neighbours hedge in my fag hideout since it would be too risky to smuggle it back indoors in view of the fact that I had no key and either my mum or my brother would have to let me in. Whilst laying in bed that night I started to wonder why they hadn't called the police throughout the whole siege, maybe there were enjoying playing cops and robbers, maybe they liked all the excitement and drama that interrupted an otherwise run of the mill boring day. At least now they could go home with a story of danger and adventure under their belts. I imagined that they were sitting down the pub telling their mates how brave they had been whilst being shot at by some lunatic. After all let's face it, going around collecting trolleys or sitting in a box distributing tickets all day falls into the "jobsworth" category and isn't the most exhilarating job in the world is it?

THE SECOND AMBUSH

About two days later the streets were knee deep in snow and the pavements were iced up and slippery. I was on my way to Rye lane with a couple of mates, and being a cocky git I decided we'd go via the alley at the back of the car park. I pointed out the meshed brickwork and the railway outpost whilst laughing and joking as I relayed the events of the other night. I always had this feeling of invincibility so was unprepared for what was to follow. As we got to the exit/entrance of the middle staircase the double doors burst open with a bang and all four attendants came charging at me shouting to create shock and surprise. This rendered me powerless for a couple of seconds which gave them enough time to surround me and grab my arms and put me in a head lock. Again they frog marched me, only this time it was towards the office rather than out of the door. I was right, they did enjoy playing cops and robbers and had obviously planned the ambush down to the last detail. Effing and blinding and playing dumb I swore blind I didn't know what it was all about. At this point the guy who had me in a head lock let go of me then went ahead to unlock the office door leaving the other three to negotiate the slippery ground as they tried to keep a grip on me. I mustered up as much energy as I could and started spinning around in circles and barging into each of them one at a time. Losing their balance one attendant slipped and fell on the ice and the other two were forced to briefly let go to prevent themselves from going arse over tit. For a split second I was free and made a dash towards a gap in the grilled fence on the left flank. I was gaining no ground due to the fact that it was so slippery on the ice. They were right behind me and chasing me with all their irate energy as though I'd just mugged their mothers. I made it through the hole and onto the street, by now the gap between them and I had opened up to about six or seven yards. I turned left on to Raul road trying to run as fast as I could without slipping over in the snow. I quickly realised that my only chance of escape would be to run through the block of flats on the opposite side of the road to the block of flats where I had originally shot them from. I Knew I would be able to lose them by running to the back of the sheds and over an old rusty broken wire fence that had been climbed on so many times it was virtually flat to the ground. Once past the fence I'd have to run down a small concrete path and would escape by quickly leaping and scrambling over a seven foot parameter wall leaving me to run off down Hanover park lane to the safety of the busy shopping area.

So with another one of my flying kicks I was quickly through the main front door and reached the gardens just as the chasing pack approached the entrance. Just as I got to the back of the sheds my break for freedom came to an abrupt halt.

"Shit" I wailed, on noticing that the once "flat to the ground broken wire fence" was now a 12 ft brand new fence recently erected by the council after complaints from the flat dwellers. Realising my number was up I collapsed with exhaustion, held my hands up and said, "alright you win." This time they were determined not to lose me again they grabbed me tightly, and after pausing for a couple of minutes to get their breath back the now shattered attendants once again frog marched me to the office.

"No chance of a drink then? I asked them. They threw me into a small empty room and locked the door shouting "Fuck off we're calling the police now." The one small window had an iron grill in front of it so I resigned myself to the conclusion that I was screwed even though I would plead the 5th and deny any wrong doing. Half an hour later the old bill showed up and while one of the coppers walked me through the office I could see the fat Turk showing them what looked like a 12 by 12 inch sheet of selotape, all the slugs they had gathered were stuck to it with the locations written in black felt (I knew there was a part of them that was enjoying all this). Protesting my innocence I gave the attendants one last cocky look as one of the coppers cuffed me and put me in the car. "We are taking you home, then we are going to search your house for the gun" they told me.

Back at home my mum was adamant there was no gun in the house and told the old bill that the only chance in hell they had of turning her home upside down to look for one was over her dead body. She was certain that her son would never do anything so stupid. "It's a riddiculas accusation," she scowled. By the time my mum had finished, the coppers looked like a couple of naughty school children who had just been reprimanded by their Head Master. So after giving me a warning they decided that my mum was more than capable of sorting me out, which she did.

I never saw the fat Turk working in the car park after that episode; maybe he thought it wasn't worth the hassle. About a year later while sitting with my mate on his garden wall in Raul road, we heard the theme tune to Popeye the sailor man blaring out as an ice cream van turned into the road and stopped 10 yards short of where we were sitting. I went over to buy my usual lemon ice cornet thinking this isn't Mr whippy who usually did this round. The driver got out of his seat and came to the open window and was taken aback slightly when he looked at me. It was the fat Turk for about five seconds we just stared at each other as though checking our feelings when simultaneously we both cracked big smiles, we shook hands and both declared no hard feelings, from that day on I saw him quite often and we laughed and joked about that eventful night. I found out his name was Metin although for some funny reason he would never tell me where he lived Ha Ha.

INSIDE
SUICIDAL

With only three weeks left to serve I was determined to stay out of trouble and keep my nose clean. I was on the final furlong and didn't want to fall off my horse 10 yards short of the winning post. But inevitably I did end up reeling off my name and number in front of the Governor again. I had been charged with dangerous conduct while in a place of work. To cut a long story short, every day in the veg-prep factory was like all out war with inmates throwing potato missiles at one another. Every time the Veg-prep screw had turned around or bent down to pick something up from the floor, we would all start lobbing cuts of spuds at anyone and everyone along the line. Although he was aware of it, the screw could never determine who was doing the throwing since by the time he looked up we were all peeling spuds like nothing had happened. We had got away with it for weeks and it would break up the monotony of peeling potatoes all day long, every now and then somebody would get hurt by taking a direct hit in the face but had to cover up the pain so as not to get anyone in trouble. This particular day the veg-prep screw got hit in the neck and finally lost his patience. There were only two prisoners working behind the shrink wrap machine which was in the direction from where the missile had been thrown, that was myself, and a mate of mine called Adrian, so he had us both nicked. The Governor added seven days to my sentence and fined me one week's wages, about £4.20, I was just glad it wasn't the 30 days he had previously threatened me with. So with four weeks now to serve I thought I was hard done by, until I heard the news that one of my friends Kevin had been arrested after a cell search when the screws found bags of heroin and various other drugs. He was due to be released on parole in two days after serving 4 years from an eight year sentence. Foolishly he agreed to hold the stash of class (A) after a dealer on his wing got a tip off that he himself was due a raid. The word on the block was that Kevin had been sent to a London bang up to serve a further 8 years. He was found guilty of possession with intent to supply a class (A) controlled drug. So he now had to serve the remaining 4 years of his previous sentence, and an additional 4 years for the drugs. I mean, the guy had two days left before tasting freedom after four years, and then had to start all over again in bang up just for doing a fellow inmate a stupid favour. Poor Kevin must have been suicidal, he had a loving wife and a nine year old daughter who were exited and so eager for him to come home. To make matters worse he would probably have to serve most of his new eight year sentence in various bang ups and the parole board would not be so lenient next time given his past record.

Anyway although gutted for him it made my measly four weeks seem like a few days, so I wasn't too fazed at getting an extra week for my crimes. After getting sacked from veg-prep I was sent to work with an outdoor maintenance group which suited me fine since veg prep was starting to get a bit claustrophobic. Ed's older brother Mark was one of three other blokes in the maintenance group. Mark was quieter and much more laid back than Ed, with a cooler and wiser head on his shoulders. He was philosophical about life and seemed to be doing his bird with apparent ease. I used to benefit from having discussions with him and always enjoyed his company. Ambling around the prison grounds changing street lamp light bulbs and repairing fences on the farms surrounding fields was a piece of cake. My old colleagues on the dairy would always stash a nice big bottle of fresh milk for us too which helped with my popularity in our four man team.

CHAPTER XV

OUT
PC WORLD

THE CRIMES I had committed in prison were schoolboy errors like pinching milk, and lobbing spuds, but on the outside they were far more risky and usually in revenge for something that someone had done wrong to me, in my opinion. As well as the Car park Assault, there was another occasion when someone had wronged me and had to pay for it dearly. So I went to see my mate Tony at his flat and this is how the conversation went.

"You chipping in for an 'enry," asked Tony as I sat down.

"Nah mate I'm on the floor, the bastards sacked me this morning."

"Why what 'append."

"I called the boss a stupid wanker when he told me I was no longer on the company insurance"

"Clever move," Tony said sarcastically.

"They've taken a fucking liberty tone," I said, as he rolled up a joint that was nearly the length of the record sleeve he was using to spin up on. "That prick told me I would stay on the company insurance until I finished paying him for the motor," I growled. After licking the sticky rim of the twelve Rizzlas he used to make the monster spliff Tony looked up and said,

"It's too risky,"

"What's too risky?"

"I know what you're thinking Rick, you've got that look on your face,"

"They fucking deserve it Tone, I've got no motor and I have to go to court for having no insurance, not to mention having to weigh off the other feller for his car."

"Ok so they're out of order, but we've only just offloaded the power tools we nicked from them the last time they took a liberty with ya, it's too hot Rick."

"That was 3 months ago, nothing's changed since then tone, and it's still the same set up"

"So what's your plan?" asked Tony giving me his full attention as he sat back in the arm chair and took a long lug on the Bob Marley type reefer.

"Well, they took in a delivery of new stock on Friday." I said rubbing my hands together.

"Bollocks to that Rick, you know how long it took us to part with the last lot of tools, and Christine aint gonna swallow keeping them in the spare room again."

"I'm sure she'll come round when you tell her it's four brand spanking new shinny computers and a photocopier."

"Four brand new computers?" Tony asked while doing mental arithmetic's.

"And a new photocopier," I said with an enthusiastic tone to my voice.

"I've spoken to Scaggy Baz who reckons his pal needs a few computers for his Jewellery business and will pay up to £400 each for the computers and we'll get at least a long'un (£100) for the copier"

Looking more and more interested Tony started pacing up and down the living room pensively.

He lived with his long time girlfriend Christine and their 2 daughters in a high-rise block of flats in Peckham. When we were skint Tony and I used to rob phone boxes and parking meters for petty cash. The parking meter's we robbed weren't the digital versions you get today, they were the old clockwork style and consisted of a heavy iron head which encased the meter and cash box. They sat on top of a thin iron scaffold pole type structure, the money slot was akin to the bubblegum machines where you'd put your coins in and twist the knob clockwise, but instead of getting a bubblegum you would get 15 minutes of parking time which would tick away like an old wind up clock. We would use a paving slab to knock the head off by resting the slab on the pole about half way down, then with two or three sharp upward thrusts the meter head would fly off the top and crash onto the pavement leaving just the pole sticking out of the ground. There was one street next to Peckham bus garage that had eight headless poles on since it was a secluded deserted road and was easy pickings for us. The only set back was trying to open the bloody things to get to the money; they were so strong we sometimes had to take extreme measures to penetrate them. This one particular meter was a stubborn git and was resisting every effort to release its silver cargo. I had an idea that eventually proved to be near fatal, I thought that by dropping the meter head from very high up it was bound to open on impact with the ground, so we made our way over the road and onto the Clifton housing estate. In the middle of the estate was a 19 storey high rise tower block so I made my way to the top floor via the lift while Tony waited on the ground in order to give me a wave when the coast was clear. After a 5 minute ascent in the lift I stepped out onto the 19th floor, the sound of the wind was haunting as it whistled and wailed through the staircase door and up and down the landing. I went through a glass door which took me to an open rubbish shoot room. The only thing between me and a 300 foot drop was a 4ft iron grill; I looked down trying to find Tony who was a mere dot on the ground. He was shouting instructions which by the time they reached me were just muffled indistinguishable noises. I could just about see him waving his hands so I threw the heavy old meter head over the grill as far away from the entrance as possible. I watched it freefall for 19 floors until hitting the ground with a loud boom. I ran down the stairs because the lift was on ground level and would have taken five minutes to get up to me and another five to get back down again. In my eagerness to help Tony retrieve all the coins that I believed must have exploded into a silver shower I began jumping the stairs one flight at a time. When I eventually got to the ground floor Tony was holding the Meter head in his arms, there was a slight scratch on one side but it was still closed. I couldn't believe it, the paving slab it had landed on was in 4 pieces but we were no nearer getting to the money than before.

"Rick we had better fuck off sharpish,

"Why?

"Some bloke and his kid came out of the lift and were on their way out of the main door when the meter landed, his kid started screaming and the geezer went mad and marched over to the police station."

"Shit, Really?

"Yeah quick let's go! As we were about to leave, the estate's caretaker came flying over dragging his wheelie bin and broom behind him.

"Are you fucking Mental? "I saw what you did; you could have killed someone you fucking Idiots." Tony dropped the parking meter on a patch of grass in the fenced of play area and we quickly fled.

"I've already called the police, and when they catch you I hope they fucking lock you up! Shouted the caretaker as we disappeared around the corner. He knew my face and knew that I was a local lad since I had grown up playing on the Clifton Estate and had come across him on many occasions in the past, so even though we got back to the safety of Tony's flat it was still going to be difficult to avoid getting some form of repercussion at the hands of the disgruntled Caretaker. Later that evening whilst walking home from the flat a police patrol van pulled up next to me with urgency and as quick as a flash out jumped three coppers. Two of them grabbed me by the arms and walked me over to the van. The third copper slid the side door open to reveal the caretaker sitting in the back.

"That's him, I hope you lock the stupid bastard up and throw away the key."

"You miserable old git," I grumbled. The old bill cuffed me and radioed for another car which arrived in no time at all to ferry me to Peckham nick. I knew that the old codger would go out of his way to identify me before he got a wink of sleep that night. Not for the first time I found myself sitting in one of the police stations miserable and depressing cells waiting to be questioned. I even noticed my name and a date was still etched in the iron door from my last spell in police custody. After leaving me to stir for a couple of hours the arresting officer took me to one of their interview suits for questioning. I described how I had found the parking meter head in the underground garages on the Clifton estate and explained that I now realise how stupid and dangerous it was to chuck it from the top of the tower block. After giving me a stern lecture on how I could have killed someone and reeled off a load of spiel about the stealing by finding law, the copper cautioned me and sent me on my way. I was surprised at how easy they let me go given that by now there were at least two roads in the area with nothing but headless parking meters on them. My latest brush with the law didn't deter us from robbing the councils cast iron piggy banks again, especially when we were desperate for a few bob.

One evening we left a full un-opened parking meter head at the flat while we went back out to try and get another one. We were hoping to accumulate enough dough for a few beers as well as fags and a five pound draw of gold seal, not to mention the Chinese take away that we had promised Christine. So all in all we needed to raise about twenty quid and estimated that two parking meter heads would be more than sufficient based on previous takings. An hour later Tony and I had returned empty handed after deeming the situation to be too risky. We decided to abort after noticing two or three cop cars cruising the area which was of interest to us. We entered the flat and found a red faced Christine sitting on the bed. She was sweating profusely after spending the last 60 minutes trying to open the impregnable cash box with a knife and fork. Tony and I creased up with laughter causing her to start swinging at us with a pillow while calling us bastards.

"Step aside," said Tony as he grabbed a sledgehammer from behind the wardrobe. It took us about fifty bashes each before we saw any coins. Christine's face was a picture when we only counted £3.50p. Yet again Tony and I fell about in stitches when Chris resumed her attack with a deadly pillow on us while venomously effing and blinding with every wallop. "I suppose I have to wave good bye to my Chinky then? She moaned before storming off to the kitchen to stick the kettle on. Well that goes without saying; Fags and booze were way above extravagant takeaway's when it came to our list of priorities.

BACK TO BUSINESS

"Seventeen hundred quid tone, we'll give a hundred pound drink to Baz for flogging them, we'll ask Tim (from the leather company) if he'll do the driving for a couple of hundred, and then we can bung Christine a few bob to keep her sweet, at worst we'll come away with a Monkey each."

Still pacing up and down Tony asked,

"What about the dog? You said they'd got a guard dog after the last time we turned them over."

"He's a Doberman cross, but as soppy as fuck and he loves me to death, I played with him every day in the yard, he does what I tell him, so don't worry about the dog, It'll be a piece of piss Tone, so what do you think?"

"I seem to remember you saying the last job was gonna be a doddle, and we ended up sawing our way into the storeroom with a fucking chainsaw!" barked Tony. While offering me the joint

"Yeah, and your point is?" I asked, as I took a lug of the spliff and blue smoke hoops at him as I exhaled. Blowing smoke hoops at people was my little way of being sarcastic.

"My point is Rick, it was a bloody Sunday morning, I don't know how it never came on top, and we must have woken up the whole fucking neighbourhood."

"We got away with it didn't we?" I asked.

"Just about" he said.

I knew he would fold, and before long we were going over the details,

I worked for a plant hire company in South East London; we used to hire out building tools, e.g. kangos, generators, compressors, pneumatic drills, Chainsaws, Angle grinders, scaffolding, etc. We were situated in a yard surrounding 3 railway arches from the rail viaduct. The offices were two Porta-cabins one on top of the other. The top one was where the manageress and her secretary had their offices; the hire and sales team used the one on ground level, it used to be our tea hut before they decided they needed more office space and we were relegated to an old shed. My roll was mainly delivering the equipment to various building sites, and when there were no deliveries I would help out around the yard. We were the sister company to a big construction firm, so we were a small outfit in comparison. I loved the job and got on well with my colleagues and manageress. Sadly after a while the construction company went bust, so the liquidators sold our company to an East end firm who bought and sold bankrupt plant hire tools and tractors. At this point most of our office workers and a couple of blokes from the yard had left, but me and another older feller stayed on and worked for the new mob along with the new boss's sons. At first not a lot changed, they kept the hire side of the company going while still buying and selling other bankrupt stock. There were three or four company cars used by the former construction company that were part of the takeover bid, the boss (Trevor) offered to sell me one of the cars for £700, a red escort 1.3. The deal was, he'd take a bully a week out of my £150 wages and keep the car on the company insurance until paid in full, and then I was on my own. We shook hands on it and that was that. I was 18 and had passed my test earlier that year; it was my first ever car and I was over the moon.

A few days later around home time one of the sons (Billy) started getting shirty with me when I refused to let him order me about, he was a prick and thought being the boss's offspring he could do and say what he wanted. We started throwing punches and ended up rolling about in the dirt, "fucking smack him one Bill" Trevor shouted, making his way down the scaffold stairs from his Porta-cabin office." Bite his fucking nose off Bill, go on," Bill had no chance of carrying out his old man's wishes since by now I had him in a headlock. Trevor grabbed me by the hair trying to drag me off his son, I tightened my grip on Bill's neck, "you fucking let go now boy or you're fucking sacked." Trevor screamed. I let go and got up; Bill had another pride saving swing at me over his brother's shoulder who was now restraining him. "Do that again and I'll sack the fucking pair of you" Trevor shouted as he walked back up to his office. After exchanging threats and obscenities Bill and I went in separate directions, I dusted myself down got in my car and drove home. I was pissed off with the whole set up, and to make matters worse I'd recently been dumped by my girlfriend Lorraine (stealing kisses in the carpets). I was 18 and she was 19 and after a great relationship we eventually moved in together, which took all the excitement out of our lives, things became mundane and we'd argue over money, shopping, washing the dishes you name it. I loved her and became insecure about her getting bored with me, so things went from bad to worse and before long I got a phone call from a geezer claiming to be her boyfriend. I was devastated, but in retrospect I don't blame her, we were young but living like an old married couple. I was naïve and thought this was how it was supposed to be, but Lorraine was a bit more forward than me and she craved excitement.

Over the next few days' things had changed at work, the atmosphere was ugly; and I knew they were probably only keeping me on until I'd finished paying for the motor and then they'd find an excuse to give me the shove.

That weekend Tony, His cousin Pat, (my Jones & Higgins partner in crime) and me decided we'd break into the yard and nick the power tools from the store room, I knew the keys were always left on a hook in the tea hut so couldn't see any problems getting in. Also on one side of the yard the fence was made from a framework of corrugated iron, and there was one sheet that would open up like a door, it was only kept closed by 3 or 4 bent nails so would provide an easy escape route to the street where we parked the car. So about 8.30am on Sunday morning we broke into the yard over a wall from a small car park nicely hidden from the neighbours. When we got to the hut the key was not in its usual place, the hut was empty apart from the tea making utensils a couple of hard hats and a petrol chainsaw. "Fuck it, let's take the chainsaw and go lads," I suggested.

"Bollocks, we aint come this far to leave with one poxy chainsaw" said Patrick (my Jones & Higgins accomplice) as he began pulling the start chord on the saw,

"What the fuck are you doing Pat?" Tony asked half whispering.

"I'm gonna saw the door off, what does it look like?"

"Pat, are you fucking mad? It's 8'30 in the morning mate, you'll bring it right on top." I said trying to make him see sense. But his last tug had started the motor, and with chainsaw roaring like an F1 Maclaren he headed for the storeroom door, and you know the rest.

I carried on working there despite the bad air between me and the new family holding the reigns. I'm sure they suspected I had something to do with the robbery, which made things very uncomfortable. They bought over a guard dog that used to patrol their old east end yard. His name was Sam, and over the next couple of months I had built up a good rapport with him and on the odd night while driving about aimlessly I'd drive past the yard and give him a stroke through the front grilled gates. By now I had already paid off about a monkey for the motor and one Friday evening whilst cruising around with a couple of girlfriends some dickhead came flying round a corner on the wrong side of the road and crashed into me wrecking the front of my car. The old bill got involved and made a report in my favour after measuring the skid marks and position of the cars. So Monday morning I went up to the office and asked the boss for the Insurance details since I needed to make a claim, and had also been given a producer, etc.

CHAPTER XVI

KEEPING SAM SWEET

"I'LL GIVE TIM a bell to see if he's up for it," Tony said picking up the phone.

"What if he doesn't wanna know?" I asked.

"I'll ask Pat,"

"Are you sure Tone, you know what Pat's like" I said rotating my index finger while pointing it at my temple. "He's fucking murder around a chainsaw."

"He can wait in the car, I'll tell him he's only the driver otherwise we'll have to cut him in on the jackpot," coughed Tony as he stubbed out the spliff.

I sighed with relief when Tony looked over and gave me a nod and a wink while talking to Tim on the blower. So Tim had agreed to drive, Christine was put in the picture and was cool and the gang about storing the goods at the flat; she was already mentally spending her sweetener as she flicked through the women's section of her Freeman's catalogue, so everything was falling in to place. I wanted to keep Sam on side, so for the next few nights I went to the yard and give him some biscuits and a stroke through the fence. On the Monday morning when I had been given the sack the computers were still in their boxes in a corner of the ground level office. Being an old Porta-cabin the door was door was a bit flimsy and still had the old Yale lock from the day's when it was the old tea hut. I knew all we had to do was pull the handle slightly up and to the right so the lock knuckle would be freed from the metal chasm on the door frame, I was confident we could rule out bringing a chainsaw into the equation again. We knew we would have to go in A.S.A.P, before they moved the computers so the three of us agreed on Sunday night.

SUNDAY NIGHT

"Where the fuck is he Tone? You did tell him to be here at eight didn't ya?"

"It's only 10 to Rick, if he aint here by 5 to I'll give him a bell."

I was energised and ready to go and waiting around was driving me mad,

Tony had prepared a hand full of roll ups and was putting them in his backy pouch when we heard the familiar growl of Tim's RS 2000 pulling up outside. Christine wished us luck as we left the flat and got in the car. Tim looked pale and nervous, this wasn't really his sort of thing, but in those days (the late 80's) 200 quid was a lot of money to turn down and the temptation overwhelmed him. He was usually a laid back and smooth character but I could tell he was shiting himself, his voice was shaky and he was twitching and fidgeting as we drove towards the yard. The plan was that Tim would park down a quiet side street next to our entry/exit point at the back of the railway viaduct. Tony and I would go over the corrugated fence, along a narrow passage way (that was over grown with brambles and various other stinging nettles,) and to the 3rd rail arch, which we would enter through an old Rotting door with one hinge holding it up. The 3rd arch was where we sand blasted all the tractors readying them for a re-spray. There were 5 or 6 pallets stacked up with bags of sand and the floor was like Margate beach. The front of the arch that lead to the yard was open to the elements apart from some long strips of industrial transparent rubber blinds whose purpose was to keep the sand from blowing in the yard. The sand blaster was very powerful and would strip a tractor down to the bare metal in a matter of minutes, so the rubber blinds also eliminated the risk of skinning someone in the yard.

"Don't be all day will you," begged Tim as Tony and I disappeared over the fence.

We methodically fought our way through the thick overgrowth of nettles, picking up some scratches and sting rashes along the way even though we were wearing gloves. The door on the 3rd arch was still in a bad way so with a little shove we were in. we crouched in the darkness behind a stack of sand bags to re-gather our composure. Tony handed me one of his pre-prepared roll ups which we smoked as we sat there planning our route across the yard to the office, we heard Tim's car start up and pull away, the sound of the roaring engine gradually faded away into the distance,

"He's fucking bottled it Rick."

"He may have seen the old bill drive past and got spooked, he'll be back, let's carry on as planned and if he aint there at the death we'll abort.

Not only did we need Tim to drive, but we also needed someone that we could pass the heavy boxes over the fence to, so without him all bets were off. We finished our fags and were about to move on to the next stage of our plan when Sam came over to investigate and poked his head under the blinds.

"Hello Sam, come on boy," I said in my soft dog friendly voice.

"GRRRRRRR" said Sam, curling his top lip and baring his flesh piercing teeth.

"Sam, It's me, come 'ere boy,"

"GRRRRRRRRRRRR, he said, while edging towards us doing his best hound of Dracula Impression.

"Rick, I thought you said he was soppy as fuck," squeaked Tony.

"Sam, come on boy? Er, Biscuit, er, walkies," Sam weren't having none of it.

"GRRRRRRRRRRRRRRRR, he said again edging nearer and nearer.

Tony started backing off towards the dodgy door in sheer terror,

"Don't worry tone, he does exactly what I tell him," Tony said, mocking my original statement.

Realising Sam probably didn't recognise me I took my gloves off, stood up and moved towards him hoping that if he still didn't realise I was his old pal reverse psychology would kick in.

It worked his tail began to wag, his head dipped and he licked my hand whilst whimpering in recognition of a friend, he covered my face in drool by enthusiastically licking my nose before making his way back to his kennel on the other side of the yard. Tony and I both breathed a sigh of relief. Staying low we ambled over to the office, I did the old door trick and it swung open. Tony got his torch out and we had a look around. There were two computers already set up on the desk and the mini photocopier was on a chair.

"Shit, they must have moved the other two computers to the office upstairs" I complained.

"Can we get in there," asked a dejected Tony.

"Not without a battering ram, it's like fucking Fort Knox up there."

"We'll have to settle for these two and the copier," he groaned.

While searching through the draws I found the petty cash box with £115 in it, which put a smile back on our faces. The boxes for the computers must have been slung. So we un-plugged all the leads and began wrapping the rest up in bubble paper left behind, we didn't want to scratch them while passing them over the fence to Tim, I stuck the kettle on and made us a cup of coffee while Tony continued to wrap. We were strangely calm and were telling jokes as we swigged our coffee while smoking another roll up. Before long we were lugging all the bits across the yard, through the arch, and down the back passage towards our exit point, Sam never batted an eyelid and was curled up in his kennel. On our third and last trip along the passage we heard Tim pull up exactly where he left us. We looked over the fence and gave him the nod, he opened the boot and we passed him the goods bit by bit over the fence, which he loaded into the boot and on the back seat.

On the way back to Tony's we pulled up at a red traffic light. To our horror a police patrol van pulled along side us. There must have been at least 12 coppers in the back and were all glaring down at us suspiciously, we sat there like statues praying for the lights to change. I was sitting in the back with the stolen property that was hidden underneath our coats. After what seemed like half an hour the lights changed to green and the old bill sped off with their blues and two's blaring, Tim threw a fit effing and blinding at us for getting him involved. We were all relieved on our arrival at Tony's flat. "Get this stuff out of my fucking motor," ordered Tim, Sending Tony and me into fits of laughter.

CHAPTER XVII

TOM FOOLERY

AFTER WEIGHING TIM off with a Long'un as payment for his part, he sped off back to the arms off his latest bit of fluff, leaving Tony and I to hide the goods under the bed in his spare room. Although coming away with half of what we originally expected, we were satisfied with our night's work Christine wasn't best happy at the fact that her sweetener was down graded to a trip to the local market, rather than a fashion spree within Freeman's glossy pages. I poured us a couple of drinks while Tony rolled up another Bob Marley. I was sat facing the front door and noticed the letterbox flap being pushed up by four black fingers, a pair of eyes appeared and then I heard "T . . . . T,"

"Let Mikey in babe," Tony said, as Christine rolled her eyes.

Mikey was a likeable character who lived in the flat above on the next landing. He called most people by their first initial, So Tony was T, Pat was P, and Christine was C, but he called me Rikki D, since R didn't have a ring to it. He came with the excuse that he wanted to show us some of the music cd's he had compiled on his brothers computer, but was really after poncing a joint from Tony.

As we listened to the music T began relaying the night's events to Mikey, and we laughed while remembering Tim shiting himself when the old bill nearly rumbled us.

"I need a computer, what make are they," asked Mikey while inhaling as much smoke as he could from the spliff Tony had passed to him.

"They're both brand new, straight out of a box, one is a Commodore and the other is an Apple," Tony and I led him to the spare room.

"How much do you want for the Commodore."?

"Being as you are a mate, we'll let you have it for three and a half," I said jumping in before Tony could answer.

"That's a shame, I've only got about £150 spare" Mikey replied.

"Never mind then," I said pushing the computers back under the bed.

"Hang on Rick, are you sure Scaggy Baz can sell em?

"Yeah, he's cock sure he can offload them by the middle of the week,"

I could see that Tony was interested in some quick cash.

"Give us a minute Mikey," said Tony opening the bedroom door to let him out.

"I tell you what Rick, I'll sell him the Commodore, and you can have the Apple and we'll go halves on the copier,"

"Fair enough Tone, but if you wait for a few days you'll double your money."

Tony was a bird in the hand type of guy, and money just burnt a hole in his pocket, he never had money for longer than a day so the offer from Mikey was gonna bank roll a day in the bookies and a night out down the pub. So before you could say Jack Robinson the deal was done. Mikey gave him £100 pound the next day, and promised to pay him the other Bull's eye within a couple of days. I asked Scaggy Baz to get the ball rolling with his buyer, and he set up a meeting to do the deal mid week.

Baz (short for Barry) was a Scag head who would nick anything to feed his heroin habit. He even stole the money from his mother's electric meter, and his name came up when Tim's car radio got nicked.

As usual Tony had spent his money in a day, and I'm not sure if Christine ever got her sweetener.

Barry took me to a small, privately owned Jewellers in the middle of Peckham's busy Rye Lane shopping centre. We were let in by a suited middle-aged bloke who changed the Open sign to Closed. After a bit of small talk he led us to a pokey little office at the back of the shop, the office was cluttered with Folders and paperwork and there were umpteen trays of Tom lying about ready for the window display, which he obviously removed before closing time at the end of the day. He introduced himself as Len and began asking me questions about the Computer. After telling him it was a brand new Apple, I reassured him it wasn't nicked in this area. Scaggy Baz was trying on a ring that he'd pulled from one of the holders.

"Barry says you want £450 quid for it," Len said as he moved the trays of Jewellery away from Barry's itchy fingers, Baz gave me a sly wink.

"Yeah that's right, it's worth at least that," I said pretending to know what I was talking about.

"Ok, give me your phone number, I'll have a chat with my partner, and let you know later."

I wrote down Tony's phone number since I spent most of my time at his flat, besides I couldn't really give him my mother's phone number could I. After shaking hands with Len, Baz and I left the shop and went in separate directions agreeing to meet up when we found out if the deal was on.

A few hours later while having a drink around Tony's gaff, I heard Scaggy Baz whistling up outside, "I'm coming down," I shouted to him. Christine wouldn't have him anywhere near her front door, since her gold earrings and a watch mysteriously vanished into thin air when he was last in the flat. I met Baz at the bottom of the stairs and offered him the rest of my can of lager while asking him if we were in business.

"It's a non runner bruv," said Baz after taking a swig from the can.

"Oh bollocks, why, what did he say?"

"I've just got of the blower with Len, and he reckons it's too hot, and his partner had already sorted out some legitimate computers for the business."

"What a fucking tosser," I said kicking the now empty can of lager on to the road.

"Sorry Geeze, I thought he was sweet as a nut, I never guessed he'd bail out at the death, said Baz apologetically.

"Well thanks for trying anyway Baz," I gave him a cockle (£10) for his trouble and after poncing a fag he left.

"What's the S.P Rick," asked Tony while I grabbed another beer from the fridge.

"Non runner Tone,"

"Wanker", Tony said sympathetically.

Half an hour later we were sitting there chatting when the phone started ringing.

"Get the phone Chris," said Tony.

"It's for you Rick, some geezer called Len," she said passing me the phone.

"Hello Len,"

"Hello Mate, look I'll be straight with you, I know what Baz is like, he's a greedy fucker and probably stuck £100 on the price for himself, if you want to cut out the middle man and accept £350 for the computer we've got a deal."

"Where do you want me to deliver it? I said in a heartbeat.

"Bring it to the shop in the morning. I'll be there about 10 am with your dough."

"See you at ten then," I said winking at Tony as I hung up the phone.

I gave Tony the good news then popped up to the super market around the corner and picked up a couple off empty apple boxes and a banana box to pack the computer in. Back at Tony's I dragged all the bits and pieces from under the bed, the monitor fitted perfectly inside one of the apple boxes, the main computer inside the banana box, and the leads and keyboard in the other apple box. The next morning I took a cab with the boxes to Lens shop. Once Len was satisfied it was all working properly he took a Roll of cash wrapped with an elastic band from his desk draw, peeled off seven fifty pound notes and handed it to me.

"I don't suppose you need a photocopier do ya," I asked him while tucking my new wad of money into my trouser pocket.

"No, just the computer for now Rick, he said offering me his hand.

We shook hands and I left. I met up with Tony later that day, and he was sulking about being skint, and kept spitting his dummy out saying that I should give him some of my winnings since he only got £150 for his and I got £300 for mine (well I did tell him Len only offered £300, hey, you have to be shrewd around Tony.)

"Tone, you couldn't wait a couple of days so that's your fault."

Still throwing his toys out of his pram and reminding me that he took a risk storing the stolen property at his house, I decided to give him and Christine £15 each to shut him up. That night I took him out on the piss to celebrate, after all he was a diamond and always generous when he had a few bob. We spent the night playing pool and getting pissed in the Star of India, and laughed as we sang Elvis Presley's "Always On My Mind" to each other. We both loved Elvis songs so would end up picking 10 of his tracks from the jukebox and most of the other punters would also sing along. Eventually we sold the photocopier for £100; we gave Tim a Bully (£50) and took a Pony each. Tony and I were pretty tight for a long time and had many other ventures together; we had shared lots of unusual and extraordinary experiences together. One example was when we went to a seedy Soho gambling club as minders for Kenny our Burmese employer who was a fly pitching burger and ice cream vendor. We had just finished a busy days work selling ice cream from our portable fridges at Camden lock in Camden Town, and were asked if we would accompany the now pissed as a fart Kenny, to a game of poker in Soho. Kenny was a short fairly stocky bloke in his late forties and used to spend the majority of the working day in the local boozer. Whatever he lacked in height, he more than made up for in bravery and spirit since he was forever getting into fights and punching above his weight. His broken English accent was laborious to understand at the best of times let alone when he was rat arsed. Tony didn't have a driving licence so he couldn't drive, Kenny had been disqualified from driving and narrowly escaped doing bird after being caught drink driving while already disqualified for the same offence. So I had to drive us to Soho in the works van which was in short supply of any legal documentation like an M.O.T to mention one. So I wasn't exactly over the moon about driving a clapped out old van and a pissed up Burmese nutcase into the heart of the West End, but I was intrigued about the nature of our destination. The prospect of going to an illegal poker game above a brothel had over ruled my sensible logic, and it wasn't long before we were shoving untold coins in a Soho parking meter, (there's no way one of those meters would have only contained £3.50p). We were met by a bloke we knew called Propaganda, well that was his nick name anyway which we had already shortened to just Prop. He was a Yugoslav burger vendor who spent most of his spare time in various seedy gambling outfits. Prop was a funny guy and a right character, he had an unkempt dishevelled appearance with a face that had "con man" written all over it so I wouldn't trust him as far as I could throw him. Anyway he led us to a black door at the end of a small dark alley behind a sex shop. Tony and I were putting on our best body guard faces while trying to look as big and tall as possible. True to form Kenny was complaining about how fucking long it was taking for some Cunt to let us in. Eventually after a lengthy discussion between prop and whoever was at the other end of the telecom system we were buzzed in. We walked up a couple of flights of stairs which led to another door and were buzzed in yet again. On the other side of the door we were met by one of the widest, lumpiest, meanest looking black feller I'd ever laid eyes on. Fuck knows how this guy could even fit into his pin striped suit let alone fit in the long narrow winding corridors which he subsequently lead us along. He exchanged small talk with propaganda which was inaudible due to the fact his voice was so deep he sounded like Barry white with tonsillitis. After negotiating a couple more staircases, hallways and locked doors we eventually ended up in an apartment which apart from being a very small casino doubled up as a brothel, evident by the state of some of the scantily clad women who were knocking about. There were another two hard core looking bouncers who worked for the owner, one was keeping order around the roulette table at the far end of the room and the other guy had the poker table covered. The "casino" boss had his own little corner of the room where he sat giving out orders to his employee's while at the same time controlling the money and chips that were being distributed between the two tables. Kenny paid the boss sixty quid entrance fee for the three of us and propaganda sorted himself out. Tony and I sat on a black leather sofa situated about five feet away from the poker table and were now feeling vulnerably insignificant as bodyguards in comparison to the heavy looking fuckers we were now surrounded by. Kenny took a seat as the 8th player around the poker table which had some very serious looking people dressed all in black like old school gangsters, and there were one or two strange looking fuckers to boot. A couple of hours had gone by in a heartbeat, Kenny was gradually getting louder and more aggressive as he continued to down double whisky chasers while losing large sums of money. Tony and I had polished off a fair amount of beers ourselves and were given permission to roll up and smoke as many joints as we pleased. Inevitably it wasn't long before we were offered a brass for £50.00. One of the suited Jamaican fellers came over and said,

"Ya wan some pussy? fifty quid fa any ting dat float ya boat."

I looked at Tony to try and gage what he was thinking, because I for one was not going to spend fifty knicker on a brass, especially seeing as I'd grafted all day just to earn sixty quid. Apart from that I wouldn't want to sleep with a prostitute anyway, well certainly not under these circumstances. It took Tony longer to make up his mind and he was busy making calculations while counting his money. I think it was mainly bravado coupled with the fact he was stoned and slightly tipsy, anyway the pimp said he'd give us time to make up our minds and told us we'd only have to give him the nod should we want fuck one of his crack hoar's.

Tony soon stuck his money away and resumed rolling up our next super duper spliff. Meanwhile things were starting to get very heated on the poker table given that Kenny had already accused one or two players of cheating and was now making allegations about the croupier. The boss had to step in and calm things down before giving Kenny a warning about his uncouth behaviour. The atmosphere had changed for the worst and was now uncomfortably ugly, the other accused players were really pissed off and began threatening to do Kenny some serious harm. The bouncers were also screwing and had turned their full attention to the poker table. Kenny apologised claiming that he must of made a mistake and promised to keep himself in check. Miraculously with a little helpful diplomacy from Propaganda and using his own brand of Burmese charm, Kenny somehow managed to win everyone back around, for the time being. The next time Kenny left the table to go for a piss Tony and I met him in the toilet and went on to tell him that if he didn't pipe down and behave we'd kick the fucking shit out of him ourselves, because he was going to get us all killed or at the very least badly hurt. He swore blind that one feller in particular was definitely cheating but nevertheless promised us that he wouldn't kick off anymore. Kenny was more than likely cheating himself, he was a right slippery fucker on the quiet, anyway he won a large amount of money over the next few hours but then lost most of it in one big hand. We managed to leave there in one piece at around six in the morning. Fortunately at some point during the twilight hours I had managed to nick a couple of hours sleep after nodding off on the comfy leather sofa, which sobered me up enough to drive us all safely home.

Other acts of skulduggery that we enjoyed getting up to was impersonating the Old Bill. A mate of ours Terry Churchill, owned and drove an ex police car, it was an automatic Rover SDI (which was the preferred old bill car at the time) and it had a distinctive sounding engine. For example if you were walking down the street or even up to a bit of mischief, you would know immediately without having to look that it was more than likely a police car from the moment you heard that engine. So we used it to our advantage, especially when we were stuck in traffic which was more often than not along the busy park lane while on our way home from a renovating job in Paddington. I would wind down the window and with my loudest piercing whistle I would mimic a police siren, and it fucking worked every time. Terry would be flashing his lights as I whistled and drivers everywhere couldn't wait to get out of the way to let us through. I even went as far as making a blue flashing light from a road works lamp and some blue sheets of Perspex. Tony would hold it on the roof as we flew through Mayfair like a scene from Starsky and Hutch. One night while cruising around east Dulwich we spotted a friend of ours called Nicky Lynch who was driving around aimlessly with his new girlfriend. We did the blues and two's routine and pulled him over whilst blinding him with a full beam. He got out of the car engulfed by a cloud of cannabis smoke initially looking petrified which quickly changed to dejection once he realised his number was up, since there was no way he could deny driving while under the influence. So with full beam still on the three of us got out of the car and made our way towards him. It wasn't until we were only a yard away from him that he began to realise something didn't add up. His brain had registered, but he looked like someone had knitted his face and dropped a stitch. We fell about laughing after seeing the look on his face, then after calling us "fucking cunts" while chasing us around the car Nick started to laughed with us, more out of relief that it was all a wind up. After five minutes of sheer rib breaking laughter we found the strength to pull ourselves together and bid Nick and his bird good night after leaving them full of paranoia about their journey home. This wasn't the only occasion I dared to impersonate the old bill, I remember back when I was around 14-15 yrs old I had acquired a replica of a beat Bobby's police hat (wooden top) from a tourist shop over the west end. So for a laugh I put on my cleanest plain white school shirt and a pair of black school trousers, I dug out a pair of black rimmed national health issue glasses that were knocking about in the house, I put a mini Scooby Doo note pad and pencil in my back pocket, I made a false moustache from my mum's black Mascara. I then made a look-alike police radio from an old black Hanimex camera which was attached to a length of black wire with one end fed through a gap in my shirt and the radio end sticking out of my top pocket. I was looking the part and was now ready to walk the beat around my neighbourhood It wasn't long before I came across my first victims while walking through the Cossal Estate. A couple of old ladies who had just left the estate community hall after playing bingo were walking towards me, "afternoon" they said politely, "good afternoon" I replied. I overheard them remarking about how young I looked for a policeman as they slowly helped each other shuffle along the path towards the elderly residence block. Suddenly I broke out into song singing Elvis Presley's Tutti Frutti complete with the pelvis dance too. I just found that sort of thing hilarious, imagining what must be going through their mind to see a police officer acting totally barmy, it just wasn't done. The two old ladies with hands now covering their mouths in shock didn't know what to make of it, knowing the effect I was having on them just spurred me on to be even more crazy so I started to do Basil Forty's Hitler impressions by marching around kicking my legs up in the air whilst holding my finger just below my nose. I could hear the old dears gasping in total confusion as I ran off Chuckling. I gathered my composure and continued to walk the beat across the estate when I noticed the little seven year old brother of one of my mates walking across the green. Although only seven he was pretty streetwise like his older brothers and sisters (big family). He was a small freckle faced cheeky ginger kid who was always up to no good. I thought I'd have some fun winding him up so with an authoritative stance I beckoned him over curling my finger at him. He changed direction and made his way over towards me with his head tilted down and swaying side to side in a guilty manner. As he stood there in front of me he could barely look me in the eye when I said in my most disguised and imposing voice, "Why aren't you at school boy? To which he replied, "it's half term sir, we've got a week off"

"That's no excuse boy, where do you live? I demanded to know. I was astonished that he still hadn't recognised me and was falling for my act hook line and sinker, I couldn't contain myself any longer and burst in to hysterics as he pointed in the direction of his house, he looked at me in the same way the two old ladies did, in total shock and disarray, I was laughing so much I could hardly speak as I tried to say "it's me" but this just confused him all the more, by now I was rolling around the floor in tears of laughter which grew more intense every time I looked up at this kid who was still totally in the dark to whom I was. He was probably trying to work out why this mad policeman was rolling around the floor in fits of side splitting laughter. Eventually I managed to pull myself together and reveal my true identity which pleased him no end since he was beginning to seriously worry about my sanity and his own safety. We parted ways and I headed for home since all that laughter had made me thirsty and I had a mouth like one of Ghandi's flip flops. Just as I was approaching my house I noticed my aunty Sue coming down the road on her 50cc moped, she used to visit at least once a day so I saw my opportunity to test my disguise for real. Twenty yards short of my door I stepped out into the road and flagged her down, she bought it, so with a concerned look on her face Sue promptly pulled off the road and parked her bike next to me. While unclipping her helmet and removing her gloves I circled the moped with note pad in hand pretending to check the tread on her tyres, "is everything ok officer? Said aunty Sue still concerned. I'm crap at keeping a straight face and crumbled before I could give her an answer and burst out laughing which gave me away immediately.

At this stage my mother came out with a camera after seeing us from the window. Sue and I posed for a couple of photo's before we all went in doors. I changed back into some normal clothes, it took me about 10 minutes to wash off my moustache. I grabbed a bottle of pop from the fridge and went back out to meet my mates on the estate. Two or three of my mates and I were sitting on a slide in the estate swing park and I was in the middle of telling them about the laugh I had whilst pretending to be a copper when two of the real local Bobby's came hurrying over, I knew them both quite well since I had spent lots of time in their company for one misdemeanour or another over recent years. We usually shared a bit of jovial banter when they came around on their beat, but this time they had urgency in their stride and a serious tone to their voices when they exclaimed,

"We've had reports that there is a nutcase going around impersonating a police officer, have you seen him? Before any of us could answer a voice came over their radio from the station giving the description of the imposter, the two bobby's listened intently and then one of them relayed the description to us, "Young man, about five foot six, black glasses, dodgy moustache" with that we all started to giggle amongst ourselves. "Come on lads this is not a joking matter, impersonating a police officer is a serious crime, have you seen him yes or no? Said one of the bobby's sharply. "Yes I've seen him, I saw him a few minutes ago" I claimed,

"Where did you see him, which way did he go? Asked the desperate bobby's. One of them spoke into his radio, "We have another confirmed recent sighting of the assailant last seen heading" . . . said the copper as he gestured to me to fill in the blank. "It was me, I am the dodgy copper" I confessed.

"You? Said the bobby's in unison with a look of disbelief on their faces. I explained how I did it and exactly what my motives were (fun), and they immediately began to relax. One of the coppers Radioed through to the station to call off the panic and to let them know that things weren't exactly how they seemed. Knowing me as they did, they were quite sure there was no malice in my actions, just innocent mischief so for my punishment they handcuffed me to a lamppost outside the Cossal estate news agent and encouraged my mates to feel free to kick and punch me while the Bobby's joined the shop keeper for a cup of coffee. At first my mates thought it was funny trying to dodge my efforts to stave them off by kicking out, they did manage to get one or two digs in here and there but soon gave up in favour of trying to help me escape. Escaping proved futile because short of ripping the drainpipe away from the wall with some sort of heavy duty motorised hacksaw there was no way out. The coppers left me to stew for about 40 minutes and after a half hearted warning and me promising never to do it again they uncuffed me and let me go. My pals peeled off in different directions as I playfully started to chase them around trying to get them back for the digs that they'd given me earlier. Well impersonating a copper and winding up the old granny's as well the freckle faced ginger kid was a normal day for me,

THE FOX

I was gutted that I didn't manage to fool Sue since ordinarily she was quite easily duped. She had fallen foul to many of my wind ups in the past like the time when a rapist, nicknamed "The Fox" was going around the Greater London and Bedfordshire area breaking into houses while the occupants were out for the evening. In their living rooms he would construct a lair in which to await his victims return. After removing the light bulbs to ensure darkness, he then moved furniture around covering it with blankets, his aim was to watch videos without being spotted by the giveaway light. As he waited, he collected dressing gown cords and cut the telephone wires and also made an escape route for himself before helping himself to food from the fridge while making a cup of tea. This behaviour became his habitual trademark and the reason behind his nickname given to him by the police.

When the occupants arrived home the Fox would pounce brandishing a shot gun or large kitchen knife. More often than not he would wear a black balaclava but on some occasions he wore a mask made out of a trouser-leg, in which he had cut out slits for eye-holes. He must have been a terrifying sight for the victims to face before being tied up and subjected to vile and horrific sexual assaults.

The Fox struck fear and sheer terror into the hearts of women all over southern England similar to the kind of hysteria that surrounded the Yorkshire Ripper. Aunty Sue was already a women that lived on her nerves and was forever relaying her fears to my mother about the proximity of the Fox's latest victims. Her overt anxiety about this particular subject played right into my evil little hands fuelling my twisted personality. I had my own black Balaclava (for different reasons than Mr Fox) and one night I sat patiently waiting outside the living room door listening for the first hint that Sue might be about to go home. It just so happened that The Fox was on the news again earlier that night and yet again was now the subject of their discussion. Sue's departure would usually follow the same pattern, which was shoving her tobacco pouch and lighter into her handbag and gathering her big old bunch of keys from the coffee table. This was my cue to sneak out of the front door and wait for her to come out while dressed in my Balaclava and wielding one of mums shinny kitchen knives. Minutes later Sue opened the door and as she took her next step I suddenly appeared.

"Come here you!!! I growled while lunging at her.

"NOOOOOOOOOOOOOO," screamed Sue as she shuffled backwards in complete and utter terror.

"NOOOOOOOOOOOOOO," she screamed again as I continued lunging towards her.

There's something I have to tell you about me, the only thing that really makes me genuinely laugh is seeing brief shock and horror on people's faces, a bit like that startled surprised look you get when someone pops a balloon. But the look on Sue's face was one of prolonged horror and sheer panic which wasn't funny at all, so I quickly unmasked myself to let her know it was just a prank. She started to hyperventilate so my mum fetched her a glass of water while I sat her down on the stairs and tried to calm her down. She eventually saw the funny side after smoking a couple of nerve calming roll ups which had been rolled by my mum since Sue's hands would not stop trembling. After a sympathetic cup of tea she eventually plucked up the courage to get on her moped and ride home. The funny thing about the Fox story was when the police eventually caught this terrifying masked monster, he turned out to be the most insignificant, small and dopey looking feller you could ever imagine. He was a Geordie who had been living with his wife and kids in Kentish Town north London.

I must admit even though 27 years has gone by, I couldn't help chuckling away whilst writing this little story about Aunty Sue and the Fox.

CHAPTER XIII

INSIDE
THE JOLLY GREEN GIANT

ONE OF MY immediate neighbours on the three's was a bloke called Steve he was about seven foot tall and built like a brick shit house. He came to the nick about a month after me, and had already spent one Christmas behind bars at the Scrubs and it looked like he would be spending one more at her Majesty's pleasure before getting out to be re-united with his two baby daughters and his ever loving wife. Steve was a genuinely nice fellow and we got on really well. He was in for GBH and had already served twelve months of a three-year stretch. He lived in Romford Essex and told me that because of his size blokes would always want to pick a fight with him after a bit of Dutch courage down the boozer since they would score points for taking on such a monster of a guy. Pissed or not I wouldn't want to try my luck with him, anyway a gang of pissed up geezers did, and before long Steve was throwing people over tables and out of window's with the help of his seven foot older brother. But you honestly couldn't have met a nicer bloke. He employed himself as my mentor and would sit in my peter while I drew portraits of his beautiful baby girls always advising me to keep out of trouble when I get out. One day after getting a knock back from the parole board, which meant he would be spending another Christmas away from his family, he returned to the wing spoiling for a fight, Just one wrong word or sideways glance would have been enough to send him over the edge, Along with Paul and another good friend Danny Webster, we tried to calm him down and pacify him whilst looking over the balcony of our landing. Every poor inmate who as much as glanced in our direction would get both barrels.

"Who you fucking looking at? Oi Sooty, I'm fucking talking to you, who you looking at Cunt," he would growl venomously. The Innocent black guy would quickly look away and dive in his Peter hoping Steve was referring to someone else. Now there were some Rock hard muscle bound prisoners in our wing, but Steve was out of control and everyone who thought they were hard and was in his firing range would get a piece of his mind. He wouldn't listen to our plea's to calm down so we all backed away from the railing and into our Peters not wanting to appear like we were echoing his spiteful comments. I went down to the Ones (ground floor) where Karl lived hoping he could have a word with Steve before he got himself into trouble. He was a lifer; and was also a seven footer and built like a Tank. They had made friends almost immediately after Steve got to the nick, and if anyone could talk Steve around Karl was the man. The plan had worked; Steve had gone for a walk with Karl and we never saw hide nor hair of either of them until later that evening when Karl came up to see me alone.

"Rick can you come and give me a hand with Steve? He asked.

"Why what's happened, has he still got the hump? I asked, thinking he was probably throwing someone around the wing.

"No mate I can't get him up, we've been on the Bong all afternoon and he's wasted," said Karl giggling. Steve had never smoked fags in his life let alone a spliff, but a Bong would hit you twice as hard as a joint, apparently they had smoked it like it was going out of fashion since Karl had convinced Steve that it was just the tonic he needed to forget his troubles. Well it certainly calmed him down because when we got to Karl's Peter we found Steve slumped across the bed in a semi coma with a fixed grin on his face. The problem was that Steve, already a heavy old lump, was now twenty odd stone of dead weight, and we would somehow have to get him past the Kanga's office and up to the three's to his Peter without them suspecting foul play. At this stage I knew we were going to have to enlist Paul and Danny to help us out. One to create a diversion and the other to help Drag Steve up the 4 flights of stairs to the three's. So after agreeing to help, the two of them came down to see what all the fuss was in aid of and fell about laughing after seeing the fixed grin on big Steve's face who was now looking green and ready to vomit. It wouldn't be long before association was over and we would be confined to our landing, so we had to get the ball rolling. Paul went to the wing office with the excuse that he needed a kit change slip, which would keep one or both of the Kanga's occupied while we slipped past with the Jolly Green Giant. Between the three of us Danny Karl and I managed to get Steve up and just about walking with his orang-utan length arms wrapped around mine and Karl's shoulders, Danny walked immediately in front of us trying to hide the fact that Steve was talking with a limp and walking with a lisp. Paul had done his job well since we had got Steve past the screw office window without so much as a raised eyebrow; all we had to do now was negotiate the four flights of stairs. Eventually we arrived at his Peter and laid him down on his bed, Karl then left and went back down to the one's, Danny and Paul went back to their game of cards leaving me with the now very paranoid Steve who kept asking me if he was fucking dying. He was actually having what's known as a white death, after smoking so much Bong for the first time his nervous system was all over the place. The symptoms were, one minute you are freezing cold and shivering violently, the next minute you are boiling hot and stripping layers of clothes. Your heart would be thumping hard and your breathing became shallow, this cycle would go on and on for about half hour and it literally feels like you are dying. Anyway by now Steve was beginning to panic so I reassured him that a mate of mine on the outside had been through the same thing a couple of times. "You are just having a bad Buzz, you'll be fine," I told him as I peeled and fed him a couple of oranges because the vitamin c was like an antidote and would help the buzz fade away. He begged me not to leave him until he got over the white death and felt a bit better so I ended up babysitting him until lights out. The next morning he looked as rough as fuck and could barely get himself out of bed for roll call, this was when the screws came round to count every inmate in their cells. He couldn't thank me enough for keeping him alive last night, (well that's the way he saw it) but I think that was the last time he ever dabbled with cannabis after having such a bad turn out. Eventually Steve had come to terms with the fact he'd have to spend another Christmas away from home, and apologised to one or two people he'd upset in the past, most of them were grateful for his apology. He was now refocused and had started working out in the gym with Karl and me. Karl was also the prison canoe Instructor and he taught me to Eskimo roll with and without the paddle. I also learned survival and rescue tactics with a canoe. Although not quite Olympic size, the prison swimming pool was fairly large and flying around in a canoe on the weekends was great fun. Karl's build bore resemblance to Dolph Lundgren, only not quite as facially chiselled and good looking, where as Steve's build was more like Richard Kiel who played Jaws, James bond's enemy in The Spy Who Loved Me and Moonraker, only not quite as ugly. So as you can imagine Canoeing wasn't quite Steve's cup of tea, although he did have his uses in and around the swimming pool. Danny, (who was quite a bit shorter than me,) and I would lunge at Steve from the poolside trying to push him into the water; we would end up getting thrown half way across the pool splashing down into the water, then we'd get out at opposite ends to launch another ambush giggling as we ran at him. Reading all this you'd never guess we were in Prison supposedly to be punished, but like I said before It wasn't always fun and laughter, and there were plenty of dark moments. I can remember one episode when still employed at the Dairy, there was an open day for the public to come and have a look around the Prison Farms. We were instructed not to talk to any of them as they wandered around with their guides; we were instructed to continue working as if nobody was there. My colleagues and I were preparing the cows bedding area by spreading fresh hay around when a group of twenty or so people entered the cowshed. The majority were young mums pushing prams, and were cautiously ambling forwards not wanting to stray too far from their guides (the screws). At that moment I knew exactly how a monkey in a zoo felt with people gawping at them like they'd just arrived from another planet. I felt like a disgusting murdering Rapist who was not fit to mingle with your average Joe public. I felt I wasn't worthy to be in the company of law-abiding citizens. It's hard to explain exactly how that whole event made me feel, it was a new experience for me and just the way they looked at you made you feel like the scum of the earth. It was obviously a new and nerve racking experience for the visitors too, after all we did have a murderer and an armed robber in our midst. For all they knew we could have all been sex offenders or mass murderers, so there was tension on both sides. After 10 minutes of ambling around in a tight huddle a young blonde pram pusher who had bravely (or stupidly) peeled slightly off from the group smiled at me and said,

"How are you? I looked over at the screws who were busy talking about the cows.

"I'm fine thanks, how are you? I replied still checking on the screws.

"We've been told not to talk to you," I told her.

"What are you in for? She asked while joining me in checking that the screws were still busy droning on about the workings of a cow farm to the older members of the group.

"Driving offences, don't worry, I said reassuringly, I'm not a danger to you." Wanting to sound as harmless as possible I told her I was here for driving offences, since possession with intent to supply was a mouth full and required further explanation.

"How old are you? She asked with her pretty smile, she was the first female I'd seen in the flesh, apart from the butch lesbian head chef from the Kitchens, and obviously members of my family on fortnightly visits. "I'm 22, I said, finding her more and more attractive by the second.

"Me too, what's your name? She asked with a flirtatious look on her face.

"Rikki, what's yours?

"Get back to work," bellowed one of the screws on noticing the proximity of a civilian and prisoner was in danger of exceeding its limit. We smiled at each other as we backed away putting a couple of yards of distance between us, then she mouthed her name like you would when talking to a deaf child, "Sandra."

"Nice name, I whispered back. I was grateful to her for being un-judgemental enough to talk to me and take away all those horrible feelings I had of being an animal in a zoo. The 30 or 40 seconds I spent communicating with her made me feel like a normal person again albeit very brief. I studied every curve of her gorgeous shapely body and every detail of her face wanting to imprint the image in my mind for as long as possible As the group were about to exit the building Sandra gave me a sexy smile and mouthed "Bye Rikki." For the rest of the day I had a grin from ear to ear and could not stop thinking about her. I think that fact that she was forbidden fruit made my encounter with Sandra much more sensational than it would have done under normal circumstances. That night my imagination ran wild with fantasy involving Sandra and me sneaking off into one of the empty stables and cavorting naked in amongst the loosely scattered hay stacks before she ran off to catch up with the rest of the group. I even wrote about my fantasy like a story you would read in a saucy magazine in order to keep the memory fresh in my mind. I imagined she lived local and would sneak in to the cow shed every day for lurid naked love making sessions. My brief encounter with Sandra kept me going for weeks and I often wondered if she was the type to fantasise about having a secret fling with a prisoner. As nice as this all sounds the thing that stuck with me the longest was that horrible feeling of worthlessness I felt in the first 10 minutes of the visitors arrival. I felt detached, like I was another species it was a feeling completely alien to me and I hated it.

CHAPTER XIX

DON'T COME BACK

W ITH A COUPLE of days left of my sentence I could almost taste freedom, the weight of prison on my shoulders was beginning to lift, the imaginary ball and chain tied to my ankle was getting lighter and almost unnoticeable, I would be leaving at 8.30 am in the morning so it was time for me to start saying goodbye to my friends. As much as I couldn't wait to get out, there was a big part of me that was going to miss this place. I'd spent nearly five months here with so much going on all the time. Out of roughly four hundred cells in the whole prison, I must have knocked on over two hundred doors to wish people well and say goodbye. Nearly every one of those people all had the same message. "Don't come back Rick, stay out of trouble," I couldn't begin to explain the emotions I went through after each hug, shake of hands, and pat on the back. I had shared an experience and a sense of camaraderie with these people that could never be repeated or forgotten. The normal practice was the night before an inmate's release; his "mates" would get him wasted, or play some kind of prank on him. I got thrown a party in my Peter with Steve, Paul, and a few others providing all the ingredients for a memorable last night. Danny had been released a month or so earlier and we did the same for him. The next morning Steve and Paul walked me down to the processing office where my transformation back to a civilian would be completed. I was given my personal possessions, and got changed into my suit. After sarcastically telling me they'd see me again before long, the screws gave me my official discharged sheet. I walked out of the office to find Paul and Steve still waiting for me, Paul had to run off to work so we shook hands and patted each other on the back, he was due for release in a couple of weeks so I told him to behave himself as he walked off. Steve's E.D.R wasn't until February 1992 so he was looking at another eight months before he would be doing the last walk to the gates. I had to choke back the tears as Steve walked the last five hundred yards with me, "Look after yourself Rick, and don't come back mate," he said as we approached the out of bounds line 10 yards short of the gate. We hugged and shook hands before he turned and walked back to the main population. I took a minute to have one more look at the place then handed the screw at the gate my discharge slip and walked out onto Civvie Street for the first time in five months. I was no longer just a number, I was Rikki again, a free man with a new start, the future was a blank canvas and I was holding the paint brush. I took a deep breath then cracked a big smile as I saw my Mum and my Nan in the car park waiting with open arms, I was so pleased to see them, and we hugged and kissed before getting in the car that my mum had borrowed. It was a white Fiat Uno. I had to drive since my mum had got flustered driving the 60 or so miles to get there. At first it seemed strange walking straight out of nick and immediately into the driver's seat. I drove straight to a greasy spoon café in the local village of Eastchurch and had a full English breakfast that I had been promising myself when I eventually got out. I also bought twenty cigarettes which seemed very peculiar, it had been a while since I last smoked a proper fag. The next few days were very strange as I acclimatized to normal life, but normal life to me was back at Stanford Hill. As silly as it sounds I wished I could go back there for a week just to see my mates. I soon realised that not much had changed in five months except a few dodgy hairstyles here and there. After a few days at home it started to feel as though I'd never been away. Now some people might be thinking, "what's he harping on about he was only in prison for five months, that's nothing compared to doing a six stretch or a life sentence. I agree it was a small part of my life on the scale of things, but those five months in a totally different world sometimes felt like a lifetime whilst serving my sentence and the experiences were personal to me. However there were many bad, sad, dark, dangerous, and very low and lonely soul destroying moments, so over all I wouldn't want to repeat it. Luckily my understanding Italian boss had kept my job open for me, so after a week I slipped nicely back into my old roll as a delivery driver for Franco's import export company. Generously he gave me an old Fiat panda to use, the engine wasn't great and Franco had repaired it using spare parts from an old washing machine, which my mate Mattie and I found out to our cost after breaking down on the M2 one night when returning home from visiting Danny where he lived in Margate. The engine had cooked; the oil and water were now mixing together and spitting out of every point of exit. We were covered from head to toe in oil and we had to push the fucking thing for about 600 yards through the coned off road works and onto the nearest bit of safe hard shoulder. Even though it was dark and pissing down with rain, Mattie and I tried our best to fix it in order to get us home, but the car wasn't having none of it. We decided to try and get our heads down for the night but only ended up sleeping for a couple of broken hours. The driver of the tow truck belonging to the company carrying out the work came over and woke us up saying he would tow us to the end of the line since our position was deemed to be too dangerous. For once I was happy that the road works were about 6 miles long, which meant we were taken nearer to our destination. By hook or crook we eventually got the car back to my local mechanic in Nunhead who had performed miracles on one or two of my other old bangers in the past. He opened the lid and had a quick look over the engine before saying, "I think I know what the problem is Rick."

"What's that then Des? I asked

"It's a Fiat Panda with a moulinex engine.

"What does that mean," I asked naively.

"You've got half a fucking washing machine in here," he said laughing while gesturing to his colleague (greasy Pete) to come and have a look. We all fell about laughing when he pointed out a couple of rubber pipes that had Moulinex written on them. So when I say nothing had changed in five months, I wasn't joking it was business as usual.

PAY BACK

One Day whilst driving along the road in Camberwell I spotted a familiar face, it was Anthony, the feller who disappeared with our money way back when. I pulled up next to him and leant over to unwind the passenger side window. "Anthony! All right mate!

"Hello Rick, when did you get out? He asked as he approached the car, he was visibly regretting the fact that he'd bumped into me. "Just the other day, Jump in I'll give you a lift," I didn't want to spook him so I played the old mates routine. He couldn't come up with an excuse quick enough to avoid getting in the car, so he got in and we drove towards Peckham. Anthony tried to create a friendly atmosphere with some small talk but I cut to the quick and asked, "why did you fuck off with our money Ant? Predictably he tried to blame his partner Mark. "Well we spoke to Mark and he swears it was you, anyway one way or another you both owe us £180.00 so let's go and ask John what he thinks we should do to sort this out." I drove straight round to Pick John up who jumped in the back of the car. "Hello Antony, fancy bumping into to you eh, long time no see, er let me guess, it was Mark who ripped us off and you had nothing to do with it, right? Asked John with a hint of sarcasm. Anthony tried to wriggle his way out of it but we weren't having none of it. "I'll tell you what, let's all have a nice little ride down to the cash point where you can draw out our dough and put an end to this fiasco," Said John.

"I've only got £100 in the bank," Claimed the helpless Anthony.

"That's ok we'll take the hundred quid and keep hold of your Tom until you turn up with the other eighty," I said after noticing a thick old lumpy gold bracelet on his wrist and a couple of rings on his fingers. John went with him to the cash point while he drew out the money, back in the car he reluctantly gave us the Tom claiming they were presents from his Nan and had sentimental value. "The quicker you turn up with our money the quicker you will be re-united with your precious jewellery, and if you aint back within a fortnight it's going in the Pawn brokers so chop chop Ant," that was the Last thing I said to him as he walked off down the street a good few ounces lighter than he was before bumping into us. It just so happened that he turned up at the flat that night with the rest of the money to buy back his Tom, John and I were happy to be up 90 quid each, so we took it no further and just told Anthony to do one. He did and left with his tail between his legs, gutted at loosing £180.00 but happy to be still walking away with about a monkey worth of Tom. The drinks were on me down at the snooker club that night, and the next day I splashed out on some new clothes and treated my cousin Tony and me to double pie and Mash and a few beers down the boozer.

Although I vowed never to do anything that would send me back to prison and prove the doubting screws right, something came up that proved too tempting to turn down and had nothing to do with making money. It was more a revenge plot with an element of job satisfaction. I was 23 yrs old and was having a drink in my local with this girl I'd met shortly after getting out of prison. It was Valentine's Day and this is how it all began.

CHAPTER XX

OUT
THE POLICE CAR POUND ROBBERY

"I HAVEN'T GOT A clue who sent it, it's probably one of my mates winding me up", I explained to my latest fling reassuringly. "I bet it's that tart down the road, I know her handwriting and if I find out it's her I'll scratch her fucking eyes out", she hissed.

"For Christ sakes it's just a bloody valentines card, stop getting so stressed about it", I said trying to make light of it. "Look lets have another half a lager and forget about it," I pleaded. Slam, went her empty glass on the bar, she grabbed her car keys and stormed out of the pub. "She looks 'appy, what have you done", asked one of my mates who was about to take his next shot on the pool table. "Nothing, she's got the painters and decorators in aint she," I said rolling my eyes. "Good luck Rick, they're murder when it's their time of month" he began to give me some examples of the drama's in his house when his wife is having her monthly's.

I was taking a risk because this girl I was seeing whose name was Katie, was the girlfriend of a well known Gangster, He was in his early 40's and he along with his many brothers were all around six and a half foot tall and drove flash cars and always wore top notch suits. Every now and then the gangster (Raymond) and his heavies would turn up at my local boozer and buy four or five bottles of the pubs finest champagne and pour drinks for all the brown noser's in the pool bar. I never joined them in sucking up to him, and when I first started seeing Katie I knew there was a rumour that she was also seeing a bloke who was a bit naughty, but since he was from Dulwich (a mile or so up the road from Peckham) I had no idea who he was. By then it was too late, we were already having a full-blown affair. I was 22 and still had this feeling of invincibility and taking risks was in my nature as you may have already worked out. Katie didn't have classical beauty but with her masses of natural blonde curly locks, a decent figure and an infectious laugh she was very attractive and oozed sex appeal. She had a certain charm about her which gave her an air of irresistibility making her a flashing light on every red blooded mans radar.

I downed my last mouthful of lager and went to try and calm her down, outside on the street I saw her speed of in her car and guessed she was on her way to my flat to look for the valentine's card, so I jumped in my motor and headed for home. It was around 9.p.m and dark. I saw Katie's brake lights in the distance as she approached the bottom of the hill and turned left along the main drag (Nunhead lane). My flat was 2 minutes drive from the Boozer, as I came to a bend in the road on Nunhead lane I heard a constant car horn sound, and then noticed about ten yards in front of me there were two cars in the middle of the road. Smashed up, motionless and lying perpendicular to the road markings. My first thoughts were, I wonder if Katie saw what happened, imagining her to have already arrived at my flat. I pulled over and got out of my car, to my horror I realised that the driver of the car nearest to me was Katie and she lay slumped on the steering wheel with her head on the Bib. Blood was pumping from her forehead, the window screen was shattered but still whole and had a head shaped dent in it. The front end of her car was completely twisted and buckled; water was pissing out onto the street. "Katie, Katie" I shouted. She came to with a start, threw her head back and started to scream. Her face and hair was covered in thick blood from a skull deep gash on the hairline of her forehead. I looked over at the other car and saw two black faces seemingly unconscious in the front seats, and two other passengers in the back seat. I couldn't tell you what car they were driving since it looked like it had just been in a game of chicken with a Bull dozer. Still screaming and in a compete state of shock and disarray Katie got out of the car and started running up the street to our left. I wanted to check on the other casualties; from my position and distance I could only see four white eyes, which looked like Michael Jackson's eyes in a scene from Thriller. As I neared the wreck I realised the driver and passenger were now awake but just staring blankly at me, as though still trying to register what had occurred. The two back seat passengers were trying to get out of the car while shouting in some African language. "You all right mate", I gestured to the driver. At this point he had half regained his faculties and was also trying to remove his seat belt, his female passenger (who I assumed was his wife) was crying but looked unhurt. In fact all four of them were unhurt on the scale of things, but would probably suffer from serious whiplash for a few weeks. The driver was out now and walking around his car scratching his head in complete bafflement. I could hear an ambulance's blues and two's getting nearer and nearer, so I darted up the street to look for Katie. After calling out her name for 5 minutes I found her hiding in the front garden of a house where she used to rent a room a few months previous. She was still in a right state wailing and acting proper weird. "Katie you've got to go to hospital to get that looked at", I told her as I tried to have a closer look at her head. "There's an ambulance down there, come on let's get you seen to", "I can't," she screamed, "I've got no Insurance and the car is registered to Ray, he will fucking kill me if the old bill start sniffing around." Let's go to your flat and I'll report it stolen tomorrow," she begged still weeping. "Katie you aint thinking straight darling, your head is really bad and you have already lost a shit load of Claret," I explained. "No, I don't care I aint going to no fucking hospital," she scowled. The gate behind us squeaked open and a copper accompanied by a paramedic had found us on the doorstep of the now uninhabited house. "She's in shock", I told them hoping that would be an excuse for her running off. "Let me have a look at your head love," asked the paramedic in a caring voice. "I'm not going to any fucking hospital, I'm fine," she replied. As you can gather Katie wasn't very eloquent and not very lady like, but I was attracted to her troublesome nature and we both knew the score, we were never in this affair to settle down as a couple, it was just a physical relationship which suited both of us at the time. Or so I thought until she went berserk over the valentine's card.

400 BENSON & HEDGES

At the hospital Katie was at her usual charming best and endeared herself to the nurses by telling them all to fuck off, and warned them they had better not hurt her while cleaning her facial wounds and re-stitching her head back together. One of the coppers who accompanied her in the ambulance was by her bed and writing down Katie's version of how the accident happened. Suspecting her of drinking and driving the copper gave her the option of a breath test or blood sample to see if she was over the limit, so after more drama's and foul mouthed obscenities she reluctantly agreed to give a blood sample once the nurse had finished stitching the L shaped gash on her forehead. She was hoping that by then the 3 or 4 drinks that she had consumed a couple of hours ago would have left her system. Bagging the blood sample and issuing her with a producer, the copper left after taking down her moody name, age, and address. Later as we were leaving I saw the driver of the other vehicle. He was having his blood pressure taken with the arm strap and pump apparatus while the same copper was taking down his details, I didn't see the other three passengers, I can only assume were being fitted with neck braces.

Both cars had been loaded on to a truck and taken to a yard where the police deposit any vehicles that required further investigation or forensic testing. The yard was situated just underneath Platform three of Peckham Rye train station and had two rail arches included in its territory, one of the arches was disused and half closed off with a corrugated iron fence. The next morning after a restless sleep I got up earlier than usual, I made myself a cuppa and sat at the kitchen table mentally dissecting the events that took place last night, It suddenly dorned on me that I had left my driving licence and some other bits and bobs including a new Dictaphone in the glove compartment of Katie's car. She had taken me to the post office to cash my giro the day before and I forgot to take them out. She was still fast asleep after having such a traumatic night so I gently woke her up. She definitely looked like she'd been in a car crash, her hair was still matted with dried blood and her face looked a right mess. When I told her about my stuff still being in the car she groaned a couple of times then pulled the duvet over her head.

"I'm not bothered about the other stuff, I just need to get my driving licence back, I wonder if they will let me have it," I asked.

"Ray is going to go ape when I tell him, and I had 400 Bensons under the seat" she moaned. "I don't give a shit about Ray or your poxy fags, phone the old bill and ask them where they took the motor," I said getting the hump. Just then Katie's mobile started to ring, she answered it with a dreaded expression on her face, it was Ray and he already knew about the crash since he was the registered owner of the car the old bill had already contacted him. He gave them a load of flannel about selling the car a few weeks ago to a young blonde woman, and he reeled off the same moody name and address Katie had given the copper at the hospital. He found out the that the motor was at the police car pound in Blenheim grove Peckham, he was more pissed off about the fact he had a folder containing his restaurant accounts still in the car, rather than the car being a write off. The last thing he wanted was the old bill sniffing around his finances. A couple of hours later Katie and I drove to the pound where they were holding her car, Katie stayed about ten paces behind me worried that one of the coppers from last night might be there. I got to the gate and the yard looked empty, I beckoned Katie over, we saw the car in amongst about 10 other cars that looked as mangled as hers. The yard was very shabby and had an old rotten four berth caravan sitting in the corner, it looked more like a gypsy site than a police vehicle pound. The gate was slightly ajar so we made our way in the direction of the car. I was taken aback when two meaty Rottweiler's came bounding towards us snarling and showing their hungry teeth. Thank god they were on the end of a chain not quite long enough for them to rip us to shreds. The caravan door opened and out jumped a burley looking feller who looked like he could do with a good bath and an extreme make-over thrown in for good measure. He had the stereo typed cauliflower ear and broken nose, the dogs must have belonged to him based on the fact that pets always resemble their owners. All though burly and very ugly he was shorter than me and I was more intimidated by the dogs than him.

"You aint allowed in here, this is a restricted area so jog on," he barked while trying to appear tough with a threatening stance. He wasn't scaring me and I thought there was a chance I could talk him round. "That's my birds motor over there mate, I just wanna get me fags and a couple of bits and bobs, is that all right Geeze" I asked in an amicable tone. I was trying to keep it light not wanting to give him the impression that there was anything of importance in there even though I was desperate to retrieve my licence.

"This is police property and if someone even see's you in here I will lose my job so Fuck off," he growled. "Look mate I don't give a shit about your job I'm just getting my salmon from the Jam jar," I snarled back as I moved closer to the car. With that he leaned in the door of his caravan and produced a lumpy big old base ball bat. He positioned it over his shoulder in a Babe Ruth manner then shuffled towards me and said, "Take one more step mate, and I swear I'll do your fucking knee caps". He was frothing at the mouth so much that he and the dogs looked like triplets. "You stupid fat bastard", I said while backing off in the direction of the gate. At this point he unhooked the Rottweiler's chains from the A bar of the caravan and with the bat in one hand and two of his look alikes in the other hand he ushered us out of the gate. After calling him all the names under the sun we left empty handed. As usual my pride couldn't let this Oaf get the better of me, but right now the odds were on his side. I dropped Katie of at her friend's house and then went home. My dog Ben had a right go at me because he was breaking his neck for a slash, so I took him for a walk over the park. On the way back we stopped at our local Chippy and I bought Ben and myself a couple of pies and a large portion of chips. We sat in the kitchen and tucked into our lunch, Bens favourite pie was mince Beef and Onion, I never fed him your run of the mill dog food because his bladder never agreed with it which I found out to my cost on many occasion in the past. My mind was working overtime trying to figure out the best way to get the upper hand on Captain caveman from the pound. I knew it would be a stupid idea tackling him head on with aggression especially whilst his twin brothers were protecting him. Eventually I decided I would kill two birds with one stone, I would break into the car pound at night, remove everything of importance along with the 400 duty free fags from the car, the Pratt with the bat would get the sack and it would be 2 nil to me. I knew it would be risky and too blatant to go in over the front gate, so after lunch I drove down to the train station to do a recce on the whole surrounding area. After a mooch about I found I could get in to the car pound from the other side of the train station, but it wasn't going to be straight forward since there were plenty of obstacles to negotiate.

PRIVATE PROPERTY

At 9.pm that night after taking Ben out for his nightly walk I got changed into my blacks, black joggers, black jersey, back gloves, and black kung fu slippers which had plenty of rubber grip but were still very light on my feet giving me speed and agility. I stuffed my black balaclava and a packet of ginger nuts in my black shoulder satchel. I wasn't tooled up so didn't have to worry about getting tugged by the old bill on the way there, although the balaclava might have took some explaining. There was going to be a lot of climbing involved in completing my mission but as I have already stated on previous occasions, climbing was one of my hobbies so this to me was going to be a straight forward in and out scenario. I guessed the three Rottwielers spent the night in and around the caravan for security purposes, and was depending on the ginger biscuits to get me out of shtook if it came on top with the 4-legged variety. As for the bruiser with the bat, I'd have to rely on speed and agility to avoid getting clubbed.

A metal company has moved into what used to be the car pound, the arches have been bricked up, the sloth

Police car pound. View from the street, the white van is parked in what used to be the car pound

I parked my car two streets away from the pound, and sat there for a while smoking a fag and mentally preparing myself for the job in hand. Whilst walking towards my first entry point the adrenalin was beginning to pump around my body, I had feelings of trepidation mixed with excitement. Being dressed in black with the satchel over my shoulder and tight to my back I felt like Bruce Lee in a scene from Enter the Dragon.

My first obstacle was a seven foot brick wall situated in the alley that led to the train station entrance, I looked about for any stragglers, the coast was clear so I ran and leapt up onto the wall and scrambled over to the other side checking for a quiet landing spot before letting go of the wall. I was now around the side of the station offices, hidden from public view. There was rubbish and crap everywhere, and although part of the rail premises this area was disused and was full of beer cans and paper coffee cups that had been thrown out of the first floor station window by commuters and the odd dosser using the station as shelter from the elements. I moved on avoiding anything noisy, as I turned left behind the main building I saw two ground level frosted glass office windows. At this time of night there would always be one or two guards still knocking around, I noticed two dark silhouettes moving about in the office. Although surrounded in darkness I didn't want to risk getting seen so I crouched down below the window sill level and methodically picked my route through the debris scattered around the bird shit covered floor. Above me was one of two bridge like structures that supported the rail lines and platforms three and four. The other bridge was situated on the other side of the car pound and supported platform one and two. Together they provided housing for about a thousand Pigeons who now had their feathers ruffled by my presence and were cooing in unison. I could also hear the disturbing sound of rats and mice scurrying around in amongst the piles of rubbish, there were rodent droppings everywhere and the stench was repulsive, it was a sour acidic smell not unfamiliar to me. Now past the office windows I had to negotiate another wall only this one had anti-climb broken glass cemented into the top row. Luckily in my favour there were a network of drainpipes all over the place and I used one to get onto and over the wall without losing any fingers. All that lay between me and the car pound now, was a corrugated iron fence about twenty feet away, it had coiled barbed wire fixed along the top edge for extra security. I sat on a Pile of old bricks that had been heavily bombarded with bird shit which didn't bother me since I used to live next door to a pigeon fancier and I was well used to birds and bird shit. I scoffed a couple of ginger biscuits then lit up another cigarette. With the adrenalin now rushing at speed through my veins I'd finished the fag in mere seconds rather than minutes and began to scale the corrugated fence. I reached the top and slowly peered through the barbed wire; about thirty five to forty feet up at the far end of the car pound I noticed the brightly lit waiting area on platform two with around 10 commuters waiting for what would probably be the last train out of town.

I was worried about getting seen by the commuters even though the car pound wasn't affected by the bright lights of the platform. In the main it was covered in complete darkness, apart from a dim light coming from behind the deck chair striped curtains of the shabby caravan which sat in the near right hand corner of the yard. There was also an open window on the main block to my left and I could see what looked like a couple of wino's standing next to it and periodically looking out while singing Oh Danny Boy. On the other side of the barbed wire to my immediate left was a drainpipe that led down into the yard. I edged over to it and descended bit by bit constantly looking behind me to see if any of the platform stragglers had noticed me, and they hadn't. On any other day it would have taken me five to ten seconds to climb down the drainpipe, but this wasn't just any other day and the consequences of getting caught would be grave so after about five minutes of doing a Sloth impression on the pipe I finally arrived on the ground and in the car pound. I grabbed a hand full of biscuits from my satchel (just in case I had a fur coat razor blade welcoming comity) and began crawling on my hands and knees in the direction of the car. Very carefully I opened the passenger door and slithered in closing the door as quietly as possible staying low to remain out of site. I kissed my driving licence and put it in my zipped jogger pockets, then started to fill up my satchel with the fags, Dictaphone, and anything else worth taking. I noticed Raymond's folder in the foot well behind the driver's seat and considered leaving it for the old bill, but then thought bringing it with me would take the heat off Katie so I put it in with the other stuff. I was about to exit the motor when I heard a grunt and the pita pata of Rottweiler's talons. My worst nightmare would be to get trapped in the car with a couple of Cujo's baying for my blood. I was playing statues on my own at this point before noticing it was one of the Devil dogs who had started to vigorously sniff around my car door. My heart was already thumping like mad but when the dog stood on his hind legs to enable him to look through my window I was close to having a cardiac arrest. I remained as still as possible and was sure the monster knew I was in there. The dog and I were literally face to face but luckily the window had steamed up and he couldn't see inside. Eventually Cujo gave up and moved on, he cocked his leg on the neighbouring car wheel, done his load then ambled back to the caravan. My heart was still pumping fast as I edged out of the door and made my way back to the drainpipe. The rail passengers had disappeared from the platform, I was so busy trying not to get pinned down by Cujo that I hadn't noticed the train pull in and out. This time far from doing another sloth impression I wasted no time climbing back up the pipe and over the barbed wire and back down into the safety of the giant birdcage. I was soon tip toeing past the frosted office windows even though the lights were now turned off. Not getting seen jumping back into the alley was my next objective, so after leaning an old palette against the wall I cautiously looked up and down the alley before making my move. I can't begin to describe the feeling of self-satisfaction I had whilst walking the final 50 yards or so to my car. It was a mixture of invincibility, accomplishment, cockiness, awe and pride. The whole operation from start to finish went without a hitch; it was a textbook execution. At that point I realised that I'd just done a Creeper, although not quite the same scenario that my prison neighbour Paul found himself in, that's not my thing. I couldn't stop grinning, I would have paid a fortune to see the gutted look on the bat wielding thugs face when he realised he'd been turned over. I pictured him with a long face as the old bill handed him his P45 for being incompetent.

I drove home, had a quick shower, changed clothes then made my way to the pub in time for last orders. I knew Katie would be there and couldn't wait to show her what a hero I had been, and tell her how I had got in and out of the lion's den without so much as a splinter. As you can tell I was on top of the world and buzzing with an overdose of adrenalin. Katie was sitting down waiting for her shot on the pool table; I walked over with a swagger and emptied the contents of the satchel on to the table. With a long sharp intake of breath Katie screeched "How the fucking hell did you get", . . . "where the hell have", ... She didn't believe my version of events at first, until we got back to my flat and I showed her the amount of pigeon shit on my gloves and clothes. Delighted about being off the hook after seeing Ray's folder and her 400 Bensons, she confirmed what I had already been thinking. "You are my hero", she confessed.

CHAPTER XXI

WHAT GOES AROUND COMES AROUND

MY RELATIONSHIP WITH Katie had run its course and inevitably came to an end. It was for the best since I ended up in countless arguments and fights whenever we went out. On one occasion while having a quiet night out at our local pub The Railway Tavern, one of Nunhead's local bullies David Muller and his pal turned up. He started trying to intimidate me expecting me to back down like most of his victims. He was a lump of a bloke and did look very intimidating with his screwed up face, but I showed no fear and went eye to eye with him. I told him I didn't know what his problem was and explained that I didn't want any trouble but at the same time letting him know that he wasn't scaring me. The truth was he'd been trying to get into Katie's knickers ever since he put her up at his flat for a couple of nights in the past, and was jealous of the fact that Katie and I were an item. Although I'd seen David around town over the years, this was the first time we locked horns, anyway he backed down after giving me a face saving warning. I had seen in his eyes that he really didn't fancy a scrap with me now but had to maintain his hard man image after already threatening to knock me out. Half an hour later I was in the pub carsey having a piss, it was a pokey little toilet but very busy. People were in and out all the time since it was situated in the middle of two bars and had a door either end, one leading to the saloon bar and the other leading back to the pool bar where Katie and I were sat, so I never noticed David come in. With cock still in hand I got walloped from behind, the wanker thought he'd get me with a lucky punch while I had my back turned and my hands full, so after quickly tucking my bits and pieces away I pushed him up against the sink and told him what a sneaky Cunt he was for hitting me in the midst of taking a piss and offered him outside for a staightener. So he went out of one door and I the other and we met outside the pub. We started to square up and he threw a punch that was so slow it could have come via a telegram and reached me quicker, I ducked the punch and mustered up as much power as I could and punched him square on the chin with all my might. His lights were out before he hit the ground and as I looked over to where he landed I was delighted to discover that he was out cold on the floor. This big old lump who had bullied most of my pals over the years was now unconscious on the floor after one punch, and half of the pub was there to witness his demise. He started regaining consciousness so I hit him a couple more times to let him know I meant business, he pleaded with me to stop and said he'd had enough and just wanted to be mates. By now I was feeling confident that if I need to I could take him out, so I let him get to his feet whilst still having my right arm and fist cocked and ready to throw another bomb just in case he got any silly Idea's of swinging for me again. David's pal Kenny was a known Scag head and used to duck and dive his way through the day by stealing, begging and borrowing to get his next fix. I was unaware that he had come out from the pub with a broken pool cue which he used to whack me in the face with while I was still dealing with David. I couldn't believe that none of my "mates" did anything to try and stop him and it took a girl (Katie) to wrestle him away from me. At that point David had managed to grab stump end of the broken pool cue, thus temporarily giving him the upper hand and an opportunity to recover his hard man reputation, or so he thought. With renewed confidence he screwed up his face again and started coming at me with the stump, **"Come on then you cunt!!!** He shouted, **"Come on lets fucking 'ave it!!!** He got louder and louder and more aggressive as he walked towards me swinging the stump to and fro. I always carried a set of Nunchuckers in the boot of my car and had been taught how to use them quite effectively when I was a youngster, so while backing off to avoid David's attempts at caving my skull in I asked two of my mates to fetch my Nunchuckers from the car. Typically they declined since they didn't want to appear to be taking sides against the bully. "Come on lads, turn it in now, your causing a scene," was the reply I got after pleading with them to grab my set of equalizers from the boot. No prizes for guessing that these were the same "mates" who left me in the lurch down the Gin Palace on the Old Kent road, and were the same "Mates" who would later set me up when some gangsters come to kill me. Why didn't I learn my lesson and dump these so called friends you might ask? Better the Devil you know is my answer to that, the day will come when they will need me and I will have a prepared script ready and waiting for them.

"Why don't you put ya fucking weapon down and fight me like a man you fat cunt! I growled at David,

"Come on fight me with your fists you wanker, you're a fucking shitter aint ya, you need a fucking weapon 'cos you know I'll knock you spark out don't ya you fucking cowardly cunt."

In between his pathetic attempts at swinging the pool stump at me I managed to land a kick here and there to his legs and body. I knew that my Nunchuckers were never going to make an appearance so I was trying to pick the right moment to land another big punch.

Just then a small Suzuki van pulled up and out jumped the 25-year-old bully's Mummy and Daddy who told him off and took him home. That was the icing on the cake; his once widely feared hard man reputation was now in tatters putting a big question mark over his future career in intimidation. So it just goes to show how it can sometimes only take one punch to change the street politics and equilibrium of an area. I even named that punch after him, The David Muller punch. Word travelled fast around Nunhead and I'd gained a bit of a reputation myself when people heard I'd knocked out David Muller, which had good and bad points. The good points were, a lot of people I barely knew seemed to want to be my mate, they were probably glad that the local bully had been bought down a peg or two, or maybe they just wanted to be on my side. The bad points were, a few of the other bullies felt threatened by me since I had taken out their top man, so they would go out of their way to make me feel uncomfortable and create an atmosphere of un-ease and would be constantly screwing me out if I happened to be having a drink in their local pub. Nunhead is a small area and had numerous amounts of boozers plotted around so although The Railway Tavern was my regular watering hole, my mates and I would also use the other pubs in the area, and other punters would frequent our pub, so we all knew each other or knew of each other. Don't get me wrong I have never tried to carry myself off as a hard man, or even thought of myself in that way.

I have never purposely started a fight or looked for trouble. I have just always been able to come up with the right punch at the right time when needed, and I rarely back down. I may have learned that from young Eric since I'd seen him in so many tear ups and he never backed down, he always went eye to eye with anyone wanting a piece of him. I wouldn't encourage anyone to fight, but there is an old saying which works in all scenarios of life, WHERE EVER THE FEAR MAY BE, LOOK IT IN THE EYE.

FACE LIFT FOR THE QUEEN BEE

Another troubled night I spent whilst out with Katie, was the one and only time I was happy for her to kick off. We were having a drink in the Crown and Anchor on New Cross road. It was a stone's throw away from the Old Den, so was a known Millwall supporters boozer. My cousin Lee used to work there as a barman a year or so previous, so I was quite used to drinking there. Katie and I sat at the bar and ordered a couple of halves of lager, it was mid evening and there was a good lively atmosphere with people warming up before heading for one of the many night clubs in the area. We were served by an attractive brunette, about 30 years old with long hair down to her bum. I vaguely remembered her from the early days, she fucking loved herself and breezed around the bar like the queen of Sheba. When I ordered our second round, I asked her for two halves of lager but she came back with a pint and a half.

"Two pand seventy!"

"I only asked for two halves love," I explained politely.

"Do I look like I'm fucking deaf? You asked for a pint and a half of lager." She tutted, grabbed the pint and emptied it in the sink before pouring out a fresh half glass, then slammed it down in front of me, thrust her hip out with attitude and said, "One pand eighty!

I knew I'd only ordered two halves because that's what we always drank, halves. As much as I wanted to pull her up about her un-professional attitude, I knew she would probably start mouthing off, and I didn't want to make a scene so I bit my tongue and paid her. Katie was strangely quiet during all this and we carried on chatting and drinking while still sitting at the bar. A little while later we were trying to decide whether or not to have another drink or move on to a club.

"It's still a bit early, let's have one more here before we shoot off a? said Katie.

"Sounds good to me, but you better order the next lot of drinks, since me and the barmaid aint exactly been getting on." I chuckled.

So Katie got the barmaids attention and politely ordered our drinks. Again the arrogant bitch slammed our drinks down and barked, "One pand eighty." Surprisingly Katie gave her a warm smile as she handed over two pound coins. The bitch came back and as good a slung the 20p change along the bar to Katie and went back to posing and strutting her way around the bar. She never once said please or thank you, her attitude was totally un-called for. Katie put the 20p in her pocket and then called the bitch over again, with another big warm smile Katie asked, "Can I just have a quick word love?

As the smarmy bitch cocked her neck to one side and leant forward to listen, Katie grabbed her head by the hair and started slamming her face into the bar. Every word Katie said equalled another whack to the bitch's face.

"Who, The, Fuck, Do, You, Think, You, Are, You, Fucking, Slag?

Still holding the now bloodied head of the bitch by the hair, Katie started to use everything on the bar to ram into her head. Bang went the ice bucket, crack went a bottle of becks. The barmaid was screaming throughout the whole ordeal but the bouncers hadn't realised straight away which gave Katie plenty of time to make a mess of the arrogant cow's face. When the bouncers finally realised that their queen bee was having an extreme make over, they came running towards us and wrestled me to the ground. I wouldn't mind, but I was just sitting there watching the action. Well they couldn't exactly start roughing Katie up so they knocked me about a bit before throwing pair of us out of the pub. I'm sure had they realised sooner the severity of the beating the barmaid had taken, they would have held us and called the police, so we counted ourselves lucky and quickly left the scene. I heard through the grapevine that the once arrogant queen bee had been brought down a peg or two since her once attractive face was now sporting a broken beak and a few ugly scars here and there. I hate violence towards women but this fucking hoar deserved everything she got that night. I'm pretty sure she would be more careful about who she abused after that.

A few months after splitting up with Katie I was in Henry Coopers down the Old Kent Road and was enjoying a night out with my new girlfriend Angie. I'd had my eye on her for a while, she was very Pretty and had a sexy smile. She was roughly ten years my senior at 33 yrs old and lived with her two children in a nice house in Blackheath village. During the couple of minutes that I'd nipped off to spend a penny Katie turned up with her latest feller and she immediately started to intimidate my other half. As I came out of the toilet making my way over to the bar, I noticed Katie was standing in Angie's face and was confessing to her that she and I were having it off every Tuesday which was credible since it happened to be my pool night and the only night I didn't stay at Angies. To be honest, we were having it off on a Tuesday night, Katie would turn up at my flat and after my initial attempts to turn her away the temptation always got the better of me. Also I was still meeting up with Michelle from time to time and I would put my hands down her knickers when we stole a moment in a dark corner of the beer garden while Angie was in the toilets.

After telling Katie to piss off I pulled Angie away while trying to convince her this girl was a fucking nutter, and she just didn't like the fact that I had dumped her. She only half bought my story and was getting upset since my jealous ex kept shouting over dates and times that were setting off alarm bells in Angie's head. I decided it would be wise to leave because I knew Katie would not give up. Besides that, her bloke was getting shirty and was itching for a chance to prove to his new bird that he was a tough guy. As we turned our back on them and began to walk away, Katie's new bloke swung a punch from behind which landed square on my jaw. Immediately I swung round with a reaction punch and hit him as hard as I could on the bridge of his nose. To my horror it wasn't the wanna be gangster reeling backwards and crashing into the DJ box, it was Katie. Her bloke had gone round the other side and was queuing up for drinks at the bar. Katie was no stranger to having a punch up whether it being with a man or woman, and like I have already mentioned she had often got me into fights in the past. Due to the fact her new bloke had been screwing me out, I just assumed it was him who threw the swinging punch at me from behind, and my reflex reaction was to hit back. Unfortunately it was Katie, and was now screaming holding her bloody nose. Hastily I headed for the door passing three or four bouncers who were angrily heading towards the scene of the crime. Now I have never hurt so much as a hair on a girl's head in my life, and have always been bought up that way. I believe any man who hits a woman is a coward and scum of the earth. So I could imagine how these bouncers wanted to rip me limb from limb after finding out I'd just decked a woman. Luckily my brother was in the club and he directed the bouncers away from me by pointing to the crowd saying, "he's over there mate," they bought it and ran straight past us leaving a clear exit. I was relieved to have gotten out of the club before they realised whom the perpetrator was, I grabbed Angie's arm and we ran to the car and sped off. I can't begin to explain how terrible I felt for Katie, as much as she was a troublemaker I knew deep down she'd only acted the way she did because she wanted me back, and was using the prick she bought with her to try and get me jealous. Also the fact that she was now in pain, and would have another horrible scar across her face caused by my hands, was breaking my heart. I know by what I have written that it sounds like Katie was a monster but when Katie was at home she could be very loving, caring and a pleasure to be around. Behind all the attention seeking bad behaviour was a lovely girl who didn't have the best start to life but always felt she had to put a brave face on.

I am a strong believer of what goes around comes around so was expecting some sort of backlash for the nightclub horror. I am not going to name names or go into too much detail, but it did come back around and resulted in a hit squad ambushing me outside the block of flats where I was living. Six burley men had come tooled up with baseball bats and cans of CS gas and were there to kill me or leave me half dead. It was a Tuesday night and about 11.30pm, I had just parked up the works van outside the high rise block where I rented a flat on the third floor, and was returning from a good night out playing pool. I wasn't drunk since I knew I'd be driving home so only had two or three halves of lager. I didn't notice anyone sitting about in any cars as I got out of the van. I had filmed the pool match that night so I was holding a carrier bag containing my video camera in my left hand, I checked the passenger side door to make sure it was locked before making my way towards the entrance to the flats. There was a pub just across the road which was already starting to send people home making it quite busy on the street so I never suspected foul play when a bloke about my age smiled and politely asked me for a light. I remember thinking that he seemed like a nice friendly chap so I couldn't wait to help him out and began searching my pockets for a lighter. As I looked up he was holding a spray can and sprayed it straight at my face, it went into my eyes and my immediate reaction was to take a sharp intake of breath at the shock of the attack. This caused me to inhale much more of the gas that I assume someone normally would under the circumstances. I heard two car doors slam shut then noticed four other fellers wielding baseball bats coming towards me. I later learned that I'd been sprayed with CS gas, this was meant to incapacitate me while the other four would give me a severe going over with their bats. Like before my immediate reaction was to attack so I laid the sprayer out with a David Muller right-hander, then I took off and started running down the road before the other four had a chance to unload. The sixth member of the hit squad was the driver who was now closing me down in his car. While running for my life the CS gas I had originally inhaled was starting to kick in and it felt like I was running in slow motion, on top of that my eyes were beginning to sting like fuck. I headed for the pavement in total panic realising my options for escape were minimal, the car was now level with me on my right hand side, then swerved onto the pavement knocking me over causing me to roll across the bonnet and fall to a heap on the ground. The carrier bag containing the video camera flew into the air and smashed into pieces after landing in the middle of the road. The next thing I knew I was being thumped with baseball bats by five out of breath blokes who were shouting Cunt! as they took turns unloading their exhausted anger and aggression on me. At this point my own voice in my head told me, "If you don't try and get up you are going to die right here right now. They stopped batting me for a split second as they allowed one of them to spray more CS gas at me, I mustered up as much energy as I could and rose to my feet throwing as many punches as possible in every direction. This bought me enough time to throw myself over the four foot high garden wall behind me. I crawled over the stinging nettles in garden towards the main window of the house and began frantically banging on the window trying to shout help, but no words would come out due to the amount of gas that was lodged in my throat. I could barely open my stinging eyes as what appeared to be an old lady opened the curtains to see what was going on. I looked at her and mouthed the words help me, and she swiftly closed the curtains again. That's it I'm fucked I thought, as my attackers began climbing over the garden wall on their way to finish me off.

The front door of the house swung open and out came the old lady holding two fierce looking angry German shepherds on a leash.

"Go away, Leave him alone," she shouted, as she edged towards my attackers with her two furious looking dogs who were snarling and eager to rip them to shreds should they get the chance. The attackers got the message and retreated back to their car and sped off. The lady quickly locked the dogs in another room while she and her husband who had been calling the police, dragged me into the safety of her living room. That brave lady had saved my life, and I constantly reminded her of that fact before passing out. The next thing I remember was regaining consciousness whilst being driven to hospital in an ambulance with an oxygen mask strapped to my bloody and bruised swollen face. Luckily although getting hit once or twice in the face, my arms and hands took most of the blows so on the whole, facially I had gotten away with it. Once the swelling and bruises faded I was left with a small scar under my eye. Apart from the affect it had on my mental state, the real damage had been done with the CS gas seeing as it stayed lodged in my throat for about a year, and my eyes would swell up and sting every time I sweated since it was impossible to wash out of my hair. On one hand I felt less guilty now about Katie's nose and felt I had got what I deserved, On the other hand I had a strong feeling that they would be back to finish the job. I became very paranoid and suspicious of any strangers and could no longer trust my so called friends when I found out that they had known all along about the planned ambush. They even went as far as providing details of times and places where I could be found, (Remember the brown nosers in the pub.) I started carrying a large kitchen knife with me everywhere I went. My mental state took its toll on my relationship with Angie plus the fact she couldn't trust me anymore, so inevitably we split up. It took a long time for me to get back to some sort of normality and ages before I could begin to trust people again.

About a year later I heard through the grapevine that a significant member of the hit squad had met his maker. Let's just say it had nothing to do with natural causes, or me.

So it just goes to prove that two important facts that I live my life by are definitely true.

Number one: What goes around comes around, and when it does come back around, it's usually ten times stronger than when it originally left.

Number two: If you live by the sword you die by the sword, your choice, you make it.

CIRCLES

To re-build my self esteem I got into bodybuilding and would go to my local sweaty gym to work out at least four times a week, I was already quite shapely due to all the heavy lifting I did working with the Italians. The thing with bodybuilding was you were never quite satisfied with your size and if you missed a training session it felt like your muscles had shrunk. It's all psychological and very addictive, I didn't realise just how big I'd got until one night down the Drovers nightclub on the Old Kent road a bloke approached me and offered me some door work as a bouncer. He left me his card explaining that he ran a security company providing doormen for nightclubs all over London, Kent and Essex. I was flattered and his offer confirmed that I was in the shape I wanted to be. But being a bouncer wasn't my cup of tea since I was always one of the lads and never got into weight training to seek power or authority like most bouncers do. My angle was pulling birds and the muscles meant that I didn't have to rely on my personality to charm them into bed. I had charisma, and good looks, so the muscles just made it even easier and eliminated the small talk. I'm not suggesting that all women are shallow and just go for looks and muscle, but there were plenty who did. By the late 90's when my baby daughter came along I was still training at the sweaty gym but had swapped being big for being fit and toned. I never usually trained on a Friday but had to one day after missing Thursdays work out. In the middle of bench pressing I heard some commotion coming from a separate room that had a glass window pained door. I went over to investigate and was immediately hypnotised by what I saw. A man who looked half Korean and half Jamaican, wearing a white Gi and a black skirt was circling in amongst eight to ten attacking students. He was throwing them left right and centre onto the safety mats strewn around the floor with no effort what so ever. I watched for about half an hour and was already hooked when the teacher beckoned me in to watch from the inside. His name was Sensei Terry and was a sixth Dan in Aikido. He invited me to join his class on Saturday morning and I gladly accepted. I spent the next couple of years eating breathing and sleeping Aikido, and although I became very efficient at the combat side of it, the philosophical side had gripped me too. Day after day if I wasn't out training I would be in my bedroom with my head buried in Aikido philosophy books. The fundamental principle of Aikido is Circles, which also relates to universal movement. Everything in life is based on a circle for example, the wheel, turning on a tap, opening a lock. Think about it, we drink from circular cups, eat from circular plates, wash our clothes in a circular spinning drum the list goes on, the moon circles the earth, the earth circles the sun along with the other circular planets, footballs, tennis balls, telescopes, atoms, protons, neutrons, athletes run around a circuit, the ring on your finger, a door or window opens in various degrees of a circle. My friends always refuse to open the circle debate with me, I wonder why? Anyway my engrossment with Aikido inevitably took its toll on my relationship with Louisa, we were practically living separate lives even though we lived in one room with our baby daughter, so things between us became rocky for a while. After a back injury at work Aikido was put on the back burner, which did improve things at home leading to the birth of our second child in 2001. I had always stated that I didn't want my kids to be brought up or go to school in Peckham/Nunhead, so by the time my daughter was five years old and nearly ready to start school I cashed in my £5000 worth of premium bonds and used some of it as a deposit to rent a house in Barnehurst Kent. We went to a local school hoping to at least come away with a prospectus or an application form. Knowing that we had left it quite late since most school places would have already been allocated we needed a bit of good fortune. Luckily the school secretary told right there and then that they had one place left and my daughter could have it. So within five minutes of arriving at the school I had paid upfront for her daily milk for the first term, and we were taken to see her new classroom to meet her teacher and classmates. It was a very good school and we were lucky to be in the right place at the right time.

A year later Louisa and I had come to the end of our rocky relationship after she had started seeing another bloke, so she moved back to her mothers in Nunhead. She met the guy through her brother who worked for him at a carwash company. He was a wanna be gangster and a coke-head who was doing his best to get in with Ed's firm who were all regulars at one of Nunhead's local pubs. The fact that he knew Louisa was with me, and he knew we had a family when he started seeing her was playing on my mind and I wasn't about to let him get away with it. I felt like he was mugging me off so on new year's eve when Carwash and Louisa were at the pub with E and his crowd, I decided I would go down there and have it out with him. I had no idea what he looked like so didn't know who I was looking for as I pulled up outside. From the moment I walked into the rowdy over crowded pub you could have cut the atmosphere with a knife. People started gathering in small groups whispering to each other, I looked for Louisa knowing that she would more than likely be with this Carwash dick head but I couldn't see her anywhere since it turned out they were in the pub garden watching the fireworks display. I noticed a couple of "mates" at one end of the cramped bar and made my way over to talk to them, I soon realised that they were uncomfortable talking to me since it was now plainly obvious to everyone why I had turned up that night. They slowly edged away or made excuses to move to another part of the pub. So I stood there alone after being refused a drink at the bar. I noticed this guy who walked past me twice nervously sizing me up, he was shorter than me and his cocaine ravished nose made him look like a weasel. The pub gangsters had obviously been geeing him up to get the first punch in even though by now he probably never fancied the job. I was still unsure if this guy was Carwash until after the third time of walking past me he turned around and tried to throw a pathetic punch. I saw it coming and dodged it, then punched him on the chin knocking him down. Before I could take my next breath people everywhere started throwing punches at me, it turned really ugly. I was throwing some hard punches back in every direction with most of them landing, but there was too much incoming especially when some of the women joined in. There were nails fists and boots coming at me non-stop, it was like walking through the tunnel of death (a game we used to play in the school playground) only these were real venomous kicks and punches and eventually I was over whelmed and kicked to the floor. At that point Ed came running over shouting "fucking get of him" as he started frantically pulling bodies away from me. Then a girl I know called Kim Furner joined in helping to pull women and men off me, I got up and shouted "all right, all right! People were already starting to back off when Kim screamed, "your all fucking out of order." I was still a bit dazed after the onslaught, Kim put her arm around my shoulder and attempting to get me out of the door which was at the other end of the pub. It was a long hard graft getting to the exit with one or two people still trying to throw punches as me as I tried to get to the door. Apparently while I was throwing wild punches in the melee, I threw a haymaker that knocked out a teenager whom I was later told was trying to help me. This prompted another scuffle outside on the street since his mum and dad wanted a piece of me. More and more people began spewing out of the pub so I made a hasty retreat and quickly left the area. From the moment I'd knocked out Carwash I never saw him in any of the fight scenes during the ensuing scuffle in the pub, proving that he was a weasel and was definitely not cut out to be a Gangster. He was worried that I might be still gunning for him and the next day he phoned me to tell me it was Louisa who was making a play for him and he didn't want to know her. Actually he never even had the bottle to phone me himself and only spoke to me after Ed passed him the phone. I told him he was a sneaky coward and warned him to watch his back. Ed phoned me back and asked me to come to the pub since he wanted to buy me a drink, then he passed the phone around the bar to other drinkers who were there the night before and they too wanted to buy me a drink. I didn't take up their offer but I did go back to the pub a few weeks later to be met by people who were queuing up to buy me a drink. Everyone wanted to shake my hand while collectively agreeing that I had shown a lot of bottle to walk in that pub alone looking for a fight. I also made my peace with the teenager and his parents.

Louisa and Carwash did end up with each other but it wasn't long before it all went tits up after he started knocking her about which eventually led to them splitting up. I knew he was a fucking cowardly cunt, and if I ever have the pleasure of bumping into the little prick in the future I'll show him what it's like to be a woman on the receiving end of a right hander.

The kids and I stayed together in Kent which suited me down to the ground given that the art of being a single parent came naturally to me and I loved our new home. I had to give up working for the Italians in January 2004 due to the fact that I slipped a disk carrying some heavy marble table tops, besides that I had recently become a single parent and the kids were my main concern. I tried my upmost to eliminate as much trauma as possible over the separation of their mother and I, which went well after I quickly introduced structured routines. My son was just over two years old, so he didn't really understand and wasn't really affected by the new changes at home. My daughter was six, and obviously had some understanding of the situation. She wasn't over the moon but I'm sure it was more of a natural progression for her to slip into my routine, seeing as I was the main influence in her life since the very second she was born.

CHAPTER XXII

REVENGE PENDING

IN 1995 MARIA Bosco tragically died after being hit by a car which had been driven by a drunk off duty policeman. I was devastated even though five years had passed since we'd split up. I won't go in to the manner of how she died but I will say it wasn't nice at all. I often bumped into her when driving through her area and we'd stop and have a little chat. Sometimes I had Ben with me and he'd go mad when he saw her and the pair of them would squeal and kiss and cuddle excitedly. The realisation that she was gone forever was hard to take. I'd never again be able to say, "do you remember this, and do you remember that? After all even though the end of our relationship turned ugly, we did share a couple of fantastic years and there were some lovely moments that we shared that only she and I would understand. Although after Maria died I was in a full blown relationship with Louisa, every time I had an evening to myself I'd occasionally drink a bottle of mine and Maria's favourite cheap wine (liebfraumilch) and dig out my tape cassette 'Tracks Of My Tears' and I'd dance with an imaginary Maria whilst crying and talking to her, strangely this gave me incredible comfort. There were many times when I found myself sitting at her Graveside talking to her with the tape playing in the car radio. Even now I have the odd private wine evenings and listen to Tracks of my tears while going over old memories with her. I still take a distant interest in how her son Jason is doing. He is a man now with his own young family.

In 1997 my estranged Dad was diagnosed with Cancer, he had recently re-married to his long time partner Kim who was kind and always welcoming to my brother John and I when we'd turn up at their door after a long hour and half journey which involved getting three buses across London to Kilburn. Dad would mumble and grumble behind the door, pissed off at getting an un-announced visit from his abandoned off spring, but after a few minutes of shuffling about behind the door he'd let us in and make an effort to make us feel welcome. Dad and Kim had a baby boy called Ryan who was about 3 years old when he lost his battle with cancer and died in the June of 1997, four months before my first child and his first Granddaughter was born. At least he left us with a fantastic younger brother Ryan who is 16. Ryan lives in Wales which is a shame since we have seen very little of each other, but thanks to today's computer technology we are constantly in touch via networking and instant messenger sites.

It's 2010 and I am now a mellowed 41-year-old father of two beautiful children. I gave up smoking a year ago and have recently ran the 2010 Virgin London Marathon where I was running for a charity called Orchid who deal specifically with Male Cancer. Apart from the charity I was also dedicating my run to my late niece Phoebe Zsa Zsa who tragically passed away when she was nine months old. I was wearing a T shirt with a large photo of Phoebe on the back and front with her name underneath. Two hours and fifteen minutes in to the race I arrived at mile thirteen (Tower Bridge) to find all six players from my pool team screaming and cheering me on. Just seeing them and hearing their encouraging words gave me an extra spring to my step as I ran on into the final 13.2 miles. At Mile fourteen my heart began to sink when I felt a twinge in my heavily strapped up left knee. I injured my knee some ten years previous and had never got it sorted, so for most of the second half of the marathon I was running/limping in complete agony as my dodgy knee began to break down. The crowds were fantastic with their shouts of encouragement, specifically for the last five miles when they were cheering me on by shouting, "come on mate do it for Phoebe" as I limped while jogging past them with pain written all over my face. Eventually I reached mile twenty five to find my fellow pool team mates and ten members of my family cheering me on from riverside on the approach to Westminster bridge. I ran over and gave my kids a kiss and cuddle before jogging off towards the finish line at Buckingham Palace. I crossed the line half jogging and half limping in 5.47 hours. Even though I was in total agony, the feelings of self achievement and pride were overwhelming, and then being given my medal at the end capped off an amazing day.

As previously stated I moved us out of Peckham and out of London when my kids were very young; it was the best move I have ever made. I loved growing up in Peckham, but I have to say there is absolutely no trace of the Peckham and its culture I once knew and felt safe in. It has changed beyond all recognition and has become an ugly place to live in. It has nothing what so ever to offer me or my children in the way of future prosperity or security. My kind, the old school cockneys have also moved away due to being considered low priority when it comes to sharing out jobs, houses, or any other public assets in the area. Unfortunately this has been widely overlooked by recent governments over the last three decades. My kids, a girl of 13 and a boy of nine are happy and doing very well at school. We currently live in a nice semi detached house with fields full of horses for a view. The children's mum Louisa is now firmly back in our lives after we straightened out our differences a couple of years ago We have the greatest neighbours you could ever imagine and all help each other out. Most of them would insist they were reading about a totally different person if ever they read this limited account of my past. People often come to me for advice about their relationships or just life in general. I am considered by many to have a wise head on young shoulders, and I attribute that to the wisdom passed on to me by my mother, and by the many diverse experiences I've had in my life. Growing up and spending 33 years of my life in and around Peckham and going through being attacked, ambushed, attempts on taking my life and threatened on numerous occasions has left its mark on my way of thinking. I tend to subconsciously weigh up situations very quickly, for example, which ever scenario I find myself in whether it be in a building or on the streets, I immediately look for possible escape routes or anything I could use as a weapon should the shit hit the fan. If I notice a gang of blokes in my proximity or just loitering, subconsciously I'm deciding which one to go for first if their intentions become ominous. I don't walk around in a state of paranoia, far from it, it's just an automatic built in survival instinct that comes from my many experiences listed above. In this book I have only written about some of the illegal things I got up to, there are plenty of other adventures that were illicit, sexy, kinky, risky, nice, happy, crime free, loving and caring parts of my life that have been omitted since I really wanted to write about my experience of prison and what lead up to me getting there. After having read this book you might think I have glamorised or made light of all the drug taking and criminal activity that went on, well I would say to any youngsters and young adults, taking drugs and getting into crime is not clever, there are consequences and somewhere along the line it will be to your detriment, trust me I know. I am committed to bringing up my children to be responsible well-adjusted and happy intelligent adults. This has been my focus in life from the moment my youngest was born, and I intend to carry this out. I haven't been tempted to cross the line to the wrong side of the law since the Police car pound robbery seventeen years ago, and would never do anything that might be detrimental to my children's well being. Although given the chance, there is one more piece of revenge I would like to carry out that has been a monkey on my back for thirty years. It has nothing to do with theft, or death, just torture in a psychological kind of way. The only thing I have left to do now, is find out where the person is, if still alive. I have always loved proverbs and wise sayings and I think to understand the principal behind this book, this next line sums it all up.

YOU CAN NEVER BE OLD AND WISE, IF YOU HAVE NEVER BEEN YOUNG AND STUPID.

WATCH THIS SPACE.

The end

R. Atkinson

Lightning Source UK Ltd.
Milton Keynes UK
14 January 2011

165693UK00002B/32/P

9 781456 822439